"Randy hits the ɪ

MW01103932

Results by Design, Inc.

"Fantastic Randy, a practical, understandable, how-to book that will help someone with no experience in Network Marketing build the business of their dreams!"

Chuck Branham, Diamond Distributor and
President's Club Member, Nikken, Inc.

"The chapter on *Choosing The Right Company For You* hits the nail on the head."

Chuck Huckaby, Publisher
Profit Now

"Candid, contemporary and accurate. Randy Gage's 'tell it like it is and tell it like it isn't' style is refreshing. Some might consider this book too opinionated. It's only bragging if you can't back it up. Once again, Gage backs it up."

Steve Spaulding, Vice President
International Mannatech, Inc.

"Finally! The Network Marketing industry has eagerly awaited a book like this for over three decades. Randy simply tells it like it is ... it's jam packed with knowledge, energy, humor, and practical real life experiences that will help you make (or create) millions too!"

Craig W. Roggow, Chief Operations Officer
Oxyfresh Worldwide, Inc.

"There are a lot of good books on Network Marketing, but Randy's tops the list. If you are serious about serious income, not only read this book — but do what it says!"

Shirley Benton, Ruby Director
USANA

"Don't buy this book! — if you think you can sponsor 1,000 people and get rich mailing postcards. Randy Gage tells it like it really is! Buy this book! — if you want a simple, step-by-step road map to MLM success — and then buy one for everyone you sponsor."

Beth Royall, President
Biogime

"The complete guide to building a large network. All the principles of success, the attitudes you'll need sooner or later. Why not make it sooner? Save yourself months, years, even a lifetime of trial and error. Read this book. No, don't just read it. Digest it and let it become a part of your intestinal fortitude."

Robert Natiuk, Director
Harmony Media

"Randy really speaks the truth about our industry. His honest nuts-and-bolts approach not only includes all of the important 'dos and don'ts' but also explains the wisdom behind the suggestions he makes. This book ranks among the best of the best for thoroughness and ease of reading. I highly recommend it to new distributors and to the seasoned distributors who haven't quite received the promise of this industry."

Lyndia Storey, Crown Performance Director
Royal Body Care

"Despite my years of experience in sales and recruiting, I learned several ideas that will be applied to my effort."

Roscoe Bunn, Division Sales Manager
Avon

"Great job! A complete Guide and Handbook for anyone in the Network Marketing industry."

Penny Loppnow, President
New Resolution, Inc.

"If getting to the top of your MLM business is your goal — then read every word in this book, and then read it again."

Jan Ruhe, MLM Master

"Who else but Randy Gage would have the audacity to write *How To Build a Multi-Level Money Machine* — and then have the book actually show you how to do just that...? Only Randy could've pulled it off. A really great book from one of the few, true, card-carrying Masters of Network Marketing."

John Milton Fogg, Editor-in-Chief of *Upline*
Author of *The Greatest Networker in the World*

"Randy Gage is one of the very few masters of building a 'forever' network marketing organization. This simple yet powerful how-to book will show you the ways and the whys of building your own financial freedom with honor and integrity."

Richard Brooke, Chairman & CEO
OxyfreshWorldwide Inc.

"A thorough, step-by-step checklist that any new distributor or leader could follow. The list only includes what to do — but why you should do it."

Tom 'Big Al' Schreiter
KAAS Publishing

HOW TO BUILD A
MULTI-LEVEL
MONEY
MACHINE

The Science of
Network Marketing

RANDY GAGE

MANJUL
Manjul Publishing House

First published in India by

Manjul Publishing House Pvt. Ltd.
Corporate Office: 2nd Floor, Usha Preet Complex,
42 Malviya Nagar, Bhopal, INDIA-462 003
E-mail: manjul@manjulindia.com Website: www.manjulindia.com
Registered Office: 10 Nishat Colony, Bhopal, INDIA-462 003

Distributed in India by
book supply co
7/32, Ground Floor, Ansari Road, Daryaganj, New Delhi-110 002
Email: booksupplyco@gmail.com

First published 2004
Third impression 2010

ISBN   978-81-86775-88-2

Cover and text design by Manjul Creative Team

Printed & bound in India by Gopsons Papers Ltd.

DEDICATION

This book is dedicated to many people. First, to all my friends who laughed at me, ridiculed me, and told me that Network Marketing wouldn't work. Having the personality type I had, it was that scorn that drove me harder and deepened my resolve to make it work. It did.

Next, this book is dedicated to my mother, Kay. She saw things in me that only a mother could see and never turned her back on me. Even when I was too selfish, stupid and ignorant to realize it.

Thirdly, this book is dedicated to my sponsors (in every program I was ever in) and the support line above them. You know who you are. Every one of you helped mold me and helped me gain wisdom. Because you had the courage to follow your vision — you gave me permission to win, as well. Most especially, to Jim Caplinides of Raleigh, North Carolina, who was the first person to draw those mesmerizing circles for me. You awakened something in me that never died. As a result, my life and hundreds of thousands of others have been enriched.

And finally, and most importantly, this book is dedicated to you, the reader. You're the agent of change who is transforming the business world. People of vision and dreams are bringing integrity and empowerment back into business. Never forget that what you do helps others. It's important. Never give up on your dreams, because without dreamers, this world wouldn't be worth living in!

TABLE OF CONTENTS

ACKNOWLEDGMENTS

I WOULD LIKE TO RECOGNIZE THE FOLLOWING PEOPLE WHO HAVE helped with proofreading drafts of this new edition of the manuscript for content and accuracy. I am greatly indebted to all of these people, as they have made this a much more powerful resource for you.

Alan Badgett

Brent Bressler

Cyndy Bressler

Lornette Browne

Art Burleigh

Dan & Nance Christy

David Geiss

Ford Saeks

Lastly I acknowledge you, the reader — for having a dream and taking the steps to build it. May you fulfill the potential of the greatness your Creator endowed you with!

INTRODUCTION

I T IS MY EXPERIENCE THAT THE "OPPORTUNITY OF A LIFETIME" comes around several times a year. Yet, most people will go through their entire life and never grasp such an opportunity. The reasons for this are many, but mostly very interrelated: low self-esteem, "lack" consciousness, fear of failure, fear of success, and a disbelief that great, wonderful things can really happen for them.

Like most people, I passed up the lifetime opportunities that came my way. Except one. Network Marketing. At first look, something resonated with me. I am one of those people who saw those multiplying circles drawn out and became mesmerized with the possibilities.

My rational side saw the impeccable logic of exponential growth. My emotional side saw the power of a dream, and the vision of empowerment. I had a dream, the drive to accomplish it, and Network Marketing was the perfect vehicle to manifest it. Prosperity was only days away ...

I just didn't know how many days. Five years later, I had done nothing, but lose money and switch companies many times. I finally came to the realization that success was possible in Network Marketing — but not without some kind of a system.

I began a study of what worked and what didn't. Learned what the long-term successful people did and why. Discovered the secrets of effective presentations, and what motivated prospects to join. And began the rudimentary forerunner of what became the system I teach today. It was only then that I began to achieve any degree of success. But it wasn't lasting ...

While I was able to conduct meetings, make presentations, and sponsor a large number of people ... most of my distributors could not. The more people I sponsored, the faster they seemed to drop out. What I did *worked*, but it didn't *duplicate*. I came to realize that success without duplication is merely future failure in disguise.

I went back to my system and fine-tuned it, simplified it, and made it easier to replicate. It not only worked, but it duplicated as well. It is that system (with continuous refinement) that has helped many thousands of people, all over the world, reach higher levels of success in Network Marketing. It is that system which I now share with you through this book.

What this book can do for you ...

This book can save you much of the frustration and failure I faced. Building upon my success, you can cut many years off your growth curve and build your network much faster. You'll learn what attracts prospects to you, and how to present to them effectively. You'll discover the kind of people you want to sponsor, and whom you would be better to screen out in the pre-approach process.

Once you're well educated in the sponsoring process, you will learn how to manage — and keep growing — a large network. How to spend your time, how to develop leaders, and how to counsel them. Most importantly, you'll learn how to empower those leaders to develop new ones. By the time you finish this book, you will have a clear understanding of a fundamental, profound truth about Network Marketing: **You don't grow your network. You grow your people — and they grow your group.**

This book will teach you exactly how to do that. You will find I'm not big on motivational clichés and "rah-rah" platitudes. I believe that if you can show people specifically how they can accomplish a desired goal — they will motivate themselves.

By the time you're finished, you will:

▲ Have an honest, realistic view of the business;

▲ Know that you really can do this; and,

▲ Have a detailed, step-by-step plan for making it happen.

My hope is that you'll view Network Marketing as the professional career it has become, and will join me on my mission, which is to continue raising the standards of this honorable profession.

Unlike corporate America — with its downsizing and rat-eat-rat competition — Network Marketing offers you the opportunity to nurture and empower the inherent talents in all those you sponsor. In this business, success means the chance to develop spiritually, intellectually, emotionally and financially, while you contribute in a positive way to others.

What you won't find in this book are canned scripts, closing techniques, or manipulative mirroring and modeling strategies. While there are many who teach these methods in our industry, these things are not how the business is truly accomplished. Real Network Marketing is about creating a culture of integrity, then teaching principles and skills that create consistency and develop character. Your success will come not from changing others, but from changing you.

As you undertake this journey of challenge, adventure and growth, you will attract others who share your vision and follow your example. You will lead them for a short time, then release them as they unfold into leaders and start the process all over again. You will feel pride, joy and a sense of accomplishment few ever experience. You will know that what you do means something — and that your community is a little bit better place because you have contributed.

Building a large, exponentially growing network is not easy — it's not supposed to be. It is simple, however. If you are coachable and persistent; if you really believe in yourself, and are willing to follow a step-by-step system — you can achieve massive, lasting success in Network Marketing. Through this book, I'll serve as your surrogate sponsor — teaching you, guiding you and empowering you to your greatest good.

I suggest you read through the book in its entirety the first time. Then use it as a resource guide as you need to refresh your memory or increase your skill level in a particular area. I believe you'll find networking to be the most rewarding vocation you've ever been a part of. You will face challenges, but none that won't lead you to the next breakthrough — onward to where you wish to go. Stay focused, follow the system, and be true to your dreams. You will achieve the success you are seeking. Never give up, because what you do is important.

As you take this journey, you will begin the process that changes you ... and then you can change things. Seize the opportunity!

— Randy Gage
Miami Beach, Florida
February, 2001

How To Build A Multi-Level Money Machine

CHAPTER ONE

WHY NETWORK MARKETING

IN EVERY GROUP OF PEOPLE, A FEW WILL RETIRE YOUNG, RICH AND worry-free. A few more will work hard and long, but finally retire in comfort. Most, however, will slog through 45 years of life in the rat race, only to eke out their "golden years" on a meager pension.

What separates these groups? And what are the secrets possessed by those in the first one? How do they get so wealthy, so fast? And what can someone do to ensure that they end up in this group? It's an intriguing question ...

One I feel eminently qualified to answer. For not only do I belong to this first group, but I've also helped thousands more to join it.

Make no mistake, however ...

I'm not referring to captains of industry, the market traders, or the real estate tycoons. For while these people have amassed great monetary wealth — they don't retire early, and they certainly do not appear to be worry free. In fact, it's quite the opposite. They're winning the rat race — but they're living like rats.

The group I'm referring to is a new breed of entrepreneur — the individual who has built walk-away residual income. What I call "drink out of a coconut" money. These people have built a multi-level money machine. One that showers them with rewards, whether they remain working, or choose to spend their days on a tropical beach, with their toes in the sand, sipping from that coconut.

The parallels of how these people reached this success are intriguing indeed ...

You might think they attained their status through higher education, but this is not necessarily the case. Many members of this group are high school dropouts (like myself), while we know that there are many people with multiple diplomas out looking for work.

And while the people in my group worked hard to attain their considerable prosperity — that alone was not the deciding factor. In fact, although I'm slightly embarrassed to admit this — most people work harder than I do, but they certainly don't receive the rewards I do.

The mechanic who tunes up my cars, the man who landscapes my lawn, my massage therapist and my usual waitress at my favorite restaurant, all work much harder than I had to — yet none of them are wealthy doing what they do. In fact, they work a lot harder, for a lot less. Not one of them shows even a remote chance of retiring early.

These people, and millions more like them, are prisoners in a dysfunctional economic system. *They are hostages in the time-for-money trap.* To receive more money, they must work harder and longer. Most are stuck in salaried positions or jobs restricting overtime, so one job doesn't even offer them the opportunity to trade more time for more money. As a result, they put their spouse or partner to work, which of course is still not enough.

So they take a second job. And sometimes, so does their spouse. The result is three- and four- income families — desperately trying to trade more time for more money. So no one's raising the kids. They learn their lessons from the television. They need mom and dad, but they're out working — simply trying to provide a good life for their children. It's a vicious cycle.

And a very foolish one ...

Because as long as you play the "trading time for money" game — **you can never reach true financial security**. The people in my group have discovered that attaining true economic freedom requires that you employ two basic prosperity principles:

1) You must employ the concept of leverage to escape the trading-time-for-money dilemma;

2) You must be able to look in the mirror every morning and know you're talking to the boss.

Once you have an understanding of these two principles — and actively apply them in your life — your prosperity is assured.

You'll see these principles in action throughout the rest of this book. You'll find both of them are foundational anchors of the network marketing opportunity. When you take the entrepreneurial excitement of working for yourself, and combine that with leveraging yourself through a network of other excited entrepreneurs — the results are exponentially spectacular. The synergistic process creates a whole that is much more powerful than its individual parts. Done properly, *the end result is a self-perpetuating, multi-level money machine.*

And you can drive it. To do so, you have to do two things.

First, you must commit yourself to one day escaping the modern-day slavery of a regular Friday paycheck. You must become the creator of your own destiny. And second, you must affiliate yourself with a solid network marketing company.

Network Marketing (sometimes called Multi-Level Marketing, or MLM for short) is one of the strongest growth industries in the world. It's practiced today in all fifty United States and more than 80 countries and territories around the globe.

3

Millions of independent distributors produce an annual volume estimated at more than 80 billion dollars. Network Marketing perfectly utilizes J. Paul Getty's three secrets for wealth:

1) Get a product everyone needs.
2) Duplicate yourself.
3) Be self-employed.

Why should you get involved with Network Marketing? There are probably as many answers as there are distributors. Usually though, it comes down to the lifestyle networking can give you. Some of the unique benefits of this business include:

▲ Choosing the people you work with;
▲ Going into business with a very small investment;
▲ Working from home;
▲ Picking the hours you want to work;
▲ Discovering unique products not available elsewhere;
▲ Reaping the rewards of numerous tax advantages;
▲ Enjoying the opportunity for an unlimited income; and,
▲ Having the chance to build your success while empowering others to succeed.

You can sum it up as "freedom from the rat race." The benefits we discussed are just not available anywhere else. Most people accept this to be true of working for someone else. But they mistakenly believe that having their own traditional business will give them these benefits.

As a former Chamber of Commerce president and owner of ten small to medium-sized businesses, I can personally attest that in many ways — owning a traditional business can be more limiting than working for somebody! Because of things like employee turnover, inventories, large investments, government regulation and market competition, you often work longer hours for less money than you pay your employees. You don't really own a small business — the small business owns you!

People today are fed up with out-of-balance work situations that rob them of their family life. And they're tired of merger mania, leveraged buyouts, and layoffs. Today they demand rewarding work situations, balance, and quality time with their loved ones.

Which is exactly where Network Marketing comes in ...

Because in Network Marketing, unlike the corporate rat race, you never get ahead by holding others back. The road to success in Network Marketing is traveled by **empowering** others. You cannot be successful without helping others to be successful. In fact, the more people you help, the more successful you become.

If you're looking to get rich quick — Network Marketing is really not for you. However, if you're willing to work hard, on a part-time basis for two to five years — you really can build lifetime financial security. The flexible hours make it a perfect business to start while you keep your current job, even if you're a student or a housewife with children. You can also start the business with a very small investment, usually $300 to $1,000 to begin.

Network Marketing has emerged as the last real chance in the free enterprise system for the average person without large capital to become financially free. It is helping yourself by helping others. Now that you have made the decision to join this empowering profession, you're in for a career of unlimited financial opportunity, and the chance to make a meaningful difference in the lives of the people you care most about. So let's get started!

CHAPTER TWO

NETWORK MARKETING VS. ILLEGAL PYRAMIDS

A S YOU MIGHT EXPECT, A BUSINESS WHERE A FARMER'S WIFE, a minister or a retired schoolteacher can make a five- or six-figure monthly income is bound to raise a few eyebrows. And simply by the magnitude of the monetary potential, opportunists and flim-flam artists are drawn to the industry like moths to a flame. It's important that you understand the difference between legitimate Network Marketing and phony pyramid schemes and money games. Let's take a look.

You might have heard me say that Network Marketing is not a sales business. Now you're probably thinking, "Wait a minute. Doesn't somebody have to sell something?" Yes. And no.

Products must move or nobody makes money. But networking is not really a sales business as much as it is a teaching and training one. In fact, non-sales types often have a natural advantage over sales types. It is not unheard of for a schoolteacher or housewife to earn more money than salespeople in Network Marketing.

How is this possible?

Because this is a business of *duplication*. A sales type is able to go out and retail a lot of product personally, but oftentimes he or she is not able to teach and train others. The non-sales types they approach fear selling, and are often put off by the sales techniques employed on them. As a result, they do not get involved. But here's the reality ...

Most sales in Network Marketing are accomplished without door-to-door or retail sales. Can you be your own best customer? Yes. If somebody buys your products wholesale, could they still be a retail customer? Yes. If they buy your products below wholesale, could they still be a retail customer? Yes. You've probably bought something from Sears or J.C. Penney below wholesale at some time or another. Obviously, selling below wholesale wouldn't be too profitable, but it demonstrates the rights you have as an independent businessperson.

Very few people involved in Network Marketing are retailing the products in a large way. Usually the products are **conversationally marketed** to friends and/or family members, and used personally. And, because of computer and delivery technologies, most network marketing companies will drop-ship orders anywhere. It's just not necessary to stockpile large inventories and be delivering products all over town. You may be using the products personally, and sharing them with a few friends and neighbors, who order direct from the main company. Meanwhile, you may have introduced the business aspect to eight or ten people, who have duplicated the process and created an organization of 5,000 people below you. You might only be making $500 a month in retail profits, and earning $10,000 a month in override commissions! Even though you're making a lot more from overrides than you are from selling — contrary to what some uninformed regulators would tell you — that doesn't mean it isn't legal. It's just a demonstration of what can happen when you employ the power of leverage.

However, this doesn't mean that every company that claims to be a legitimate network marketing program is one. They're not. There are some telltale things that can signal a program is not legitimate. Let's look closer at some of these factors.

As a practical matter, it's impossible for regulators to predict and legislate all of the infinite variations of legal and illegal marketing programs. For that reason, multi-level and anti-pyramid laws are drafted and interpreted very broadly. This allows regulators to encompass all of the possible variations of illegal schemes and have a jurisdictional basis to close them down. The problem arises when the regulators themselves are not educated as to the differences between legitimate Network Marketing and illegal pyramids. More about that in a minute.

For now, let's look at the two major distinctions used by knowledgeable regulators to determine if a program is a legitimate multi-level opportunity.

The first focus is *the conceptual design of the compensation plan.* More specifically, does it compensate participants:

a) Merely for introducing others to the program? or...

b) For the sales of goods or services to the end consumer?

If the plan focuses on rewarding participants for recruiting — it is a pyramid. If the commission structure is geared on product/service sales to the end consumer — it passes the first phase of the test.

The second analysis is on *the actual operation of the program.* Regardless of how the compensation plan is designed, regulators look at what the distributors actually spend their time doing. If the emphasis of the program is on recruiting rather than product or service sales — it still can be determined to be a pyramid.

Only a few sophisticated states have statutes that specifically define and regulate Multi-Level Marketing.[1] Most states do have anti-pyramid laws. There are no comprehensive defining

---

1   At the time of this writing, they were Georgia, Louisiana, Maryland, Massachusetts, Wyoming and the Territory of Puerto Rico.

laws on the national level in the United States, and many other countries. In the U.S., federal regulation comes primarily as the result of administrative and judicial decisions that have come as the result of lawsuits from private parties and the Federal Trade Commission (FTC).

Piecing together these decisions along with the definitions created by the state legislators gives you the eight elements that define a Multi-Level Marketing program. Table One below describes them and gives you a checklist to see if your program meets these requirements:

Table One

Elements of a Multilevel Compensation Plan	Does Your Program Meet These Elements?
1. A person, firm, corporation or other business entity	

2. which
    a. sells;
    b. distributes; or
    c. supplies	

3. for consideration	
4. goods or services	
5. through independent agents, contractors or distributors	
6. at different levels	
7. participants may recruit other participants	

8. compensation to participants is paid as a result of
    a. the sale of such goods or services; or
    b. the volume produced by the distributors in
       your organization.	

From an anti-pyramid standpoint, the most important determination in state statutes is whether or not the money participants earn is contingent upon recruiting others into the program. Thus, pyramids, endless chain schemes and chain letters are illegal. As long as a Multi-Level Marketing plan does not fit all of the four elements in the table below, it is permissible (at least from an anti-pyramid standpoint). See Table Two.

Table Two

Elements of a Pyramid	Does Your Program Meet These Elements?
1. A scheme, plan or program;	
2. For which a participant renders consideration to join;	
3. For the right or chance to receive compensation or other things of value; and,	
4. Which is contingent upon the introduction of additional participants into the scheme, plan or program.	

From a federal standpoint, the determination level is slightly different. While Canada has passed national anti-pyramid legislation, most countries have not. This is changing, however. Many central European and other countries have been victimized recently by large-scale pyramid schemes, which naturally have failed. This is causing many nations to adopt legislation.

Here in the U.S., there has been no anti-pyramid statute passed by Congress. Most Network Marketing companies have developed their programs based upon the case law of Federal Court decisions and, more frequently, the decisions of the FTC.

The most cited decision used to define pyramid schemes is the FTC's ruling *In the Matter of Koscot Interplanetary, Inc.*[2] In that decision, the FTC held that "entrepreneurial chains" are characterized by "the payment by participants of money to the

---

2   86 F.T.C. 1106, 1180 (1975)

company in return for which they [the participants] receive (1) the right to sell a product, and (2) the right to receive in return for recruiting other <u>participants</u> into the program rewards which are *unrelated* to sale of the product to ultimate users."

The key here is the words, "rewards which are *unrelated·* to sale of the product to ultimate users." Meaning: Do you make money from things other than selling products personally, or overrides on products sold by your people? If you're making money for these other things, such as signing up recruits, or selling sales aids, you're likely to be determined to be illegal. See Table Three for the elements of pyramid according to federal decisions.

Table Three

Elements of a Pyramid – Federal Decisions	Does Your Program Meet These Elements?
1. Payment of money to the company;	
2. The participant receives the right to sell a product (or service);	
3. The participant receives compensation for recruiting others into the program;	
4. The compensation is unrelated to the sale of product (or services) to the ultimate user.	

The preceding information and tables are a good example of the pyramid issues facing the network marketing industry. Because a company complies with the literal terms of the law does not guarantee that it will overcome all legal challenges.

Because states have different legislation, a program may be legal in one state and found to be a pyramid in another. In addition, judges may interpret a statute in a matter not consistent with its literal terms.

And many underpaid government regulators are quite uneducated in this area and are not up to speed on case law in this area. In fact, it would appear that some of these regulators (and in some cases — judges) have never read the Constitution. Here's a perfect case in point, *Capone vs. Nu Skin.*

First, the background: This was a class action lawsuit initiated on behalf of Nu Skin's Canadian distributors. Nu Skin filed for a summary judgment from the court. (In this case, the U.S. District Court for the District of Utah.) In March of 1997, the court's Memorandum decision held that a Nu Skin distributorship might constitute a security!

Nu Skin, of course, maintained that this was ridiculous, being that the entire investment involved was purchasing a $60 distributor kit. The court, however, agreed with Ms. Capone that in order to "meaningfully participate in the Nu Skin marketing plan, it is necessary to purchase products every month to meet the personal volume and group volume requirements."

The court justified this by claiming,

> "... a key feature of the Nu Skin Canada Marketing plan is that **every distributor**, in order to receive commissions from down line distributors, **must purchase 100 "points"** (equivalent to approximately $100.00 [U.S.]) worth of Nu Skin products. Similarly, distributors who become "Executives" must account for $3,000 worth of product **purchases** every month among their distributors to be eligible for commission. Moreover, there is **evidence which suggests that commissions are paid regardless of whether the distributors actually retail the products they purchase.**"

Of course, there are two problems with this convoluted logic. First is the fact that distributors are not required to "pur-·

chase" products, but rather *produce volume*. It is certainly not unreasonable for Nu Skin or any other company to expect a distributor to produce a certain amount of personal volume to get paid overrides. In this case it was $100. And distributors do not have to "purchase" it themselves. They can certainly market that much to their friends and relatives, which many do.

The second problem is the court suggesting that commissions, rebates, or overrides should be paid only on products that are retailed, and not including those purchased by distributors who are their own best customer. There is absolutely no basis in law for this — it's simply a case of uneducated jurists trying to create new law.

Furthermore, the court went on to maintain that Nu Skin was a security because distributors could make "big money from building a sales force, becoming financially independent and the like." The court went on to state that the "promise of lucrative rewards for recruiting others tends to induce participants to focus on the recruitment side of the business at the expense of their retail marketing efforts, making it unlikely that meaningful opportunities for retail sales will occur."

In simpler terms, the court maintained that any program that potentially pays a distributor more from his group overrides than he makes retailing product personally satisfies the elements of an investment contract — and is then a security. Of course this is ludicrous.

At the risk of overstating the obvious — the courts sometimes forget that they are not supposed to "make law," but interpret it. Not only are courts making law, but they're making bad law too. Lone federal judges are creating legislation faster than any congress or legislature. Several recent decisions, such as this Utah one, clearly show the complete lack of understanding the courts have of MLM case law, and even the Constitution.

While this Nu Skin case is obviously an abuse of government power, for the most part, regulators are honest, hardworking people simply protecting the public from unscrupulous schemes. Ultimately, the regulators will look to substance over form. Even if a program uses all the correct "buzz words" in its marketing materials — but does not enforce those policies that protect the public — the program will be treated just like one that does not have safeguards built in.

An example would be inventory front-loading. True, legitimate Network Marketing is not about pyramids, chain letters or garages full of water filters. As you now know, *products have to be reaching the end consumer*. There should be no large up-front investment required. If someone tells you to buy a huge quantity of inventory to qualify for a certain level, you are being front-loaded. Legitimate companies will never want you to purchase more products than you can use and/or resell in a month or two.

Technically, in a front-loading situation, everyone is compensated solely for the sale of products. In reality, this is a subterfuge. The emphasis is not on the sale of products to the actual consumer, but rather on recruiting new distributors with the goal of "loading" them with as much inventory as possible. It's quite improbable that the average distributor would be able to use or resell these products or services in a reasonable time. Because of this, the courts have consistently held that these types of transactions are actually a "headhunting" or "recruiting" bonus, and thus constitute a pyramid.

When it's all said and done, there are many inconsistencies among the state and federal laws. Ultimately, there are three major factors that both federal and state regulators look to when conducting a pyramid analysis. And while these criteria are not embodied in a comprehensive statute, they are generally used because complying with these three criteria does protect the public from the dangers posed by pyramids. They are:

1) **Substantial sales of products or services to ultimate users.**

The key here is ultimate users. If someone gets front-loaded into buying $5,000 worth of water filters and storing them in his garage — he is not an ultimate user. As mentioned earlier, this is a subterfuge, not in the spirit of the law, and definitely not legitimate Network Marketing.

However, when product is getting to the end consumer — even if a large percentage of these consumers are distributors — this does meet the literal requirements of both the FTC Koscot decision and the spirit of the law. Don't be confused by the one or two misguided federal decisions holding that distributor usage does not qualify as products to the ultimate consumer. These are quite obviously cases of judges attempting to actually write law, which tells us they slept through Constitutional Law 101 in law school.

2) **Commissions paid only on product usage — not "headhunter" fees.**

As we discussed earlier, your income must come as bonuses and overrides based on the sales volume produced by your organization. If you're paid simply for recruiting, or for selling training, distributor kits or training materials — then you're in a pyramid.

3) **Inventory Repurchase Requirements.**

Most of the states with actual Multi-Level Marketing laws require companies to repurchase inventory that is returned by their distributors. These states also require this policy to be stated in the distributor application (agreement).

In most cases, this buy-back requirement becomes effective only when the distributor terminates his or her distributorship. In other states, the company must repurchase any returned inventory simply if the distributor was unable to resell it within 90 days of buying it. (In both cases, there are some specifics. Usually, the buy-back is for 90 percent of the purchase price; the products must be resalable; and any commissions paid on the sold products may be deducted.)

Companies that comply with these three criteria are in line with both the letter and the spirit of the law.

Another option to beware of is the so-called Buyer's Clubs. These programs advertise "no selling required" and stress signing up everyone to buy wholesale. The FTC and attorneys general take a very dim view of such closed marketing systems, considering them pyramids. Here's why:

You can start a wholesale club, just like Sam Walton did, and it's perfectly legal. But take a wholesale club and put a multi-level commission structure on it, and it becomes illegal in most cases, because the product retailing option is simply not there. This system is only a closed club of wholesale buyers, and thus illegal. Since everyone is a member, there's no one to sell to.

But, probably the biggest fraud in networking is programs masquerading as legitimate companies by pushing substandard or overpriced products. Some of these are quite obvious, like the mail-order recipe and mailing list clubs. These are simply chain letters. Others, such as discount clubs, tout products or services that are of questionable value. Several of these types of companies got into trouble when regulators found that the discounts they were promoting were no more valuable than those available to anyone who simply shopped around, or were members of organizations like AAA and AARP.

The product or service must be a legitimate one that people would buy at the retail price on the open market. (If no one would likely buy the product or service without participating in the compensation plan — you are looking at a pyramid.) If you are counting on the lure of the business opportunity to so excite your prospect that he will not notice that he is overpaying for your product — you will be greatly disappointed. A strong retail base of happy customers (who are not distributors) is one of the best indicators of a strong company.

For now, you should know that a great number of people you offer the business to, who choose not to become business-builders, should elect to become customers. If you're not having this happen, it is a real danger signal. It means one of two things:

1. Your products are not a good value. People not receiving a check simply don't find them desirable at the price offered.

2. Your presentation is too wrapped around the business opportunity, and doesn't showcase the benefits of the products.

Look first at possibility two. Keep in mind the results your sponsorship line is getting. If they have a standardized presentation and they're not having any difficulty getting customers, then the problem is likely not with your products, but with the way you're presenting them. Work with your sponsor (role playing if necessary) to punch up the product portion of your presentation.

If, however, it seems that virtually no one in your company has retail customers, then the problem is probably caused by the first instance. The only solution to this is to find a different company. **There is no compensation plan and no amount of hype that can sustain a company long term with over-priced or substandard products**.

This doesn't mean your products must be cheaper than what's available elsewhere. But, they must be of an exceptional enough value that non-distributors still want them and are willing to pay for them. We'll look at this issue deeper in the chapter on selecting the right company.

This is not to say that your distributors won't be much better customers than non-distributors. They will. You will find that distributors have much higher volumes. They understand that anytime they buy a "Brand X" product, they are taking money out of their own pocket. Hence, they always make sure they have an adequate inventory, so they never run out of product. You'll also find they use the products more liberally, because they're better educated about them; they find it easy to order the products; and they appreciate the savings of buying wholesale.

There's another big factor that figures in here ...

Compliance. Especially if you're in a program with nutrition or weight management products. Because distributors have a vested financial interest in the results, they are much more likely to follow the proper use guidelines, exercise, and make any other necessary lifestyle changes. So distributors are much better customers.

There is one more area we need to address — the so-called "Gifting" clubs. They are having a renaissance as I'm writing this second edition. Their whole argument is that they do need products, because the participants in the program voluntarily give "gifts" of money to the sponsorship line. Gifting programs are nothing more than cheap imitations of illegal chain letters. Only idiots get involved with them.

> **Note:** Because I'm not an attorney, none of the preceding information is meant to be legal advice. Please consult with a lawyer for specific legal matters. What I've tried to do is give you a layman's understanding of the differences between legitimate MLM

and illegal pyramids and schemes. This should be quite sufficient to the average distributor.

For company executives, or those wishing to start a network marketing company, by all means you should seek out a law firm which specializes in the industry. I can strongly recommend **Grimes & Reese**, an Idaho firm that works extensively with Network Marketing. They were extremely helpful to me during the writing of this book, and the tables in this chapter came from their publication, *Legal Aspects of Multi-Level Marketing.* Reach them in Idaho Falls at **(208) 524-0699** or FAX them at **(208) 524-5686**.

There is one more thing you can do to protect yourself, whether you're a distributor or a company. Please get a subscription to the *mlm-metro.com newsletter.* It's a non-biased newsletter that focuses on training issues, and it also serves as the watchdog of the industry. They name names and expose companies that have legal actions pending against them, don't pay their distributors, or are outright scams. They accept no advertising, so they will tell you the truth. They issue Distributor Advisories to protect you when new scams pop up. They can be reached at **(316) 942-1111**.

They also run a website that serves as the hometown for network marketers all over the world. As a subscriber, you'll have access to the restricted areas of the site where new Distributor Advisories are continually posted. You'll find lots of other great stuff like chat rooms, forums, guest speakers, recruiting materials, online courses, and lots more. Check them out at www.mlm-metro.com. Once you think you've found a legitimate MLM company, it's time to move to Chapter Three, and see if you have what it takes to succeed in this amazing business!

CHAPTER THREE

YOUR PREREQUISITES FOR SUCCESS

NETWORK MARKETING HAS PRODUCED SOME OF THE MOST amazing success stories in America and around the world. Virtually every company has its "rags to riches" stories of everyday people who went from modest or even poor beginnings to earning more money in a month than most people bring down in a year. Those stories range from a farmer's wife in Utah, to an almost bankrupt minister in Texas, to a young man in Taiwan who rode his bicycle to opportunity meetings. These people, and thousands more earning outrageously delicious incomes, have their own unique stories to tell.

Yet, across the industry and around the globe — you will find striking similarities in the ultra-successful people in all companies. These common traits are the prerequisites for long-term success in the business. Network Marketing is perfect for everyone. Everyone, however, is not perfect for Network Marketing.

So, while I would certainly urge anyone who desires a better lifestyle to consider Network Marketing as a career choice — before you commit to this course, it would be wise to study the following prerequisites and see how you stack up. If you don't possess these attributes, then ask yourself if you are willing to develop them. Fortunately, there's nothing you need to do for networking success that you can't learn if you want it enough.

The four types of networkers ....

Your organization will contain four groups. The first of these is the **wholesale consumers**. Technically, they really should not be distributors since they don't retail product or sponsor others. But many people initially sign up as distributors, and then decide they don't want to do the work the business entails. They remain distributors, however, because they like the savings of buying wholesale. Others circumvent the system and simply join the program to get the wholesale price. They really have no need or desire for the business aspects of the program. This group might make up anywhere from five to ten percent of your distributors.

The next group is the **active consumers**. Like the first group, they have more of a product focus. However, unlike the first group, they understand the benefits of referral marketing. Chances are good they're telling their friends and family about the products with the hope of making enough overrides to cover the cost of their own products. It's likely that this group will make up about 30 to 40 percent of your network.

The third and largest group is what I like to call the **weekend warriors**. They're building a business part-time, usually evenings and weekends. While they may be entertaining visions of a six-figure income, more likely they are happy to earn an extra $500 to $5,000 a month. They will be involved in the sponsoring process, but not in a massive way. They use the products themselves and usually share them with their friends, neighbors and relatives. This part-time force may account for 35 to 45 percent of your network.

The fourth and smallest group is the **entrepreneurs,** or **power players**. Usually accounting for less than five percent of the distributor force, these are the people who bring in the five- and six-figure monthly incomes. They attain these income levels not by selling large quantities of the product personally, but by building huge organizations with thousands of distributors (who, of course, market massive quantities of products or services).

All four groups are necessary to a stable, secure company. The power players bring in the masses; the weekend warriors move the most products; and the consumers feed both groups. You can fit into Network Marketing on whatever level you desire. I'm assuming that because you're reading this book, you want to be one of those who are building a big business. If so, here are:

The prerequisites for success...

The first attribute you find in all successful long-term Networkers is <u>the ability to submerge their ego</u>. You might find this surprising. Most seem to be strong-willed individualists. They have reached levels of success the masses only dream of, and have done this as sculptors of their own destiny. They are in positions of leadership, and they influence the lives and careers of thousands of others. Yet, the networkers who attain success *and keep it,* have a healthy ego, but don't let it run amok.

At its very soul, Network Marketing is a business of duplication. *One in which what you can do, is subservient to what your people can duplicate.* "Lone rangers" never make it longterm. You must be willing to edify and duplicate your sponsor, who in turn must be willing to edify and duplicate their sponsor, and so on — letting the process continue to the person who must be willing to edify and duplicate the parent company. As you'll learn in Chapter Four, reinventing the wheel can be fatal to your business. A big part of the business is the ability to follow the successful patterns, strategies and systems developed by your sponsorship line. It means less personal glory, but more personal security, because your business is not so dependent upon you.

The second prerequisite is <u>the willingness to do business in a whole new way</u>. Network Marketing isn't about memos, cubicles, office politics or committee meetings. It's a radical, unique approach to doing business.

A large part of this new way to operate is empowering others. It's about going deep into their psyches — locating their innate abilities, talents and natural success programming — then nurturing them through the unfolding process of bringing these to light. Network Marketing is about the new business paradigm that believes success can only come from making others successful.

Most people equate security with a 9-to-5 job. They see the rat race as a necessary evil in life. Network marketers suffer from no such delusions. They see a 9-to-5 job as an insidious trap — one that gives you just enough income that you are afraid to forego it — yet not enough to achieve independence or security. They look at people clawing their way up the corporate structure with the detached wonder and amusement you would expect to see on the face of a ten-year-old child watching the workings of an ant farm. They know that we need ants in this world, and we need rats, but they don't choose to be one. Network marketing professionals know that life is meant to be an adventure, and they live it as one.

Most people strive to maintain the appearance of having a good job, even if it's one they despise, because that is what society expects of them. But networkers dream of a career of personal development and spiritual growth, and then work until that dream becomes a reality. Most people look at "real" jobs and the status quo, and just accept them as necessary evils, because "that's the way it is." Network marketers look at the rat race and wonder why people would forego human dignity in the pursuit of a buck.

Make no mistake. If you need someone checking over your shoulder, you can't seem to motivate yourself, or you desperately seek the security of a Friday paycheck, then Network Marketing is not for you. Network Marketing is for entrepreneurs. Business people, but business people with vision and a sense of adventure. If you're tired of memos, committee meetings and not being able to use your ideas, then you'll find this business to be a refreshing, rejuvenating tonic to your career.

The next talent you need is <u>the ability to keep your confidence and maintain your self-esteem in the face of peer pressure and challenges</u>. *Most of us have surrounded ourselves with people who give us permission to stay the way we are.* In fact, they actively encourage it. You're likely surrounded by negative people. You might even be married to one.

So when you proudly announce to the world that you have joined a network marketing company in search of a better lifestyle, the people around you are likely to assault you with all the reasons you shouldn't ... they wouldn't ... and you couldn't possibly succeed in such a venture. Then these "well-intentioned" souls will regale you with one horror story after another — stories of people who tried Network Marketing and failed, bought a garage full of products in the dream of instant riches, or contracted an almost fatal case of hives from using some MLM skincare product.

In my years of working with nutrition companies, I learned a very valuable insight. <u>Many people are not willing to be healthy</u>. Being sick is who they are. They believe it gives them love, attention, or a reason to be. Likewise, I have learned that <u>many more people are not willing to be wealthy</u>. They have been raised with "lack" consciousness. They subconsciously believe they are not deserving of riches; they mistakenly believe there is something spiritual about being poor; or they have discovered that becoming wealthy involves a degree of work.

It's highly likely that these kinds of people are all around you. And nothing is more threatening to these people than to think that someone they know is becoming successful. <u>They will do anything in their power to dissuade you, and in some cases, actually sabotage you</u>. These people subscribe to the Oscar Wilde theory:

it's just not enough to succeed — your friends must also fail. I could make quite a case for changing some of the people in your life, but that is another book entirely. As a beginning network marketer, you must remain steadfast in your convictions in the face of such negativity.

Another mandatory requirement for long-term success is <u>conducting your business with integrity</u>. Although there are many examples of people bringing down big-dollar incomes instantly by filling someone's warehouse with water filters (or diet cookies, or whatever), those incomes don't last. It's only a question of time before these people run out of prospects to front-load and must find a new program to work where they can start the process all over again. Likewise, it can be tempting to try to pirate away another distributor from a non-related line. The burden of negative energy you place on yourself far outweighs the limited economic gain you experience. Long term, these kinds of practices will ultimately destroy your business.

For reasons unknown to me, it has become fashionable to conduct business without integrity. Timeshare salespeople are taught how to pressure couples into buying units they can't afford; salespeople celebrate pulling a bait-and-switch on an unsuspecting customer; secretaries are taught to lie about whether or not their boss is actually in; and bookkeepers are trained to lie about the check being in the mail. We've spawned an entire cottage industry of trainers teaching neuro-linguistic programming techniques to others so they can coerce people, who really don't want their products, to think they want them. The Delta ticket agent will look you in the eye and maintain that your flight will probably leave on time ... even though it's ten minutes prior to departure and the incoming plane hasn't landed yet.

Television and movies present dishonest businesspeople as likable rogues — role models to be emulated. People brag about returning a dress to a store after they've worn it to a gala event, or scamming the insurance company by fixing an old dent in a new accident. A man's word used to be his bond. Now it means what he tells you is true — unless something better or more convenient comes along. If you accept this current lack of ethics, you will find Network Marketing quite frustrating.

In this business, when you sponsor someone, you are, in essence, his or her partner and mentor for life. Even after they learn the skills you teach them and become high-level executives, they will always look to you as a compass for the moral fiber, accountability and work habits of the organization. Much, much more than traditional business, Network Marketing revolves around the trust between the sponsor and his or her distributors.

Properly functioning, this is the strongest recruiting asset you possess. Millions of people are fed up with the dysfunctional relationships, gossip, office politics and lack of accountability in the corporate world. The honesty, accountability and sense of community in Network Marketing will attract them even more than the money, cars and trips. If you ever lie to your distributor — even thinking it's for his own good — you will destroy the bond that is the foundation of the business. You will also eliminate one of the most powerful enticements that attract people into the business. Distributors who have built lasting success have learned that their word must be their bond, and integrity is sacred.

Another important prerequisite for Network Marketing super-success is good teaching skills. Here's why. About ten percent of any group of people are sales types. They like to sell; they're good at it; and they don't fear rejection. About ninety percent of the population rank selling right up there on their list of things to do along with jumping into a pit of rattlesnakes. The mere thought of rejection sends them scurrying for the cover of their comfort zone. If you make cold calling, knocking on doors and assaulting strangers on street corners part of your recruiting strategy — you will scare away ninety percent of your prospects instantly. Why? Because they cannot see themselves doing those things.

In fact, only one person in a thousand will be successful with those types of approaches. Worse yet, because they are not duplicatable, they will have to keep sponsoring massive numbers on a monthly basis just to keep their income steady. All the "rah-rah" hype they can muster will not change this. They have no residual income security, and will have to rally and rebuild lines every few months.

By contrast, <u>successful network marketers concentrate on simple, duplicatable actions that they can teach to anyone</u>. Their number one priority is making sure that their organization knows everything they do. They do not knock on doors like encyclopedia salesmen, but rather become their own best customer. <u>They will develop retail or wholesale customers through default of the people who are not interested in building a business</u>.

While others will advocate the opposite — finding business-builders from the ranks of people whom you have been selling products to — I recommend against that. The reason, of course, is the group of ninety percent non-sales types. They won't want to do your business because it involves selling to strangers. *You'll find schoolteachers, professors, karate instructors, piano teachers, and anyone with good teaching skills usually excel at Network Marketing.* (We will look at this issue more deeply in later chapters.)

Another common trait among the successful is <u>a quest for lifelong learning</u>. They set aside daily time for quiet reflection and self-development. It's important that you continually sharpen your saw. Books, videos, cassette tapes or online seminars — the medium is not important. <u>What matters is that you dedicate yourself to always being a little better today than you were yesterday</u>.

Initially, my biggest mistake in the business was thinking that success would come from changing others. I soon learned that success comes from changing yourself. The actions you take and the examples you set create a ripple effect that impacts everything around you in a positive way. To change the world — you must first change yourself. I believe an integral part of the system you utilize should be a structured, ongoing, self-development program. More about this later.

Finally, the last important attribute to have is <u>a sincere desire to help others</u>. The rules of the corporate world don't apply in Network Marketing. In this business, you get ahead not by "beating out" other people or holding them down, but by helping them to grow. The more people you make successful, the more successful you become. A corporation has room for one president, a few vice presidents, more middle managers, and then many of the low-level jobs. In Network Marketing, you encourage everyone to reach for the higher levels of success. There is no limit to the number of people who can reach the top of your compensation plan.

If you approach the business with an attitude that focuses on what you are going to make off those you sponsor, they will receive those signals and you will face many challenges. Focus instead on how you can help others, and success will readily seek you out.

Let's summarize the prerequisites for your long-term Network Marketing success:

▲ **The willingness to submerge your ego**. Edify your sponsorship line.

▲ **An openness to doing business differently than the status quo**. Conventional wisdom is neither.

▲ **A strong self-confidence in the face of challenges and negative people**. Never let anyone steal your dream.

▲ **Integrity**. The patience to build a solid foundation and initially grow slower, but do the right thing and know that ultimately, greater rewards will be there for you and your people.

▲ **Good teaching skills**. Keep the business simple and duplicatable, so either a salestype or non-sales type can do it.

▲ **A commitment to lifelong learning**. The best teachers come from the best students.

▲ **A desire to help others**. Empower others and your success is assured.

Now that you know the prerequisites for success, and you already possess them or are willing to learn them — turn to the next chapter and discover how to choose the right company for you!

CHAPTER FOUR

CHOOSING THE RIGHT COMPANY FOR YOU

O NE OF THE MOST IMPORTANT DECISIONS YOU WILL MAKE IN your Network Marketing career — and possibly, your life, believe it or not — will be the company you choose to work with. Unfortunately, most people spend less time selecting a company than they do buying a new refrigerator. In fact, most let the company select <u>them</u>. In other words, they join the first opportunity that's presented to them. There are two schools of thought on this.

First, if you're presented an opportunity by someone you know and trust — and they'd like to sponsor you and are committed to work with you — there's a good deal of power in that. It's not necessary for you to go out and discover every other network marketing company in the industry and do a side-by-side comparison. You would spend two years on research — and about the time that you should begin receiving walkaway, residual income — you'd be just getting started.

However, the company you join does play a dramatic role in your chances for success. You need to do enough due diligence to select a good one. Let me give you two questions to ask first. This will simplify things for you a great deal. Any company that you don't get a positive answer to both of these questions, you can cross off your list.

Question 1: If you were not involved in the business opportunity, would you buy this product or service anyway?

Be honest with yourself. If the answer is no, find another company. If the opportunity you're involved with is not centered on products you believe in and will personally use — it is highly unlikely that you will be successful with this company. Network Marketing is driven by the enthusiasm and personal testimonials of the people involved. Two of the first questions your prospects will ask you are, "Do you use these products?" and, "Are they any good?" If you can't answer with a positive yes, then they are not likely to get involved. Now, if you can answer yes, you can move to...

Question 2: Would you buy that product or service <u>at that price</u>?

If you wouldn't pay the price for your products on the open market, it's unlikely anyone else will. Don't think people will pay more for a product simply because they might get a bonus check. It's been shown time and time again they won't.

Your success in MLM is based upon product getting to the end consumer, who actually uses it and wants more. People who buy products to get a check end up stockpiling them in their garage and will eventually stop buying when their garage is full or their credit card is maxed out. <u>People must want to use your product and be willing to pay the retail price for it</u>.

Don't be misled by hype and attempt to market an overpriced product. Like any industry, Network Marketing has a small segment of opportunists with no integrity. They're very good at fueling the hype machine, creating what appears to be legitimate excitement and momentum, but is actually a carefully orchestrated front.

For example, let's suppose they are promoting a company that sells a cup of coffee for $4. They made a sweetheart deal with the coffee company who gave them some extra money and other up-front goodies. Then they come to you with this

31

"hot" deal. You're skeptical. *"Four dollars for a cup of coffee,"* you say. *"Isn't that expensive?"*

"Are you crazy?" they reply. *"Everyone is buying this coffee. Look at my bonus check. I made $5,000 my first month! This month I'm going to make $8,000."*

Four dollars for a cup of coffee seems awfully steep to you. But $5,000 his first month? You begin to think that if all those other people are buying that coffee, it must be something special. You've just been seduced by the dark side of the force. The allure of fast cash clouded your judgement and you let greed overcome your common sense.

The next thing these opportunists do is convince you to buy in at a big dollar level. They convince you that you'll get a head start and *start as a director,* or *can be car-qualified in your first month,* and other such nonsense. So you buy $10,000 worth of coffee. You make $2,000 your first month and receive a $500 car allowance. Pretty cool, right?

But where did that $2,500 come from? From your $10,000. But you're not thinking about that. Because your sponsor just showed you his latest check and he's now up to $20,000 a month. Now, of course, what he neglected to mention is that he's making that kind of money because he gets suckers like you to buy $10,000 worth of cups of coffee (which are sitting in your garage ... and the coffee's getting cold)!

Now there are people all over town with $10,000 worth of cups of coffee cooling off in their garage, and they're feverishly working to get in new people ... so they can unload all of their cold coffee. More people join, the meetings get bigger and bigger (they take on a revival air), and the hype machine kicks into high gear ...

People keep paying the $4 for a cup of coffee, because they have dreams of getting a $5,000 bonus check their first month. Sooner or later, however, someone will say, "Are you nuts? Four bucks for a cup of coffee? I can get it at the diner for a buck."

Now the hype deflates like a punctured balloon. Attrition starts at the bottom and moves up, level...by level...by level. In the end, lots of people have $10,000 worth of coffee in their garage, which they're now desperately trying to sell at the flea market as iced coffee. What a rip-off, and what a tragedy. All of which could have been avoided if you had just asked yourself, "Would I pay $4 for a cup of coffee if I were not trying to qualify for a bonus check?"

Now, don't be mistaken. <u>This doesn't mean your MLM company must have products cheaper than what's available somewhere else</u>. **It means that they must be of such value that you and other people are willing to pay the price for them.**

In fact, many Network Marketing companies have products that cost much more than similar products available elsewhere. But due to their high quality, effectiveness or concentration — they are actually a better value to the consumer. Network Marketing companies have introduced a number of breakthrough products to the market. The conversational marketing nature of the business is perfect for higher-priced or new, not well known products that might not sell well on retail store shelves, but move quite well with a little education of the customer. Network Marketing has brought many specialty products to the market that are so unique, they require a story be told. Of course, the other tangible advantage is the personalized service and attention a customer receives from MLM distributors. Customers are willing to pay a little more for personalized service and convenience.

So don't ask, "Is this the cheapest product on the market?" But rather, "Would I buy this product if I were not trying to qualify for a check?" and, "Is it a fair value?" I believe if people would ask those two questions, they would eliminate 90 percent of the programs they look at, and prevent a lot of disappointment and frustration.

Now, we'll suppose you asked those two questions and found a product line that you like at a fair price. Let's look at the other product variables you should be considering as you evaluate a company.

Are they unique and exclusive? Ideally, you want products that are only available from your company, so your customers can only get them from you. If your products are available from retail stores or other outlets, you're likely to face more challenges, unless your price point is dramatically lower.

Are they consumable? I'm biased here, but I think consumable products (food, nutrition, skin care, etc.) work better long term than non-consumables, like water filters or jewelry. I know the industry is filled with nutrition, household products and personal care companies, but there's a reason for that. They work. If your people use up shampoo, laundry soap, or vitamins on a continuous basis (as most people do), you're likely to experience more frequent orders. This means higher volumes and bigger residual bonus checks for you.

What kind of monthly volumes are likely to be produced by the products you market? This is an important question, because a great deal of your volume is going to be produced by the personal consumption of your network participants. And, of course, the rest will come from the monthly consumption of their customers. The higher the monthly average is, the bigger your profit potential will be.

Suppose you're in a company with only one product, an energy drink that sells for $40, and the average person uses one bottle a month. With 100 distributors and customers in your organization, you would get paid on a volume of $4,000.

Now, suppose you're in a company with an energy drink, meal replacement bars, a multi-vitamin, antioxidants and fiber caplets. And the average monthly volume per family is $100. With the same 100 distributors and customers, you would be receiving override commissions on a volume of $10,000. All things being equal, you're going to make more money in a multiple products company. Of course, this means you would make more retail profits as well.

This doesn't mean you can't make money in a one-product company. If the product has a high-dollar monthly cost, or if people need to buy it a lot during a month, you'll produce and get paid on higher volumes. **But here's the bottom line. The higher the average monthly volume of product usage — the greater your profit potential**.

These product questions are the foremost considerations you should have as you choose a company. <u>Real long-term organizational growth is driven by product demand. The compensation plan, company leadership and other factors are all secondary to the product.</u>

There are opportunists and even some trainers out there who will tell you that the products don't matter. They insist that the compensation plan is what drives growth. This may be true initially (when the hype machine is in full swing), but you cannot sustain your business longterm if your products are not a value to the consumer. This is a lesson I learned personally ...

About 15 years ago, I was just starting to make some money in the industry. I attended a seminar put on by an author who had written a book on MLM. In a private conversation, he told me that the products were really irrelevant; it was the comp (compensation) plan that drove growth. Figuring he was the expert, I took his advice to heart.

At that time, I was working with a program that allowed you to buy gift certificates in lieu of a monthly product purchase. Since the monthly volume I needed to qualify was $100, I bought a gift certificate for that amount each month.

This was when I still smoked, and in the days when you could do so in public places without getting shot or arrested. So each month, at my biggest opportunity meeting, I would light a cigarette with a gift certificate and let the audience watch it burn up. What a showstopper!

I would explain that I had paid $100 for the gift certificate, and tell them how much my check was that month (which was a whole lot bigger than $100). I went on to say that as long as I bought $100 worth of stuff — even if I burned up a gift certificate or bought products and threw them in the river — I would get a check! I thought this logic was unassailable. It was. *Except for two slight problems.*

Number one, <u>it was illegal</u>. Any deal where people buy simply to qualify for a check is a pyramid, illegal in all states in the U.S., and most countries around the world.

And number two is the fact that <u>it completely diminishes the value of the products</u>. People view products simply as a means to get a fast paycheck, so they never even use them. They don't bond to them, and they're missing the emotional connection so critical to long-term success. **It is this emotional connection to your company's products that motivates people to grow, and also keeps them from jumping to the next "hot" deal that comes along.**

But I didn't know all this back in 1987. So I burned my gift certificates and preached the power of the profit incentive. And, of course, my front-line leaders duplicated me. Heck, even some of the non-smokers took up the habit so they too could burn certificates at their opportunity meetings!

Everything worked great for about five or six levels down. Because these people were all making, or about to make, more than their $100 monthly expense. The problems began on the lower levels, where people were not yet in profit ...

The end of the month came and went, but these people never placed an order. When the bonus checks came out, their surprised and frustrated sponsor would call them up, demanding to know why they hadn't ordered anything.

"'Cause I didn't have anyone under me," was the reply.

Well, of course, the next month those sponsors might not order, because the people under them might not be ordering, because they didn't have volume under them. Attrition started at the bottom and began to work its way up, level by level. This organization, which had taken me over a year of work to build, looked like it was going to self-destruct in a month or two.

It took a lot of frantic scrambling to stop the bleeding. I got back to personally using the products, and conducted product workshops and other activities to show the value of the products to the end consumer. I learned my lesson well. <u>The products matter</u>. They must be the driving catalyst for the company.

An interesting side note ...

I came to learn that the "expert" on MLM, by whom I had been so influenced, was actually just another opportunist with no regard for others. He used his books and seminars to raid other organizations of their people. He was actually in 20 or 30 companies at a time. He would roll all his people into a new company, taking himself to the top of the pay plan within a few months.

Meanwhile, all the other distributors in this new company would be wondering how he had accomplished this growth so fast. So they'd buy his books and tapes and go to his seminars, hoping to learn his secret. They would follow the methods taught in the materials, only to find that they didn't work. They were theories. The trainer himself never actually used these methods to build a group. He built his groups by raiding the organizations of others.

About the time the people in this new company discovered that his methods didn't work, our trainer was ready to move on to the next company. He would explain that the reason his methods weren't working was because the opportunity was flawed. But, fortunately — he had just discovered a better

37

one! So off he would go to another new deal, taking some of the people from the old one with him. And bringing his larger group to this new deal would shoot him up to the top of the pay plan once again ... and he would duplicate the entire process all over again. Believe it or not, there are actually so many startup companies always popping up and closing down that he's done this for more than 20 years. He's made millions selling books, tapes and seminars to unsuspecting souls.

There are a couple of lessons here. First, find a company that makes sense and stick with it. Never turn your ethics and reasoning ability over to anyone else. If something doesn't make sense to you, or seems unethical ... pass it up. The only free cheese is in the mousetrap. This doesn't mean you can't learn things from outside experts. It <u>does</u> mean you should discuss what you learn from them with your sponsorship line — because they have a vested interest in your success.

Okay, let's assume that all of the product issues are resolved. What are the other factors important in selecting the right company for you?

Begin with your sponsorship line. **Select them as you would any business partner.** They are going to be your coaches and your support structure, and you're going to be spending a lot of time with them in the years ahead. You'll be working very closely with them for the next two to four years. After that, hopefully, you'll be spending the next 20 to 30 years attending functions, retreats and getaways with them around the resorts of the world.

There is a pervasive belief that if you are a moral person, you are compelled to sign up under whoever sold you that first bottle of product, or first mentioned the name of the company to you. That makes as much sense as saying you are morally obligated to build your franchise on the first vacant property you see, even if it is out in the country. This is a serious business in which you need to make intelligent, well-informed choices.

It's important that your sponsor be someone you like, trust, and would enjoy working with. Don't think you must sponsor in with someone who's necessarily making a big check or is a "heavy hitter." The qualities above are much more important. In fact, in cases of rapid growth ... the best sponsor might be someone who's not yet making $300 a month! This is because in an organization that is "moving on" (the kind you want to be in), it's not unusual for it to go down four or five levels in depth in a single month. These new people don't yet have experience or big checks, but they have the drive, vision and enthusiasm necessary to build an organization. Find a sponsorship line with a system, one that's willing to teach you how to get started, train you on giving presentations, and excited to make your first presentations with you, and you've got a good one.

Let's look a little deeper at the issue of your sponsorship line having and using a system. Although the next chapter explores this issue in greater detail, it will be useful to understand a little about it now.

By a system, we mean the step-by-step process by which someone builds his or her business. This information should be specifically spelled out and available to everyone in the organization. It should explain what action to take and what materials to use at each step of the recruiting and sponsoring process.

This is important to you for two reasons:

First, it will greatly speed up the time it takes for you to build your group. By having a system which outlines exactly what to do — you won't spend time wondering what to do next, or waste valuable time pursuing strategies that don't work. Such a system includes only the methods and techniques that have proven themselves and stood the test of time.

The second reason a system is so important to you is it ensures that the people you introduce into the business will be able to duplicate your success. Their education level or their business experience ceases to be an issue. They simply follow the system exactly as you (and your sponsorship line) did.

If the company you're looking at has a system, but your potential sponsorship line doesn't follow it, then your group will forever be receiving mixed messages and growth will be difficult. If the company doesn't have a real system (and most don't), but the sponsorship line does, then you can achieve success fairly readily. The perfect situation is finding both a company and sponsorship line that follow the same duplicatable system.

Finally, after all these other factors are addressed, you can start to look at the specifics of the company. Conventional wisdom says that you should look for a seasoned company, one that's at least five years old and debt free. Let's look at that.

The truth is most new Network Marketing companies will go out of business within two years. Of course, it's also true that most new restaurants, dry cleaners and valet parking companies will go out of business within two years. That's the nature of business in the entrepreneurial system — 90 percent of start-ups fail. Network Marketing is no better and no worse. So, does that mean you should avoid startups? Maybe.

The odds that a start-up company will go out of business are greater than those of a ten-year-old established one. Yet, there is a certain allure to start-up companies, a chance to "get in on the ground floor," that attracts people. If the company has a founder's club, or similar program, then you could get in early and build lifetime financial security.

A company that's new and not yet known has a tremendous growth potential. You have the possibility of greater risk, but the corresponding opportunity for greater rewards. On the other hand, working with a household name like Amway or Shaklee gives you a certain amount of credibility to begin with, and you're likely to face less skepticism.

I've worked with an established company; I've ridden a relatively unknown company to success as it became established;

and, I've gotten in on the ground floor only to learn later that there was a basement! Which option is right for you depends a lot on your personality.

If you're not adverse to a certain degree of risk, you may enjoy the challenges of a start-up opportunity and the chance to cash in big time as you ride a new company to the top. If you're more conservative and looking for greater security, go with an established company. You'll face less risk and probably experience more stable growth. Choose the situation that best matches your personality.

Now, let's deal with this issue of being debt free:

Truth is, about the only companies that advertise this are start-ups with growth so slow that they don't need to be in debt. And half of them are lying. Just about every company that experiences rapid expansion will experience cash flow problems and need a line of credit to continue to grow. This is not just Network Marketing ... this is any industry. In fact, due to the exponential growth often experienced in this industry, you could argue the case that there's even more reason to have a line of credit in Network Marketing.

In the early 1990s, I was building a program that put in more than 25,000 new and <u>active</u> (meaning they had product volume) distributors and customers in one month. Two months later, we put in 40,000 new and active people in a month. And a short time later, 60,000 in one month.

The kinds of demands made on the parent company during exponential growth like this are mind-boggling. To expand phone lines fast enough, to find and hire enough employees, and to simply locate and lease office space fast enough are monumental challenges.

Now, figure what it takes to keep up with production in manufacturing products. Factories can't be built in two months. It can take a year to find the right site, draw up the plans and pull the permits. Realistically, you have to start planning a factory three to five years before you need it. Depending upon the breadth of the product line, machinery at the factory can cost tens of millions of dollars.

So imagine having to add 80 or more employees a month; pay for all the phones, office space, desks, computers, training, etc. that they require; <u>and</u> having to invest tens of millions of dollars more in a factory that you won't need for two years. This is the challenge Network Marketing companies face. The company that can finance this kind of growth out of cash flow is one in a million. You could actually argue that to do so would leave the company's assets too tied up to handle any unexpected challenges that arise.

I hate debt. I was burdened with it for too many years. Nowadays, I try to encourage my people to pay cash for everything, including their cars, and even pay off their mortgage. Yet, it still makes sense to keep a line of credit or some credit cards. While you may not use it, it makes sense to have the credit available.

Imagine the dilemma placed on a Network Marketing company in the heat of exponential growth. Being completely debt free might not be a good idea at all. I have seen this happen time and time again — companies grow so fast, they grow themselves out of business. Even as fast as they're growing, the money coming in is simply not sufficient to adequately finance the massive ramp-up in physical plant and operations that's necessary.

This does not mean the company shouldn't be properly capitalized. I believe the days when a successful network marketing company could be started in a basement or on a kitchen table are over. It takes at least $15 million in start-up capital to launch a company today, because the Internet makes the whole world a neighborhood marketplace. Even with this kind of start-up cash, it's likely that when the company hits "critical mass" and enters the exponential growth curve, it will need a line of credit or an infusion of more money to keep ahead of demand on production, personnel, manufacturing facilities and offices.

I might also mention that the reason a lot of companies are debt free is because they cannot get credit. A company with some debt and creditworthiness with a financial institution is a good sign. So all told, finding a company that's debt free is simply a non-issue. As far as the other things to look for from the company standpoint, here are what I think is important:

Management Depth.

If the entire corporate staff consists of five people, the company will be hard pressed to give any meaningful type of distributor support. A credible company should have a president and CEO (which may be the same person), a chief financial officer, a chief operations officer, an administrative manager, a distribution center manager, a data processing chief, a customer service manager, and a marketing vice president or manager.

Some of these positions, even in a brand new, start-up company, will require assistants and line employees. There may be nothing for them to do when the company first opens. But the whole point in business is having the resources you need before you need them.

I especially look at what kind of marketing staff a company has. Do they have a marketing VP or national marketing manager? Do they have corporate trainers who travel around to the functions and conduct training? Is there a support staff to back up these people?

It's important to know if anyone on the corporate management staff has any successful Network Marketing experience. Networking is dramatically different from traditional business, even direct sales. If a management team doesn't understand the unique nature of Network Marketing, it will be quite difficult for them to guide the company. When I consult with companies, this is the biggest issue they face. They have a management

43

team with corporate experience, who try to force selling techniques in a network marketing culture.

COMPENSATION PLAN.

While there are numerous types of plans, there are four major types of compensation plans in use today:

1. Stairstep-Breakaway
2. Matrix
3. Unilevel
4. Binary

Let's look at them in turn:

The **Stairstep-Breakaway** is actually a combination of two plans: the Stairstep Plan (which is used to pay you on the volume of your personal group) and the Breakaway plan (which pays you for the people who "break away" and head organizations of their own).

See Illustration One and Two:

ILLUSTRATION ONE

Director				20% Rebate
Manager			15% Rebate	5% Override
Supervisor		10% Rebate	5% Override	10% Override
Trainer	5% Rebate	5% Override	10% Override	15% Override

Sample of how a Stairstep plan is structured. Participants receive an override based on the difference in their own rank and the rank of those they sponsor.

ILLUSTRATION TWO

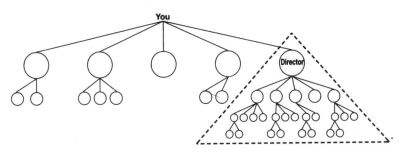

In a Breakaway plan, once someone reaches a certain rank (often called Director) – they "breakaway" from your personal group. You then receive an override on the volume produced by their entire group.

This type of plan received a lot of criticism in the nineties for a variety of reasons. Primarily, you will hear people disparaging the plan because a small distributor sponsored someone who then broke away and built a massive organization. As a result, the small distributor did not have a large enough group left over to qualify for overrides on the distributor who had broken away.

In reality, this is the way the plan must be structured. To access depth, distributors must be required to build width — the wider you go, the deeper you access. This provides you with both income and security, and gives everyone an incentive to keep building. With a well-designed plan, leaders can stop at any time to receive the residual income they've already earned ... but there should be continuing incentives so they realize they will be leaving a lot of money on the table if they don't build wider. This should be true for each rank of leadership right up to the top one.

Like any plan, however, there can be good variations and bad ones. Some of the bad comments about Breakaways stem from bad constructions ... usually, they are what I call "top heavy" plans.

Examples might be plans for companies that have only one or two products, but have a high dollar level (like ten or fifteen thousand dollars a month) that someone must maintain to receive overrides on the directors that break away. Due to the lower average volumes that they actually achieve, 99 percent of the distributors will never consistently qualify. So the overrides they would normally receive roll up to a few "poster boys" and "poster girls," or are considered "breakage," and the money washes up to the company.

This can produce high six-figure monthly incomes for these poster boys and poster girls at the top of the plan. But for each of these big earners, there are tens of thousands of distributors not making a monthly check big enough to take their families to the movies. These big distributors can wave their mega checks around to hype growth initially, but ultimately most distributors will move on once they discover that they are not likely to earn any serious money. They will leave with a bad taste in their mouth and believe that MLM doesn't work.

On the other hand, "bottom heavy" plans will not work long term either. These are plans where virtually anyone who joins can get up to $1,000 in monthly income right away. They are designed in a way that OVER rewards new people, with the hope that this will attract distributors from other companies to jump ship and come to the new company. This excites people initially, but in the long term, the top leaders cannot make the incomes they deserve. You only have a finite amount of money to pay out. If you're overpaying the people on the bottom, it's coming out of the pockets of the people at the top. They look at other plans and realize that with the exact same volume and same organization ... they would make a lot more money in another company. This creates a leadership drain that ultimately prevents a company from succeeding.

To really balance a plan is a science. Yo
ning distributor to be able to start earning pr
possible, yet have the plan allow leaders tc
keep, big-dollar incomes. Depth should be p
to width. Breakaway levels must be carefully (
upon the number of products the company
realistic average volume should be. A small distributor who
mainly retails may not always break away, yet, breakaway
qualifications must be achievable with a fair amount of effort
by a serious business-builder.

If this plan is properly constructed, it will contain all of
the necessary elements to promote growth and pay people in
proportion to the work they've actually done. However, it is
vitally important that it be constructed in a balanced manner
and that safeguards be in place to prevent "buy-ins" or front-
loading at expensive levels.

Now, let's look at the other types of plans.

A plan that gained prominence in the 1980s is the **Matrix**.
This plan actually limits your group to a specific configuration.
For example, a 3 x 3 Matrix means that you (and everyone in
the company) can sponsor only three people on your front level
(the first three), and you will get paid on the volume produced
by three levels of distributors (the second three). So, in this
example, you would have three people on your first level, nine
people on your second level, and 27 people on your third level.
You would earn commissions on the volume produced by these
39 people only. Anyone from the fourth level on would be out
of your pay range.

A 3 x 5 Matrix means that everyone can have three
people on their frontline level, and get paid through five levels. A 5 x 7 Matrix would mean five on your front level, and
you would get paid through seven levels. See the Matrix in
Illustration Three:

ILLUSTRATION THREE

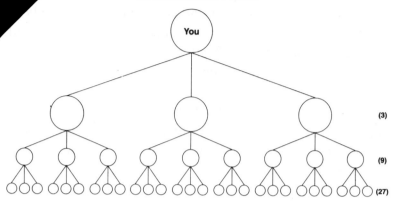

Here's an example of a 3x3 Matrix. Each participant can only sponsor three people on their first level and receives overrides for three levels of distributors. Anyone from the forth level on would be out of the pay range

One problem with this type of plan is that it limits the number of people you can put on your front line. Once the front line is filled — you end up putting new recruits on the lower levels. This can be a problem if you place someone too far down, as it can cost you thousands of dollars a month in income if that person really takes off.

This was one of the factors that caused this plan to run into regulatory troubles in years past. People were just placed in the Matrix by the computer, relative to the order they came in. The authorities viewed this as a lottery and went after companies with Matrix plans. Nowadays, Matrix companies allow a distributor to determine where each new distributor is placed, so this is no longer a problem.

Even though you now determine where to place your new enrollees — if your first levels are full, you'll be forced to place them on the lower levels. This leads to another challenge you can have with Matrix plans — the welfare mentality that is sometimes created.

Here's what I mean. Because you can only put a finite number of people on your first level, it stands to reason that top producers will sponsor extra people, who must be placed on the lower levels. The problem comes when others advertise this fact as a recruiting tool. Prospects are encouraged to join early so they get the results of "spillover." They're told, *"Just sign up and we'll build your group for you."* This attracts a lot of un-motivated people who sit idly by, clogging up the Matrix, wondering when someone above them will spill over enough people into their organization to make them rich. Unlike a Breakaway, where you can just open another line, if you end up with one of these do-nothing distributors on your first level, it can dramatically hurt your earnings.

So, if you join a Matrix plan, don't encourage this hype about spillover. You'll do better longterm if you just present the rewards to be earned from working hard. The other issue with Matrix plans is they blur the sponsorship lines. You might have to put someone you personally sponsor on your fourth level. This can create problems when it comes time to do your monthly counseling, which we'll talk about in a later chapter.

Most companies that begin with a Matrix graduate to an-other plan after a few years. It's also worth noting that at the time of this writing, there is only one company in the world over five years old and doing at least $300 million a year using a Matrix. And it is a modified Matrix. Once you develop a cer-tain number of leaders in your group — you are allowed to expand the Matrix and open more frontline positions. So, real-istically, it is a Matrix in the beginning stages, which then later incorporates aspects of a Breakaway.

Now, let's look at the next type of plan, the **Unilevel**.

Unilevel translated means "one level." Which is exactly what a Unilevel is not. Most companies that use a Unilevel type plan actually pay from five to nine levels. In this plan, there are no breakaways. You can go as wide as you want, but you only get paid on a fixed number of levels. It may help you to think of it as an "infinity times a certain depth" Matrix. For example, in a plan that pays five levels deep, you could think of it as an infinity x 5 Matrix. See Illustration Four:

ILLUSTRATION FOUR

YOUR RANK	Commissions you're paid on each level				
	1st	2nd	3rd	4th	5th
Trainer	5%	10%			
Supervisor	5%	10%	10%		
Manager	5%	10%	10%	10%	
Director	5%	10%	10%	10%	10%

A Unilevel plan has no Breakaways. You can sponsor as many people on your front level as you like and you receive a fixed percentage based upon what level people are on.

The issue you want to watch out for here is that most of your leaders will come from depth. Some Unilevel plans, like Matrix plans, offer no compression. If you have four levels of distributors doing exactly the minimum volume necessary to qualify — and a Diamond Director on your fifth level — it's conceivable that you could earn no more than two or three hundred dollars in monthly overrides on that line.

Here's what happens in reality. If you're a leader, you're working directly with that Diamond on the fifth level. The four levels in the middle are probably basically consumers, or people who thought they were going to build a business, but found it was too much work. They would quit, but they have so much easy money coming from the Diamond beneath them that they stay. They're not getting rich — but they make more than their product costs, so they stay active, doing the minimum to stay qualified each month. This keeps any meaningful volume from compressing up to the leaders. These leaders can get frustrated at the low paydays and move on to another opportunity. You can protect yourself from this by making sure your plan pays on more levels, or has some kind of compression built in.

Just as with Breakaway plans, you must watch against "bottom heavy" Unilevel plans. These are sometimes offered by start-up companies trying to attract distributors from other companies with promises like "no Breakaways" and "you'll never lose your group." Beginning distributors like them because they can get into profit quickly. They will quickly become disenchanted, however, when their organization starts to grow. Make sure the plan you work is balanced to get new people some money, but not at the risk of losing your leaders.

Let's look at our last plan, the **Binary** ...

This is another offshoot of the Matrix plan. Think of it as a "two by infinity" Matrix. You can sponsor only two positions on your front level, as can everyone else. Thus, you can have two positions on your first level, four on your second, eight on your third, 16 on your fourth, and so on.

There are three unique features of Binaries. First is the fact that you don't really sponsor people. You sponsor positions, or "income centers," as they are sometimes called. Income centers are determined by volume. For example, if an income center equals $250 in volume, someone entering the organization with $750 in volume would actually take three income centers. So, if you sponsor Mary, who has this $750 in volume we just discussed, she would actually be your first-level position, and two of your four second-level positions.

The second unique feature of Binaries is that the sponsor can reenter his or her own organization. So, in our previous example, if you had $500 in volume, you could reenter with one more position under Mary.

So your organization would look like Illustration Five:

ILLUSTRATION FIVE

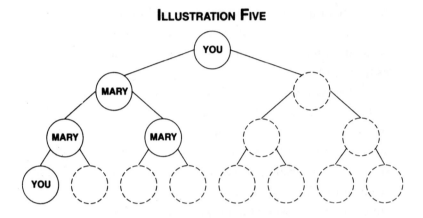

Which leads us to the third unique feature of many Binary plans. You only get paid on the volume that is equal between your two lines. So, in the example we just mentioned, although you have $1,000 in volume in your left line — you have no volume in your right line — so you wouldn't get a check. Obviously, like the other plans, there are a lot of nuances, but you get the main idea.

The Binary plan offers many opportunities for abuse that, of course, leads to many regulatory problems. I believe the basic problem is the income center system. By its very nature, it's ripe for abuse. In some cases, people are encouraged to purchase $5,000 or $10,000 worth of income centers to instantly qualify for the higher ranks, commissions or car bonuses. This is just another variation of the front-loading that was practiced by unscrupulous Breakaway companies in years past. Much like a Ponzi scheme, this plays on the prospect's greed, which impairs his better judgment, and, in all the hype and hoopla, he does something stupid. Also, sometimes a distributor may spend big dollars buying income centers to equalize the volume with a stronger line. In either case, once new distributors start investing large amounts of money, you raise business opportunity issues and a whole new set of problems.

Like the Breakaway plan, the Binary plans can be designed as top heavy plans to reward the company and a few top distributorships. Because most Binaries pay weekly and any volume that is not matched in your other line is "washed" (meaning you don't get paid on it), this can produce a rich company, a few rich distributors, and a lot of little people who don't make a dime, (and then have a tainted view of Network Marketing).

The plan is perfect for hype, because you can immediately purchase many income centers and get a big check your first week. Of course, most of that check is from your own money, but your prospects don't know that. Big distributors can claim that they have 50,000 people in their group in only six months. In actuality, they may only have 3,000 or 4,000, many or all of whom keep reentering the organization. And, because people can reenter the organization, this can make counseling and managing the network more difficult. It inherently leads to cross-lining, which is bad for business.

Much has been done in the last couple of years to improve the Binary. There are several companies that have done some modifications to greatly improve the Binary, and ensure that abuses don't occur. Probably the two most important modifications are one that prevents extra volume from being "washed" at the end of the week, and safeguards that prohibit distributors from buying in at large dollar levels. So if you are looking at a Binary plan, make sure that it has those two factors covered.

Another trend I'm seeing today with compensation plans is a lot more hybrid plans, which combine elements from several (or all) of these plans. By combining plans, companies are able to eliminate some of the abuse potential of individual plans, and create a fair and balanced income opportunity for distributors.

To sum up this section, I think it's important that you know the ins and outs of the compensation plan you're considering, so you can act accordingly. No matter which plan you choose, the ultimate qualification for your success will be the effort you put into your business. Don't lose sight of that.

Now, let's look at some other considerations you should take into account when choosing a company.

SUPPORT STRUCTURE.

What kind of support structure is in place? Does the company you're considering put out a monthly newsletter? Does the newsletter list achievements, feature products and have business- building information? Or is it simply a collection of miracle cure product testimonials that are likely to get the company closed down by regulators? Is there an annual convention, special pin-rank distributor training, and other events hosted by the company?

Does it have a voicemail system, demand conference, or regularly scheduled conference calls? Are the materials professionally prepared, benefit-driven, and effective from a marketing standpoint? This is where I see most companies fall down. And I do mean most companies, not just the start-up ones. There are two major problems, which I see repeated time and time again.

PROBLEM NUMBER 1:

All of the company materials are completely devoted to the products — and the business opportunity is either not mentioned, or mentioned as an afterthought. You see this a lot, because most Network Marketing company managers don't understand the true nature of the business. They don't comprehend the concept of duplication (though I have yet to meet one who will admit this), and they think it's a sales business. As a result, they keep producing pretty product brochures, videos and audios, and exhorting their distributor force with silly platitudes like, *these products just sell themselves,* and other such nonsense. There's nothing to tell the prospect how the business works, how money is made, or even what the business is. The next time someone tells you, "These products just sell themselves," you might reply, "Well, in that case, you won't be needing me!"

PROBLEM NUMBER 2:

All of the marketing materials are feature-driven, not benefit-driven. Here's what I mean by that. Anything about your company, products or comp plan is a <u>feature</u>. Anything about the prospect is a <u>benefit</u>. Prospects are motivated to action by benefits. Yet, interestingly enough, in 90 percent of the marketing materials I see — you couldn't find a benefit in them with a search party.

Look at the materials of the company you're considering. Is the first thing you see the company logo? A picture of the founder? Pictures of the building? Are they filled with inane blather about how great they are, how old they are, where their officers went to school, and where they travel to get ingredients for the products? These things are all features and mean nothing to your prospects.

Does the company video show the machines that make capsules, the machines that put capsules into bottles, the machines that cap the bottles, the machine that boxes the bottles, the machine...? Well, you get the idea. These things are all features, also. Marketing materials, in order to be effective, must be about the prospect. This means benefit-driven, not feature-driven.

If your brochure says, "We're an established, eleven-year-old company..." that's a feature. If it says, "Your future is secure, because we're an established, eleven-year-old company," now, we're getting into benefits.

If your materials claim, *"We have an automobile fund ..."* that's a feature. If they say, *"When you reach the Gold Director rank, you'll get a new car for free ..."* that's a benefit.

> **NOTE:** For more information on this topic, review my audiotape albums, *How to Earn at Least $100,000 a Year in Network Marketing* and *Confessions of a Marketing Genius.*

I simply cannot understand why so many companies make one or both of these mistakes, but most do. The effectiveness of the marketing materials you have to work with will dramatically impact your success, so evaluate them carefully.

The final factor to consider when choosing a company is:

Accountability of the Company.

If a company does not ship product in a timely manner — and pay commissions on time every month — my advice is to move on. My experience is that if a company does not have the capital and resources to pay bills and stock product early on — then it will only get worse as the company gets bigger.

Even the best companies experience problems with inventory keeping up with demand from time to time. While no one enjoys problems, this is the kind you like to have. If a company is generally well run and ships out *the vast majority of its orders* on time, an occasional miscue should be overlooked. But, a company consistently not shipping in a timely manner or paying its bills or commission checks is a sure sign of trouble.

Final Thoughts on Selecting a Company:

You'll notice in every case, I used the singular version — not plural. <u>I don't believe anyone can build two programs</u>

simultaneously. This is a big issue with MLM "junkies." They're in so many crazy deals all the time that one or more of them is in the process of going bust. They use this as evidence that they should be in yet more deals — to diversify and protect their income. And, they offer all sorts of convoluted logic to support this position.

"Company A has nutrition products — Company B has household cleaners, so they don't compete with each other. You need to use the phone for both of them, so Company C — a long distance program — is the perfect complementary program. And Company D offers a free car program — which is perfect — because Company E has car polish!"

Even having two companies with which the products do not compete — the business opportunity does.

A Shell service station franchisee wouldn't open an Exxon station across the street. It would be foolish. Why compete with yourself? Although there appear to be people building multiple programs successfully — a closer look shows otherwise.

One example is our aforementioned industry expert and trainer. Although he's in several dozen programs at a time — this won't duplicate for you for several reasons.

First is because those programs are not his primary source of income. They're just the gravy that comes after selling training materials and seminars. And, second, you don't have those training materials and seminars to recruit with like he does. And, finally, he forever has to look for the next "hot" deal every six months to a year. What you're looking for is walkaway residual income security.

Now you can find people who get income from more than one program. But my experience is that if it is substantial income – it was produced working only one program at a time. In other words, they built up one program and retired. Later, they joined another company and built a new network, never touching their people in the first organization. If you want to build a vacation home — it doesn't make sense to use the boards from your existing house.

Working more than one program can look tempting. Discounts on all those products. All those different bonus checks coming in. All those different cars, trips and awards you're going to win ...

But, in actuality, those things don't happen. Each company's system contradicts the other's. There are so many materials to buy, functions to attend and training systems to learn that your distributors become so confused, they're paralyzed into inactivity.

Here's the reality. I tried building more than one program simultaneously, as have some of the finest minds in Network Marketing. But, we all failed. In fact, if you discard people who roll over their existing organization into another company — I know of no person who has ever built two successful programs at the same time in the 50-plus-year history of Network Marketing.

My advice: take the time necessary to select the right program for you — then give it everything you've got, exclusively.

CHAPTER FIVE

A SYSTEM FOR YOUR SUCCESS

IN THE 1970S, FRANCHISING REVOLUTIONIZED THE BUSINESS WORLD. The concept, which was quite controversial at the time, was that the parent company (franchiser) would design a complete business plan, including site selection, operating procedures, purchasing requirements and employee training. The parent company offered this expertise and complete system for an up-front investment and some kind of royalty on sales.

The person who licensed the business (franchisee) would give up a percentage of his or her profits, but dramatically increase their chances of business success. These were "turnkey" operations. In other words, you turn the key, and you would be open for business. There were step-by-step procedures to follow for each facet of the business, from the simplest detail (what brand of straws to use) to the most complex (how to lay out the kitchen equipment for maximum productivity).

McDonald's, of course, is the consummate example of that. Go to any store, anywhere, at 7 o'clock in the evening, and you're likely to find it being run by a 19- or 20-year-old who just recently graduated from teenage acne. It's also possible that this 19-year-old has a mother who won't let him borrow her Volvo, because she doesn't trust him with it. Yet, this same 19-year old is successfully running an operation that does in excess of $3 million a year in sales. What's the secret?

A system.

One of the most complete, specific and tested systems ever developed. A system that can turn any 15-year-old into an effective, efficient and productive employee. One to three items go in this bag; four to six items go in the next size bag; here are the napkins you use; here's where you get them from; here's what day of the week you order them; and here's when they'll be delivered.

You see the same thing in the military. Eighteen-year-old kids are flying fighter jets that cost more than the gross national product of developing countries. But there's a pre-flight checklist, an in-flight checklist, a post-flight checklist, and probably a checklist just for the checklists.

Having this kind of system to follow created a quantum leap in the success ratios of start-up businesses. Today, as then, franchises have a dramatically higher level of success than independent businesses.

In the 1970s, a former beer truck driver from North Carolina was to revolutionize the network marketing industry the same way. This occurred when that driver, a fellow named **Dexter Yaeger** joined the Amway Corporation. Although Amway had been established for many years, it was basically a collection of small-time retailers, many selling soap door-to-door. Yaeger had a vision for the possibilities of building an organization.

At the time he joined, the Amway Corporation had no real system for organizational growth. Its system was exclusively devoted to retailing. Dexter's survival instincts and business savvy led him and his wife Birdie to develop a duplicatable system for their organization to replicate. Yaeger set out to construct his system, and the rest is history. Last year, his organization, which numbers in the hundreds of thousands worldwide, produced retail sales in the neighborhood of several billion dollars.

Other Amway distributors, most notably **Bill** and **Peggy Britt,** and **Ron** and **Georgia Lee Puryear,** have created similar environments for their distributors. These distributorships are a prime example of the power of creating a duplicatable system and reaping lifetime residual income. Find an organization with a complete, duplicatable system to follow, and a lot of work is already done for you.

Now, let's look specifically at what a system is, and why it's so important to you ...

A system should completely delineate and spell out the entire process that a distributor will follow: from where to find prospects, how to approach them, how to sponsor them, and how to train them to reach the higher pin ranks. (For the sake of simplicity and your understanding — I'll use the term "pin ranks" throughout the rest of this book. This term refers to people who reach the top levels of your compensation plan, whether they're called Diamond Directors, National Vice Presidents or Master Coordinators. The name comes from the fact that distributors receive a pin upon achieving these ranks.) Each stage in this process should be clearly defined and taught to the distributor at the appropriate time.

> **NOTE:** What you get throughout the rest of this book is my generic system. If you find discrepancies between what I teach and what you're currently doing — check with your sponsorship line before making any changes.

Here's a breakdown of the steps that might be included in a system. This is not meant to be the be-all, end-all. In fact, your system may be quite different. I offer this example so you can see the kind of structure I'm talking about.

Step One — The Pre-Approach

This is the qualification step — the one that determines whether you have a suspect or an actual prospect. This can be done simply with qualifying questions, or qualifying questions combined with a pre-approach packet. This packet would include materials designed to screen out people who are not good candidates for the business. (We'll look at this in more depth in the following chapters.) Pre-approach means *before the approach*. In other words, this step will determine whether or not you would approach them about the opportunity at all.

Another way to do this is with a brief mini-presentation. This is a quick overview, usually about 30 minutes or less, to see if your candidate is a serious prospect. This is usually done one-on-one in a non-threatening environment (example: in the prospect's kitchen or at a coffee shop). When you first begin, you should do this as a two-on-one, which means you and your sponsor together presenting to your prospect. This can also be done in a small group meeting in your living room.

In either case, the interested prospects would be given a specific set of materials to study, which is usually called a take-home packet. This packet would have a breakdown of how money is made in the business, along with some supporting materials on the products, usually a brochure or catalog.

Step Two — The Presentation

This is where the prospect takes a second look at the presentation, which is usually at a larger home or hotel meeting, but it can also be done one-on-one. Like all steps, there should be a clearly defined set of specific materials (the *Follow-up Packet*), which should be given to the prospect. This is usually more detailed information than the previous packet.

STEP THREE — THE FOLLOW-UP

This step might involve getting the prospect to another, bigger presentation (like a large hotel open meeting), or simply bringing one more packet of information to the prospect and encouraging them to make a decision. Check with your sponsorship line. In either event, the packet of information and the procedures followed should be exactly the same for every distributor on every level.

STEP FOUR — THE ENROLLMENT PROCESS

This is the step that takes place after the prospect says "yes," and is ready to become a distributor.

> **NOTE:** This can happen at step two, or step three. Each prospect comes in at his or her own speed. It's important that even if a prospect is ready to join at step two (that's great!), you can still expose them to the information in step three to preserve the integrity of the system.

Like our other steps, the enrollment process should be completely spelled out, step-by-step. The training that you receive should be the same, exact training that someone on your 25th level, five states away, will receive when joining your organization.

These four steps are the foundation of your system. No matter which program you're in, it should generally parallel this process. Again, though, check with your sponsorship line for specifics. The later steps of the system will vary more greatly from program to program. They involve managing organizational growth and developing leadership skills. We'll explore them in more depth in the *Building Depth* and *Leadership Strategies* chapters. We'll also flesh out the specifics of these first four stages, and I'll show you the rest of my generic system in greater detail in the following chapters.

Overall, however, visualize a system as a complete, step-by-step process that anyone who joins your organization — whether they're a doctor or waitress, Ph.D. or high school dropout — can duplicate. It means you should be able to fly to a city 3,000 miles away — work with someone on your 50th level that you've never met — and be teaching the same principles and specifics they've been hearing from the person who's on your 49th level.

Why is this so important?

Two reasons. One, for your benefit. Two, for your organization's benefit. Let me explain.

The reason a system is so important for you is that it ensures walkaway residual income. When you have a system in place — you no longer remain essential to the process. Even if you disappear, the system keeps perpetuating itself.

Most people, even the successful ones in Network Marketing, don't have a system. It's because they built a network based upon their sales talents, or because they give great meetings, or simply through the sheer strength of their personality. They mail 20 cards a day; they call all of their key people five times a day; they hold "rah-rah" rallies all the time; or they're 24-hour-a-day sponsoring machines. I know of a person who prospects 30 people a day. These kinds of people sponsor dozens and dozens of distributors a year — which they need to do to replace the dozens and dozens who drop out. They walk across the stage at their company conventions; they make lots of money; they live in nice houses; and, they drive nice cars. But they certainly aren't living the lifestyle of freedom and controlling their own destiny. They've traded enslavement to a boss for enslavement to a business.

What these people do works. It just doesn't duplicate. They work hard and mean well, but <u>the average person cannot duplicate what they are doing to build their businesses</u>. Now, granted, they're probably making a lot more money in their networking enslavement than they were making in their job — but they're still enslaved. More importantly, they can't show other people how to escape the rat race, because they're still trapped in it.

With a complete duplicatable system, anyone — sales type or non-sales type, shy or outgoing — can do the business. The most important axiom in the business to remember is this: it's not, "Does it work?" But, "Does it duplicate?"

Let me give you an example. Let's suppose you took an ad during the Super Bowl to sign up new distributors. You could sign up 10,000 distributors in one night. But, how many of them would have the two million dollars it takes to run a commercial during the Super Bowl? Maybe one or two of them. And you know what they would do between now and the next Super Bowl? Nothing. <u>How you bring in your people is how they will bring in their people</u>. So this scenario *works*. It signs up 10,000 people. But it doesn't *duplicate*.

Having a duplicatable system protects your people — from themselves. Here's what I mean. Suppose you're in Shaklee and you sponsor a chiropractor. He thinks, *These are great nutritional products. They will help all my patients. I'll sell them in my practice.*

That works. But it doesn't duplicate. What you find in this scenario is that our doctor will retail a lot of product. But, it's likely that he won't duplicate down three levels. Here's why:

Even though he may talk to people about the business, 99 percent of them will never get involved. On a subconscious level, even if the business sounds enticing — they'll be thinking that to do this business, they'll first need to become a chiropractor and have 30 to 40 patients a day to prescribe products to.

Likewise, the same is true of the dentist who joins Oxyfresh and markets the dental care products in his practice. Or the radio talk show host who joins a program and promotes it on her show. Or the personal trainer who joins USANA and sells the products in his gym.

These things work, but they don't duplicate very well. If these people worked a system (asking a qualifying question, giving a pre-approach packet, giving a presentation, etc.), they would more likely bring in more distributors and duplicate better. So, you see, a system is not just for your own benefit — but it helps all of your people, as well.

Let me give you one more example.

Ten percent of the population are sales types. They love to sell; they know how to sell; and they love to hear *no*. They know that after a certain number of *nos* — they're going to get a *yes*. Sales types have no compunction about cold calling complete strangers to present them the business ...

Some of whom will sign up due to our sales type's savvy sales techniques. And, of course, of these people he signs up ... 90 percent of them will be non-sales types, who wouldn't make a cold call to a stranger to save their life. So, they join, do nothing, and eventually drop out.

Sales talents, techniques and methods are great — for sales. But remember that Network Marketing is really not so much a sales business as it is a business of teaching and training — a business of duplication. Using sales techniques — which work great on the used car lot — will often backfire in Network Marketing.

When sales types join your program, and you have a system for them to follow — it actually prevents their sales skills from working against them. You and your people have greater security if you follow a system, and a lot better shot at walkaway residual income.

Let's go back to our example of the successful network marketer who doesn't follow a system. They're succeeding based on their dogged determination, sales skills and personal strength. They make a lot of money, and they look successful to their group.

But, if they took a month off — their income would immediately drop. If they took two months off — their check would be down 30 percent. If they took off three or four months — they wouldn't have a business to come back to. When you build with a system, once you secure a line, you can walk away and it will continue to grow. You set the system in motion, and once it's in motion, it goes on without you. It's the consummate example of using the leveraging power of Network Marketing.

Here's the important thing to understand about a system. Unless you're the head of the organization that creates it — you must follow it religiously and never change it. Here's why: Let's suppose that you don't particularly care for the tape used in your company's take-home packet. You know of another tape that you think is perfect. So, you switch. Now, your front level people see this. And, they learn that it's okay to change things in the system.

Now, they don't particularly like the brochure used in the follow-up packet. So, they swap it for one they like. Now, for the person on your third level — there is no system. The message they got was, "choose the materials you like and design your own system."

This creates two major problems:

1) You cannot go down and work in depth in your organization, because what you're teaching will contradict what they've learned from their sponsor; and,

2) Prospects are much less likely to join your organization, because one of the primary benefits — a step-by-step system to follow and an entire sponsorship line to teach it to them — is no longer there.

Following the system set up by your sponsorship line can offer you a lot of benefits and save you a great deal of work. Your sponsorship line is where you want to be, and they want to help you get there. If you don't follow the system — they can't effectively help you. One of the secrets to network marketing success is learning how to edify your sponsorship line and put them to work for you. If you don't follow the system, you're effectively tying their hands. They can't come down and train in your organization without contradicting you...which is a lose-lose situation for everyone.

It's necessary that you follow the system — even if you don't like it — until you reach your company's highest level pin rank, and you are prepared to completely administer your own. <u>That means creating the system, providing all training materials, and providing all the functions</u>. This means your organization would be hosting its own conventions, leadership conferences, rallies, etc. — because your people can no longer go to the ones provided by your sponsorship line, since the training would be different. **This is a major jump — one that should only be contemplated when you reach the highest levels in your compensation plan, and are prepared to develop an entire support structure that creates materials, administers functions, schedules speakers, rents auditoriums, and the like**. <u>I strongly recommend against this, unless you simply have no other alternative</u>.

Final thoughts on the subject.

Some of you reading this are right now working programs with no duplicatable system in place. It's very tough to develop residual income in this situation. This gives you two choices, neither of which is easy.

1) You can quit what you're doing and find another program with a system. Know that this will mean

starting over, and you will likely lose many of your people along the way.

2) You can take charge of your business and determine that the system will begin with you. It's a tremendous amount of work, but it can be done. I have had to develop systems several times. Throughout the course of this book, I will be sharing with you my system. I've also referenced the generic materials I've developed, which will help you create one.

Should you go the route of creating a system — I suggest you put a copy of this book and my *How to Earn at Least $100,000 a Year in Network Marketing* audiotape album in the hands of your sponsor. The more levels of the sponsorship line you can enlist — the easier it will be for you. When it's all said and done, however, the final responsibility for your success rests where it belongs ... on you. You can proclaim yourself a victim and decry your lack of a system — or you can do something about it. If you are ready to do something about it, then turn to the next chapter, **Getting Started Fast**.

CHAPTER SIX

GETTING STARTED FAST

THERE'S A MAGIC MOMENT IN THE SPONSORING PROCESS — when your prospect catches the vision and makes a decision to join the business. But, there's another magic moment — one even more important. This happens when your new distributor really understands **how** he can make his dreams come true in your program.

When people drop out, it's usually because this second magic moment was never reached. What happened was your distributor had second thoughts. Those big checks, free cars and trips sounded wonderful ... for you. But your distributor just didn't relate to how **he** could get those things for himself. Unless you show him how he can reach his dreams through your program, he won't have the frame of mind to persevere through the challenges and reach success. If you make this connection — you'll have a distributor forever.

Here's the usual sponsoring process. You make a presentation and sponsor a new distributor. He's excited and dreaming about all the money, trips, cars and other goodies he's going to get. He already has his first five distributors in his mind. So, you send him home and tell him to make a name list.

Since he already knows the five people he wants, he doesn't bother with the name list, but calls all five people and invites them to the next meeting. Now, he sits back and relaxes — waiting for the big bucks to roll in.

The night of the meeting arrives, and what happens? With luck, one person shows up. Your new distributor is devastated. Hopefully, he will recover. Then, he will spend the next five weeks re-inviting those four people who never came. Every week, they have even better excuses.

What your distributor doesn't realize is that these people DON'T WANT TO COME. They just don't know how to tell him. So, by the end of his second month, your new distributor tells you, "I just don't know anybody else."

Rather than having to face more rejection and frustration, your distributor has given up the ghost. It's highly likely he will quit. If he stays with it, there's a good chance he may come to meetings for the rest of his life, but he will never bring a guest. **His fears are greater than his dreams.** He now sees those big checks, trips, etc. in the abstract — they sound good and look good, <u>but he doesn't actually believe they are ever going to happen for him.</u>

To turn fantasies into dreams, and dreams into commitment — **your dreams must be stronger than your fears**! Motivation, positive thinking and hype will only last so long. <u>Unless your distributor has a believable, logical plan for attaining his dreams, the fear will take control</u>. The same holds true for you, too. The purpose of this chapter is twofold: to get you off to a fast start — and to teach you how to work with your new distributors as they sponsor into the business.

There are two requirements — and only two — to build a big business. They are **a dream** and **the willingness to trade seven to ten hours a week** for that dream. You need the dream, because that's the only way you'll find the seven to ten hours. You need the seven to ten hours, because that's how much time the business takes to start. This chapter will show you how to put these two things together.

Here's what I've discovered: <u>you will make or break your new distributors during their first two weeks in the business</u>. Here's why:

We are creatures of habit. We replace old habits with new ones. You and your new distributors are already using all 24 hours of each day. Probably in the same way, week after week. Having a dream gets you to set aside the necessary time. The way you or your distributor spend that time during those first two weeks is the new habit you create. If you spend those two weeks analyzing brochures, watching the company video one more time, and getting ready to get ready — then the two weeks go by and nothing has really happened. Your excitement fades and your dream gets farther away.

Now, if, during your first two weeks, you're learning the business, taking action steps, having some small successes, and actually getting people into your group — then momentum begins and your excitement level rises. Good work habits are created ... which are rewarded with positive results ... which encourages more good work habits.

The best place to start is knowing your dream. And, making sure it's a big one. Something about the presentation you saw excited you. You need to find out specifically what that was. When you have a big enough *why*, the *how* comes easy. So, you've got to know your dreams.

Now, many people don't like to talk about dreams. "Too corny," they say. Not me. I love to talk about dreams. The kind you have with your eyes wide open. I can think of no good innovation, invention or situation that didn't begin with a dream.

Maybe your dream is to bring your spouse home from work. Visualize that. Plan for it and set a goal for it to happen. Picture having his or her "freedom party" with all of your new network marketing friends. Imagine at 4:45, just before your spouse is ready to get off from work on his or her last day. A long stretch limo pulls up with three dozen long-stem roses and you in the back seat. Fifteen other cars filled with your group are lined up behind you with streamers and cans tied to the bumpers.

Your spouse's co-workers look out the window. *"Who's getting married?"* they ask your spouse. *"Oh,"* he or she replies, slightly embarrassed. *"Those are my friends waiting for me. We're on our way to my freedom party."*

Maybe your dream is for <u>you</u> to quit work. Set a date, make plans, and rehearse the speech you'll give the boss when you tell her that you can't afford to work there anymore. Picture the day after your last day of work. Your alarm clock goes off at the usual time. You wake up, pick up a hammer, and break it into a million pieces! Then, you climb back into your cozy bed, snuggle back up to your spouse, and go back to sleep!

One of my dreams was to be able to support my church in a meaningful way. Thanks to Network Marketing — I was able to introduce a weekly class on prosperity, serve as Board president, and tithe more money than a lot of people make.

Your dream may be to help out at a shelter, adopt a child, or support the fight against muscular dystrophy. Or, it may be all of those things. It could be getting out of debt, becoming a millionaire, and spending more quality time with the people who bring quality to your life. Whatever it is, you need to know <u>exactly</u> what it is.

Maybe one of the reasons you selected your opportunity was because it has an automobile fund. It's not enough to say you want a new car. You need to say you want a BMW Z-3 roadster, light blue with black leather interior and a CD player. Then get a brochure of one and put it on your mirror. Better yet, have your picture taken sitting in one.

I believe in having lots of dreams, big and small. I think you should have dreams for things you want (like cars and houses); things you want to do (like helping your temple, synagogue or church; and feeding the homeless or coaching your daughter's little league team); and things you want to become (like a foster parent, high pin rank or volunteer coordinator at a local charity).

You need to have a dream big enough to encompass the dreams of your group. If your dream is too small, it might restrict the dreams of your group. For instance, let's suppose your dream is to make $200,000 a year in your Network Marketing business. On the surface, that seems like an ambitious dream. But, if you have five people on your front line whose dreams are to each make $200,000 — then your dream is too small to encompass theirs.

Don't be afraid to have BIG dreams. When I was 17, I decided I was going to become a millionaire. Nobody took me seriously. "Be realistic," they said. And truth was, that looked like quite a stretch. I came from a poor family, a single mother who raised three kids, and I was a high school dropout. But I had a dream! And, if you get nothing else from this book, get this — <u>when your dream is big enough, you mold the universe to your will</u>.

In my case, the things I was doing (like working in the restaurant business) were not very conducive to my becoming a millionaire. But, my dream was always there. So, the vehicle to fulfill my dream — Network Marketing — found its way to me. I seized the opportunities offered me and made my dreams come true. You can too, if you know what your dreams are. So, as you begin your networking business, start by looking at your dreams.

Now, let's go through some of the other steps you'll want to take to get started fast. (I've created a booklet, entitled *FIRST STEPS: Getting Started Fast in Network Marketing,* that you can use to work along this process. You'll find it quite helpful to give a copy of this booklet, along with the "Getting Started" training materials I'll mention later, to the people you personally sponsor.)

Here are the things to do immediately when you first sign up:

PLACE YOUR FIRST ORDER.

You must use the products or services personally so you can get excited about them. How much should you order? Somewhere between what you need — and where you're nervous.

I say this only halfway in jest. You see, we've found that "just what you need" is not enough. You'll need some inventory for reselling to new distributors, extras for temporarily out-of-stock items, and samples for personal marketing. You certainly don't want to have a garage or warehouse full of products. But, make sure you have enough products on hand to build your business.

Some years back, I was working in a program that offered organic household cleaning products. One of the things I did with new distributors was to go through their house with them — removing all the "Brand X" products from their bathrooms and kitchens. We'd place all these in a shopping bag — replace them with the good stuff — and give away the old stuff to a good cause. This concept will work for most programs, no matter what your products are.

SCHEDULE YOUR "GETTING STARTED" TRAINING WITH YOUR SPONSOR.

Ideally, this should take place within 48 hours of the time you sponsor in. Schedule between two and four hours for this training and follow along in the booklet. Long distance, this can be done by phone.

BUY A DAILY PLANNER OR APPOINTMENT BOOK.

Bring this to your "Getting Started" training meeting. There is a planner, called the *PowerLine Planner,* created specifically for Network Marketing. I recommend it strongly.

Begin your Prospect List.

Don't talk to anyone about your business at this point. Do that only after you have finished the Getting Started training. For now, begin writing down the names and phone numbers of anyone and everyone you can think of in the *Getting Started* booklet. (If you don't have the booklet, this can be done in a notebook.)

Make a commitment to your business.

Success does not come overnight. It takes work. I suggest you make a one-year commitment to your business. Accept the fact that there is a training period. Just like any job or occupation, Network Marketing requires learning new skills. It does not take years or cost thousands of dollars, but you do need to learn some new things. Of course, you will "earn as you learn," but it's still a good idea to consider your first six months a learning experience. For the average network marketer — working your business only seven to ten hours a week — a one-year commitment is a realistic approach. I·believe that if you follow this duplicatable system for that time, you will be so pleased with the results you will be networking for the rest of your life!

Review the "Getting Started" training materials you received from your sponsor.

These will be different for each company.

NOTE: If your company doesn't have a system, these are the resources I recommend you give to your new front-line distributors.

▲ *What You Need to Know First* audiotape
▲ *The Greatest Networker in the World* book
▲ *Getting Started* audiotape

▲ *FIRST STEPS: Getting Started Fast in Network Marketing* booklet

▲ *Secrets of a Dynamic Day* audiotape

(To purchase these materials, contact Prime Concepts Group at (316) 942-1111, or log on to www.mlm-metro.com.)

IF YOUR COMPANY OR SPONSORSHIP LINE PROVIDES A VOICE MAIL NETWORK — SEND IN YOUR APPLICATION.

This is another aspect of your support network. You'll get meeting updates, training tips from your sponsorship line, and inspirational messages. Get connected now!

These are the things you want to do as soon as you sponsor in. Within 48 hours from that time, you'll want to hold your "Getting Started" training with your sponsor. This is your opportunity to map out your plan of action for your business.

This ensures you get off to a great start in your first two weeks, and have a strategy laid out for where you'll go after that. The following ten steps are part of the "Getting Started" training:

1. SET YOUR GOALS.

You must decide what your ultimate goal is from your networking business. Are you just interested in getting your products for free? Are you looking to make a few hundred dollars to cover your car payment? Or, do you want to develop complete financial freedom? To reach your goals, you must first determine what they are — then, set a timetable to reach them. This is your chance to make plans for the dreams you have.

Write them down. Goals are dreams with a deadline. That means they must be written down. You also want to make sure they are specific and measurable.

I believe that the average person, following a system, can achieve financial independence in this business during a two-to-four-year time period. Think about what you want to do right away. Then, think about what you'd like your two-to-four-year plan to be.

Dream-build with your spouse and your sponsor. Reawaken those wants and desires you used to have, but probably lost somewhere along the way. Sometimes we get so busy in the bustle of everyday living that we lose sight of our dreams. It's important that you discover your "burn." It's this burning desire that will keep you focused and motivated during the early development stages of your networking career. This is the secret to staying self-motivated. Then, fill out the goal form in the *First Steps* booklet, or write down your goals on a sheet of paper.

2. SCHEDULE YOUR APPOINTMENT BOOK.

This is a business of your word and a business of appointments. To build effectively, you must plan your work and schedule your time in a manner that best suits building your business. You're already using all 24 hours of every day. To change your life, and what you're getting out of it, you must change the way you're using your 24 hours. You must carve out at least seven to ten hours a week exclusively for building your business.

Work closely with your sponsor to determine how to schedule your seven to ten hours for the first few weeks of your business. Find out the dates of all upcoming functions for the next 90 days, so you can schedule your work and other obligations around them. Also, learn the dates of any annual conventions and conferences. These are major events critical to your success, and you want to make sure you're at them.

3. LEARN THE BASIC COMPANY PROCEDURES.

To be truly independent, and proactively build your business, you must be able to operate without your sponsor's assistance for day-to-day minor matters as soon as possible. That means learning some of the basic company procedures as soon as you can.

These include:

▲ How to order products

▲ How to fill out distributor applications, order forms and requests

▲ How to transfer volume

Set aside a few hours of quiet time (Sunday evenings are ideal for most people) to read your entire distributor kit. Learn which sections to go to for specific information, and familiarize yourself with all the forms. Study the rules and regulations, and learn the Code of Ethics.

4. ORDER YOUR BUSINESS CARDS.

If you're in business, people expect you to have a business card. Check with your sponsor for the style of card you need and where to order it.

5. OPEN A BUSINESS CHECKING ACCOUNT.

To run your business in an organized fashion, you must have a separate checking account. This should be used exclusively for your business. It's vital for good record keeping, and it will really help you out at tax time.

> **NOTE:** When you order products for your personal family use, buy them from your own business at retail. For example, let's suppose that the wholesale price of one of your products is $7, and the suggested retail price is $10. You would write a $10 check from your personal account to your business account. Of course, you already paid a $7 check from your

business account to your company. The difference
— that $3 — is really retail profit that should be
credited to your business. <u>You want to be your own
best customer and have all your people do the same</u>!
Following this procedure helps you and your people
appreciate the <u>true</u> value of your products.

6. Purchase the Business-Building Materials You Need to Get Started.

Check with your sponsor to see which particular tools you
need to get started right. Some companies or sponsorship lines
have a specific system laid out that uses certain tools. Others
do not. If your company does not have a specific system to
follow, I would recommend the following items:

Ten Pre-Approach Packets:

Lifestyle Freedom Pack. (This is my generic pre-approach
packet, which includes a Special Report on Network Marketing and my *Escape the Rat Race* audiotape.)

Five sets of "Getting Started" training materials:

▲ *What You Need to Know First* audiotape. (This is
  information that will take five years off your growth
  curve.)

▲ *Secrets of a Dynamic Day* audiotape. (This is designed
  to be listened to every morning — to help you plan
  your day and create a positive mindset.)

▲ *Greatest Networker in the World* book. (A great book
  to explain the essence of the business.)

▲ *Getting Started* audiotape. (This takes you through the
  ten-step process outlined in this chapter.)

▲ *First Steps: Getting Started Fast in Network Marketing* booklet. (Use this to work along with the *Getting Started* audiotape.)

(To purchase these materials, contact Prime Concepts Group at (316) 942-1111, or log on to www.mlm- metro.com.)

Five sets of your "Company Materials" pack:

▲ Product catalog or brochures

▲ Business plan brochure

▲ Company audio or video and presentation pack

▲ *Your Destiny* book, or *Future Choice* book

(Check with your sponsorship line for specifics.)

Several sets of your "Follow-up" pack:

▲ Testimonial-type audios or videos

▲ Article reprints

(Check with your sponsorship line for specifics.)

You greatly enhance your chances for high-level success when you have all the resources you need to compete effectively. Make the investment in yourself.

7. Learn the Core Qualities of a Network Marketing Leader.

There are nine key qualities that every great network marketer possesses. Some, or even many of these, you have already put into action. To be a leader, and set an example that others can duplicate, you must practice all of them.

To live all nine core qualities means you've made and honored a commitment to "Go Core." To develop your business, you must identify and work with the people in your organization who are willing to make this very same commitment. Let's take a look at each one of these core qualities:

Use all of the products.

To "Go Core" means that if your company has a product, you would never buy a competing product for any reason ... ever! A "Brand X" product purchase takes money out of your business, and puts it into someone else's. This kind of practice will put you out of business quickly. A core person never buys "Brand X," regardless of sales, convenience, or for any other reason. It's simply bad business. You must use all of your company's products that apply to you — and be able to talk knowledgeably and enthusiastically about them — to effectively build your business.

Develop a consumer group.

Your business is driven by the volume produced by sales to the end consumer. A great deal of those sales will be to distributors who "buy from their own store" and use the products themselves. But, there are many other people who will benefit from your products or services, but will not be interested in building a business at this time. These people will become your consumer group.

It's critical that you develop this consumer group. This is good business, because you:

1. Service the people who aren't distributors, but need your products or service;
2. Earn retail income;
3. Develop consistent income you can count on from regular customers; and,
4. Build personal group volume — volume that can keep you qualified to earn other lucrative bonuses and incentives. It's a good goal to develop a base of at least ten retail customers when you are just starting out.

NOTE: Please, don't go out and try to sell products retail first, and then attempt to sneak the business in the back door. Present the whole program — business and products — and let your prospect decide. <u>Get your retail customers from the people who choose not to participate in the business</u>.

Make regular presentations.

Like every business, Network Marketing requires consistently taking action steps. One of the most important of these is making regular presentations. Realistically, you need to be making three to five presentations a week when you start your business (working seven to ten hours a week). As your business grows, you will want to increase this number. When you reach what I consider "full time" in this business (about 25 hours a week), you will want to be making five to eight presentations a week. Of course, not all of these presentations will be to new prospects that you want to personally sponsor. Many of them will be presentations you are conducting for your people as you train them and build depth.

<u>You must consistently make presentations if you want to grow your business</u>. Don't be misled into thinking you're growing your business with "busy work" (reading manuals, going to seminars, filling out forms, etc.). These things are important, but they are support functions to the real business — which is making regular, successful presentations to prospects.

Attend everything.

Functions are the glue that holds your business together. Attending them helps you grow your business, gives you crucial training, and keeps you focused. In your regional area, you will have the chance to attend opportunity showcases, product workshops and rallies. If these are within two to three hours driving distance, then you will want to attend. There will be other events, such as conventions and leadership conferences, which are held annually. These are major, often life-changing events, and you'll want to schedule your vacation time around them, so you'll never miss one.

Spend daily self-development time.

If I've discovered one fundamental truth, it is this: your business will grow only as fast as you grow. You will have to develop new skills as your business progresses. Initially, you will need recruiting and training skills. Later, you will need time management and organizational skills. Ultimately, you will need leadership, communication and empowerment capabilities. In order to develop others, you must first develop yourself.

It's important that you set aside specific time each day for self-development. For most people, this is best done in the morning before the day starts. You might meditate, exercise, listen to inspirational tapes, or read anything that helps you grow your mind, body and soul. Set aside this time and stick to it.

Invest in audiotapes, books and videos that help your personal development ... and make sure half of this is specific to your network marketing business. Keep tapes in your car to play at every opportunity you have throughout the day. Get a portable cassette player and use it when you go walking or cycling. Also, don't end your day by watching the late news and then going to sleep. Make sure the last input you receive before going to bed is positive — even if it's just reading one paragraph from an inspirational book.

Many companies or sponsorship lines offer programs that provide positive, inspirational and/or instructional material on a subscription basis. If you're in such a situation, you are quite fortunate, because much of the work of finding and getting good material is already done for you. Sign up right away and make sure your people do, as well.

NOTE: If your company doesn't have such a program, or you would like to supplement your program, I'd like to suggest that you consider a subscription to my *Dynamic Development Series.* Each month, you'll receive a one-hour tape dedicated to exploring the frontiers of body-mind development.

Be teachable.

If you want to build your business in the fastest manner possible, you must be teachable and be willing to be coached. You will find Network Marketing is quite different from traditional businesses. Things that work great in sales, sometimes do not work well in Network Marketing. Your sponsorship line has learned the methods, strategies and techniques that work best in your business. They will work with you and teach you everything they know ... without charging you a penny. Your sponsor is the repository of all the experience of many generations of distributors — all the way to the company. Learn from them.

Practice accountability.

For years now, chain letters and money games have been masquerading as legitimate network marketing programs. This means those of us in true programs must be beyond reproach. We must set a standard of integrity much higher than that of the corporate world. Network Marketing is a business of relationships, and relationships operate on trust. To earn and maintain that trust, you must be accountable.

You can never tell a lie to your distributors or customers and be accountable. Accountability also means that when you write checks, they're good; when you promise to work with someone, you follow through; and when you commit to attend an event, you're there — on time.

Accountability means that when we have a product display with 24 products, there will still be 24 products at the end of the night. It means never approaching someone else's prospect or attempting to steal distributors from another line.

You create the culture of your organization. If you do it right, it will mean you can hold a function, and 800 women can leave their purses on their chairs, come back, and find everything exactly as they left it!

Edify the organization.

Savvy distributors learn that they must edify their sponsorship line. By "edify," I simply mean to build up. When you point out the success and accomplishments of your sponsors — it makes those sponsors more effective when they come to work with both your prospects and distributors. Many times you will find it difficult to be a prophet in your own hometown. Sometimes your friends and relatives aren't yet ready to accept that powerful, positive concepts can come from you. By edifying your sponsorship line — then bringing your prospects to them — you'll have support to hold you over until you develop some initial success and credibility. Likewise, your sponsorship line can help you when you're working with your new distributors.

This was a lesson I had to learn the hard way. I was so ego-driven in my early years in the business that I would never edify my sponsor. In fact, I did quite the opposite. I used to complain to all my people how weak my sponsor was, hoping I would look strong by comparison. (Of course, it did just the opposite, but I couldn't see that.) In any event, when my sponsor would come to town, do a training, or conduct a meeting — none of my people would turn out. So, when I needed someone to give me credibility, there was no one to provide that. I never got any of my close friends or family members into the business. I still today believe that the reason is because I didn't edify my sponsorship line.

Follow the system.

Leaders understand that "lone rangers" can be successful initially — but will not enjoy long-term success. For residual income, and walkaway security, you must follow a step-by-step, duplicatable system, and you yourself must be duplicatable.

This means that everyone in your organization must use the same marketing materials, employ the same training, procedures and follow a standardized presentation. This way, the method you use to bring in your new people is the same method they use to bring in their new people. You are completely duplicatable. Regardless of someone's previous job experience, their education or confidence level — they can do the business in exactly the same, successful way you did.

Your sponsorship line has learned what works and what doesn't. They have created the system based upon that experience. Follow the system, and you'll have the resources of the entire sponsorship line working for you. If you change the system, you lose the benefits of having all those resources at your disposal. Also, when you change the system, (substituting a different tape, changing the presentation, etc.) you send a message to your people that it's okay to change the system.

This is the problem. Your first-level people change the system a little, so their first-level people change the system a little, and so it goes down through the entire group. After a few levels, there is no system, so you have no security and no potential for walkaway residual income. Always follow the system — no matter what!

Go Core!

These nine Core qualities are what separates Network Marketing leaders from the people who drop by the wayside and never reach long-term success in the business. Practicing all the Core qualities isn't easy — it's not supposed to be. But, you must practice them if you're truly interested in building a network where others can achieve the same success as you.

"Going Core" means doing all nine actions, not just the ones you like. It also takes a substantial investment in you. But, you will discover that the people who invest in "Going Core" reach dramatically higher levels of success than those who don't. As a leader committed to empowering others, you have a responsibility to go core yourself, and create this culture throughout your organization.

8. Complete Your List of at Least 100 Names.

This is one of the most important steps. Do not skip it, and do not do it halfway. Just start writing down the names of everyone you know.

Do not prejudge people. *Well, he makes a lot of money. He won't be interested. She's a sales type. She wouldn't look at this.* A mistake like that can cost you tens of thousands of dollars down the road. So, do not prejudge. Just get down the names.

On your list of 100, there will be one or two pin rank executives, three or four mid-range executives, and 30 to 40 people who will want to use the products as a consumer. You don't know who's who ... and it's usually not who you think it is.

Begin with the memory joggers list in the *First Steps* booklet. Then, look through the business cards you've collected. Go through your address book and your holiday card list. Finally, skim through the Yellow Pages, and scan all the occupations listed there as a reminder of people you know. Start with accountants, barbers, and contractors, and go all the way to x-ray technicians and zoologists.

Don't make the classic mistake of thinking of five or six people who will be interested and stopping there. You will certainly be disappointed. Make sure you get down at least 100 names, so we can let people sort themselves into the right categories.

9. GET AT LEAST TEN "PRE-APPROACH" PACKETS IN CIRCULATION.

This is where your planning ends and your actual business-building begins. Now, you'll begin to discover who's just a <u>suspect</u> — and who's really a <u>prospect</u> for your business. A Pre-Approach Packet is a pack of materials for conducting the initial screening of your prospects. This will determine whether or not you move forward to make an actual presentation. If your company does not have a Pre-Approach Packet, I have developed one called the *Lifestyle Freedom Pack* for you to use. It's an attractive album that includes an *Escape the Rat Race* audiotape and the *Money For Life: Creating Wealth in Network Marketing* Special Report. Check with your sponsorship line for the correct pre-approach procedure to follow and materials to use. Not all lines use Pre-Approach Packets. Some count on intense training and strong motivation to help their people overcome rejection, and go right to inviting them to meetings.

10. SCHEDULE YOUR FIRST PRESENTATIONS.

This is where the actual building begins. The business is built in the living rooms and dining rooms. After you pre-approach someone and get a positive response, <u>you must set up a presentation as quickly as possible</u>.

Initially, your sponsor should accompany you so these are two-on-one presentations. **As soon as possible, you must learn to do the presentation yourself.** The two-on-ones and one-on-ones should lead to living room meetings for the prospect's second look. The home meetings should lead to larger, hotel meetings. (We'll look at this in more depth in later chapters.) For now, know that you want your new distributor to have success as soon as possible. This comes from one-on-ones — which lead to home meetings — which lead to hotel meetings.

NOTE: In cases of rapid organizational growth, your sponsor may not yet be qualified to make a presentation. If so, that's okay. Go further up the sponsorship line, and you will find someone to help you.

This is a critical part of your training. As you watch and listen to your sponsorship line make your initial presentations (taking good notes, I trust), you will be learning how it's done. The sooner you learn to conduct a presentation yourself, the sooner you'll be on your way to independence. You can then duplicate this process with your people. By following this system, you will be building secure lines with the potential for walkaway residual income.

As you can see, this procedure is time consuming and a lot of work. Most people would rather sponsor by mailing postcards, by making phone calls etc. But remember that <u>the easier you build a line, the easier it is to lose it</u>. By taking time at the beginning, you will be saving yourself and your new distributor countless hours of wasted, unproductive time down the road.

Your new distributor will see specific action steps she can take to build her business. Rather than hype, she will see a believable plan for attaining her dreams with networking. Her dreams will be greater than her fears. And, you will have a committed distributor and a secure line in the making!

Remember that all of the information in this chapter has a double purpose: to get you started fast, and to also teach you how to conduct "Getting Started" training for the people you sponsor.

Before we move on, we need to address the issue of distributors who want to do the "small business." Small-business distributors are not that interested in sponsoring others and duplicating. They are most excited about the products, and want to concentrate on marketing them. They won't commit to going Core, or spending seven to ten hours a week building their businesses. Their only desire is to use the products themselves and retail products to a few friends. They won't want "Getting Started" training, and probably won't attend one, so it's counterproductive to schedule one for them.

Instead, with your small-business distributors — simply spend an hour or two with them when you sign them up, explaining where to find things in the distributor kit, how to order products, and the other procedural things they will need to know. Let them know about the event schedule and that they're always welcome, but don't pressure them to attend everything. Not everyone is interested in the big business. Advise them that you won't be pressuring them, but you're always available when they have questions or need help.

And then — the most important part:

Let them know that it's likely they will encounter people who want to do the "big business" (sponsoring and duplicating). Advise them to bring these people to you. Big-business-builders are going to need help with presentations, training, counseling, and other things that their small- business sponsors cannot give them. When you get a big-business distributor under a small-business distributor, you will work with the big-business distributor as though they were on your first level.

NOTE: When this happens,. it would be wise for you to suggest that the small-business sponsor may want to reconsider becoming a big-business-builder. They are already doing most of the things required. By adding a few more presentations, they could upgrade to the big business and receive even greater rewards. Inevitably, small retailers will stumble across people who want to build a big business, and they will leave a lot of money on the table if they

91

don't upgrade at some point. But, don't pressure them! If they are happy to do the small business, be grateful for them and support their decision.

Now, as you've probably deduced by now, I'm a maniac for having a system. But, this is most certainly not the only way to build a business. There have been many successful people who have built large networks without following a system. They are happy to let each person find their own way, and experiment with different approaches to the business. They have some people sending out bulk e-mails, others who only advertise, and yet others who only prospect by phone. They are popular with their people because of the freedom they give them.

Tom Schreiter, author of the "Big Al" book series, and I have fought over this for years. Tom is a class guy, and one of the people I most respect in the business. He believes that you should never hold back your people, and should let them build the business in any way that is comfortable for them. He's built a strong organization on that principle. Following a system like mine can create some friction, particularly with strong-willed people.

I won't lie to you. I've had some real drama and attempted mutinies from leaders in my organization over the years. Now that I'm retired from the business, I can look back and reflect on whether or not I made the right moves. I think I'd give myself a B- grade. I probably was too strident about my system and the way I enforced it. I believe, in retrospect, I should have given my people more latitude.

Overall though, I still do believe that part of your job as a sponsor is to practice "tough love" with your people. I also believe that a lot more ordinary people have reached extraordinary levels of success in the business, because they have the structure of a system to guide them. Having said that, let's go to the next chapter and look at an overview of the entire sponsoring process ....

CHAPTER SEVEN

WHAT A PROSPECTING PIPELINE LOOKS LIKE ...

O NE OF THE BIGGEST MISTAKES BEGINNERS MAKE IN THIS business is thinking that sponsoring is a one-shot, all-or-nothing event. Actually, <u>sponsoring is a process</u>. One that takes different amounts of time for different prospects. Your goal shouldn't be to "sell" or "close" anyone, but rather to give the prospect enough information that they can make the best decision for them. Unlike in sales, where often you are taught to manipulate or close people, in Network Marketing, we are looking for people motivated enough to take action themselves. We simply want to expose them to the opportunity, and see if they are open to it. Some people are open to new concepts, and others are stuck with the preconceptions they've been taught. You want to look for the open ones.

Professor **Stephen Hawking** opens his brilliant book, *A Brief History of Time,* with the story of a well-known scientist who gave a public lecture on astronomy. The scientist described how the moon orbits the earth, the earth orbits the sun, and how our solar system orbits around the center of the galaxy. When he finished, a little old lady got up and said, "What you have told us is rubbish. The world is really a flat plate supported on the back of a giant tortoise."

The scientist gave a knowing smile and replied, "What is the tortoise standing on?"

"You're very clever, young man, very clever," she replied. "But it's turtles all the way down!"

We all know people like that little old lady. (Actually, I know quite a few.) The point is, why try to convince them otherwise? If they believe that the universe is a big stack of turtles — or that all Network Marketing opportunities are illegal pyramids — nothing you present to the contrary is going to change their beliefs. True prospecting in Network Marketing is pretty similar. It's not so much about convincing people or changing their beliefs, as much as it is about finding the people who are open to what you have. It is a sorting process, divided into stages, wherein the prospect indicates their level of interest and commitment at the appropriate level. You will meet people who believe all network marketing opportunities are pyramid schemes. Why spend all your time trying to convince them otherwise when there are legions of people who are open to what you have?

Take a look at the illustration on the following page. This is the basic process I taught to my group when I was still building. I include it here to give you an example of what a systematic process might look like. It is by no means the only way to build. Because, among the many different opportunities and different sales tools for each, individual systems will differ. Check with your sponsorship line for the specifics in your company.

The objective of your sponsoring process should be to sort out the non-prospects, and get the true prospects the information they need to make a decision. Everyone we know and meet is a suspect. They may be a candidate for the business; they might be a retail customer; or they may be neither. The first step of the process is to separate the prospects from the original group of suspects. I did this with a pre-approach step. We did this by asking qualifying questions, or, giving the prospect a packet of materials. (I developed a pack especially for this purpose. It's called the *Lifestyle Freedom Pack,*

The Sponsoring Sequence

Step One — Qualifying Question/Pre Approach

☐ Prospect is interested   ☐ Prospect is not interested ➡   Get them as a product customer

⬇

Step Two — Abbreviated "First Look" Presentation

☐ Prospect is interested   ☐ Prospect is not interested ➡   Get them as a product customer

⬇

Step Three — Complete Presentation ("2nd Look" Home Meeting)

☐ Prospect is interested   ☐ Prospect is ready to join   ☐ Prospect is not interested ➡   Get them as a product customer

⬇   ⬇

Go to step 5

Step Four — Family or Crossline Meeting (Prospects 3rd or 4th Look)

☐ Prospect is interested   ☐ Prospect is ready to join   ☐ Prospect is not interested ➡   Get them as a product customer

⬇   ⬇

Additional Follow up

⬇

Step Five — The Enrollment

"Get Started" Training

and it can actually take the place of doing a one-on-one to pre-qualify your prospect.) This would help us discover whether or not the prospect was interested in the business. If they were not interested in the business — then we would want them as a customer. If they have no interest in either, then they would stay as a suspect until something in their life changes. (They could become a prospect tomorrow, if their boss yells at them, but, for right now, they're still a suspect.)

From the larger universe of suspects, you have now narrowed down your search to a much smaller list of prospects. These people go to a brief (approximately 30 minutes) "first look," which is usually done as a one-on-one, or two-on-one with your sponsor. Your goal here is simply to find out whether or not your prospect has enough interest to want to explore it deeper. Most will. Others will make a decision that the business is not right for them. If they tell you this, then you will suggest that they become a customer.

Of the people still undecided, this process will repeat itself in steps three and four, during the follow-up. Some will join the business; others will choose to become customers; and yet others will decide they're not interested in either. What you need is a yes or a no. The only thing we can't live with is a maybe. Remember, we don't want to close or convince people — we just want to get the appropriate information in front of them at the proper times, so they can make the right decision for themselves.

Some of our prospects will turn into distributors, and some will turn into customers. Technically, this is the end of the sponsoring process. But, you can see that there is one more level we aspire to. We want to turn the distributors into leaders. This is done as part of your training system: the functions, the self-development programs and materials. We'll study this process in later chapters.

Once someone becomes a customer, your goal is to turn them into a committed regular customer. If your company has a customer-direct ordering plan or an auto-ship program, then this is where you want them to be. (Auto-ship plans are where a customer signs up to automatically receive a certain order every month.) If your company doesn't have this type of program, then you at least want them to the point where they feel the product is one they want to keep in their life, and they would only buy it from you. You do this by superior customer service.

You should be letting them know when to order product, so they never run out. Check back with them on a regular basis to make sure they're using the product correctly. Make sure they're satisfied with it, and answer any questions they may have. From these happily satisfied customers, a number of business-builders will eventually develop.

Now, let's go back to the original process and look at it in more depth. This is the most critical part of the business, and it's essential that you understand it completely. The pre-approach, or qualification stage, is usually the most difficult for new distributors to get started with. Some of them will need your help with this initial stage. They may need you to get on three-way calls with them as they ask their first qualifying questions, or even to role-play with them. Help them until they are able to do this unassisted. <u>A new distributor can never build a business until they are able to qualify prospects and get materials into their hands</u>. We will devote the entire next chapter to this prospecting process.

Here's the secret of the sponsoring process. <u>Every time the prospect sees the presentation — it should be a bigger "event" than the last one.</u> We'll look at this again in the chapters on presentations and meetings, but I want you to understand the broad outlines of the process now. You'll want to check with your sponsorship line for the specifics in your particular program, but here is how I manage the process for myself.

The first time I see prospects for a presentation, I want it to be a non-threatening occasion where they feel comfortable. I will conduct it either at their home, or meet them in a coffee shop (during non-mealtime hours). I prefer their home, because there are fewer distractions, and I have a better chance to get both spouses together. <u>You must have both spouses present if you want a successful conclusion to your presentation</u>. When I make the appointment, I will always use language that conveys how important it is that both spouses be present. (More about this later.)

When I arrive, I will attempt to take control of the situation. Rather than chitchat, I will explain that I know their time is valuable, so I'd like to get right to business. I'll ask if we can turn off the TV or stereo, so they won't be distracted. Expect some raised eyebrows on this. Most people turn on the television the second they walk into the house, and leave it on for every waking moment.

But what you have to say is important — they need to hear it uninterrupted. I will also ask if they can disconnect the telephone or put it on the answering machine. Usually, by now, the spouse I didn't get the appointment with is looking at me as if I had just asked them to donate a kidney. Sometimes they'll shut off the phone, sometimes not. Either way, it's better that I asked. The ones who turn the phone off won't be disturbed; the ones who won't now know that I consider this very serious; and, in the event the phone does ring — they usually keep it short. If one party does take a call, stop your presentation until they're finished and get back to you.

I remember doing a presentation once that was going great. We were almost done; they were very excited; and then the phone rang. The wife took the call, which was her mother — so she insisted she had to take it, but that we should proceed. The wife stayed on the phone until the end of my presentation. I finished and the husband wanted to know how he could get started right away. The wife jumped in with, "Don't you think we should talk about this first, honey?" I knew I was in trouble. I offered to redo the second half of the presentation for her, but she declined. She assured me that her husband would explain it to her and they would get back to me. Of course, they never joined.

There are two problems with this scenario. One, a spouse can <u>never</u> explain it to the other one. They've only seen the presentation once, so there's no way in the world they can do it justice. Second, look at the dynamics of the situation. If one partner in a relationship makes a decision for the couple — what does the other one immediately do? Protect the couple from the overzealous, impulsive decision of the other member. They immediately begin to attack the decision, looking for the holes in it. Many times, if they can't find any — they'll make some up. The negative spouse will put a wet blanket on the presentation, and your prospect doesn't join. Better to find this out now, rather than sign them up and think you have a real business-builder, only to have them quit within the first month. <u>When a couple views a presentation and makes a decision together ... it's one they'll stick with</u>.

On a better note, sometimes the negative spouse (and, it can be either one) will not want to do anything, but will agree to let the other partner try it himself or herself. This is a good start. If you can just get the negative spouse to attend a few major functions — they'll usually come around sooner or later. In any event, for all the reasons above, you can see why it's critical that both spouses be present.

In later years, when I arrived at an appointment, and found that one of the spouses was missing, I would try to reschedule it. The other option is to make a presentation to one member — and let's say they like it and want to join — make them promise not to try and explain it to their spouse. Just set up an appointment when you can come back, and present it to them together.

Now, let's go back to our home presentation example. After I've asked about the television and telephone, I'll request that we go to the kitchen table so I'll have something to write on. I try to sit at the end of the table with the couple together on one side. This way I can present so they both have a good view and I can make regular eye contact with both of them. From here on out, the procedures I follow are the same whether I'm presenting in someone's kitchen or meeting them in a coffee shop.

For this first, one-on-one presentation, I will do an abbreviated version of the presentation. I will cut back the first section (which is devoted to how the economic system isn't working and how most people are living lives of quiet desperation). There are two reasons I do this.

First, most people are not going to feel comfortable admitting to me, at the first meeting, that their life is not working, that they're deeply in debt, or that they hate their job. We live in a very plastic, superficial society. Most people want others to think they are doing better than they actually are. If I touch too strongly on this at the initial meeting, then it's likely that they will get defensive and tune me out. You never want to attack a prospect's position, so skip the information on layoffs, time for money trap, etc., and get right to the benefits of the business. Show how it works, and talk about your products or services.

The other reason I drop the first part is because I want to save some info — so there's new material the second time they look at the program (the next step in the process) — making it more of an event than the first time. Depending on your program, this first presentation should take from as little as 30 minutes to no more than 45 minutes.

I'll make very clear at this first meeting that they will definitely want to take a second look at the program, and that they will get a lot more out of it the second, or even the third time. This is where you edify your sponsor. *(You've got to see Matt do this presentation — he's a real rising star with the company.)*

Now, if you're using my Pre-Approach Packet or just the Rat Race tape, the prospect is already programmed to see another look at the presentation, because I've made that quite clear in the tape. So, if they're interested, they will expect you to be taking them to a live presentation.

You want the next stage, the second look, to be a bigger event — so, you bring them to a home meeting. The prospect will hear the same basic presentation, but it's a bigger event. It takes longer, there's more information, and, more importantly — they see other people who are involved. Now, it's starting to look like a much better opportunity, because they now see others participating. Even if you bring them to a meeting at your house, and there are only six other people there — it's still a bigger event than their initial, one-on-one presentation.

For the next stage of the process — I want to dial it up a couple of notches. I want to take them to a small family meeting (family, meaning my or my sponsor's organization) or to an open, cross-line meeting. (Cross-line means that more than one pin-rank leader has their organization participating. By working together to produce an open meeting, each organization gets the benefits of having a much larger, higher energy meeting.) This meeting might have 200 people or 2,000. Now, when you bring your prospect here, this is a <u>major</u> event. The more people at the event, the more likely they are to join. My experience is that once your meetings reach a level of 300 people or more — virtually every prospect that comes to one gets involved. There's just some kind of social proof mentality at work here.

This will happen provided they have <u>already</u> seen the presentation at least once before. You do not want to bring a cold prospect to a large hotel meeting. They could get very negative and influence many other prospects. Open hotel meetings should only be used for second, third, or even fourth looks at the program.

Of course, at open, cross-line meetings, only the most successful distributors make the presentation. They've given thousands of meetings, so they're witty, charming and highly effective. This is a crowning event in your sponsoring process. The prospect sees a vibrant, growing organization that seems to get bigger every time they see it. And, of course, at each stage, the odds increase that they'll meet someone who does what they do (*"Oh, this must be a good business for computer programmers."*), or see someone they know (*"Isn't that Tim and Monica from church? Wow, if we'd gotten in sooner, they could have been in our group. I was just thinking about them!"*).

If it seems like I am overly concerned with controlling the process at every step — it's because I am. Either you control the process, or it controls you.

The magic is in the process. Or, more specifically, the way the process expands the presentation each time the prospect sees it. Think about the mind of the prospect as they go through this process.

Someone they know, like and trust — you — asks them if they're interested in developing a second income with residual possibilities. That sounds intriguing, so they agree to review some materials. They're impressed enough with the materials to want to learn more. But, they're still guarded, maybe even a little skeptical. So, you offer them a chance to learn more in a very non-threatening way. You go to their house, or meet them for a cup of tea at the neighborhood coffee shop. You run through your shortened version of your presentation, leaving out the broken economy information and stressing the benefits for them. You honor your word, keeping it to under an hour, leaving them hungry for more. You send them home with another packet of materials that will reinforce what you've just told them and deepen their interest level.

But not before you set the next appointment, and explain how much more they're going to get out of it the second time.

You let them know how sharp your sponsor, is and you let them know that your sponsor will be the one conducting their next presentation — which you book with them.

On the night of your home meeting, they arrive to find six or even ten other people present. Now, on a subconscious level (or sometimes conscious), your prospect is thinking, *Wow, this deal is getting more popular.* They may join right then.

For the sake of you understanding the process, however, let's suppose your guest still isn't ready to join after the home meeting. You'll send them home with the follow-up packet, making sure you've scheduled the next meeting. They then go to a meeting with 30 to 60 people. They can't help but think the deal is catching steam. Now, they go to another meeting, and this one has hundreds of people at it. At this point, usually within 15 seconds of entering the room and estimating how many chairs are set up — they've made a subconscious decision to join. If not, they will almost certainly join by the time your guest pin-rank speaker finishes their presentation.

Understand this: <u>your prospect is looking for a cause to be-lieve in</u>. We've lost our sense of community — even family. Most people miss this, and are desperately looking for something to replace it. They're looking for a cause, a community, a move-ment, something bigger than themselves that they can believe in. To see 200 or 2,000 positive, proactive people together in a hotel ballroom ... sharing an experience and having fun ... is such an intoxicating experience for most people that they simply can't wait to be a part of it. The fact that every time they see the pre-sentation there are more people involved creates this kind of feeling in most prospects. If your prospect doesn't join by this point, give up. They aren't right for the business.

In reality, most people will join by the second or third look at the program, or remove themselves from consideration. Of course, even when your prospect joins in the early stages, you still continue to move them along this process so that they experience the bigger meetings anyway. This just serves for re-confirm to them that they made a great decision, and increases their already high enthusiasm. Of course, the best part is <u>you can help them conduct two-on-ones with their prospects so they can actually be bringing guests and signing up new distributors at these later meetings</u>. Now, you're talking exponential growth!

Make no mistake. **This is a powerful way to build the business.** The one-on-ones in the kitchens and coffee shops, which feed the home meetings in the living rooms and dens, which feed the bigger family meetings, which feed the open, cross-line hotel meetings.

It's when you don't follow this process that challenges occur. <u>If you don't use a powerful Pre-Approach Packet, or you skip the one-on-ones, you'll find that most prospects never show for the house meetings</u>. It doesn't matter that they answered the pre-approach questions positively and promised to show.

Like many people nowadays, their word probably means nothing, and if there's a good show on TV, they'll probably blow you off. If they've seen a one-on-one and realize that there's something in this opportunity for them, they're much more likely to show up for the home meeting.

After all, they know you; they know your house — it doesn't seem so threatening. The potential upside (getting rich and being their own boss) outweighs the downside (actually missing an entire evening of cable TV).

Likewise, <u>you will see the process break down if you don't do home meetings</u>. You will see that the large hotel meetings will lose steam and attendance will drop off. If distributors aren't doing the home meetings, it means they don't have a steady stream of prospects coming through the "pipeline," so they aren't that motivated to get to the meetings themselves. Fewer people come; the meetings get smaller; fewer prospects sign; and the deterioration continues in a vicious circle.

Don't let this happen to you. Take it by the numbers. Pre-approach people or give one-on-ones to the real prospects. Then, bring them through the pipeline. Remember to follow two critical factors:

1. At the end of each step in the process, always schedule the next meeting.

2. Every time the prospect sees a presentation, let it be a bigger event than the last.

By structuring it in this manner, you will achieve the most positive results. Your prospect will get information in digestible doses; there will be momentum created; and those that are real prospects will develop a sense of urgency.

If you consistently make three to five presentations a week — one-on-ones leading to home meetings, so you're in the living rooms three or four nights a week — you'll become very successful indeed! Now, let's move on to the next chapter and see how to prospect successfully.

CHAPTER EIGHT

HOW TO PROSPECT SUCCESSFULLY

O NE OF THE BIGGEST MISTAKES PEOPLE MAKE WHEN THEY JOIN the business is they start to think, *who can I sell this stuff to?* This is completely off base — the opposite of what a successful distributor should be thinking.

Here's the reality.

Every Monday morning at 6:00, 6:30 and 7:00 a.m., alarm clocks all around the world are going off. People are groggily hitting the snooze button, desperate for another five minutes of sleep. They get up at the last possible second, rush through their shower, and then either microwave breakfast, skip it or buy it in a drive-through window on the way to work.

We know that 80 percent of people are going to a job they don't like, or actually hate, and 99.9 percent of them think they should be making more money. Most of them will slog through the day in a comatose state, and grab dinner at another drive-thru window on the way home. Then, they will plop onto a sofa or recliner, and spend the night rubbing the hair off the back of their heads, drinking cans of rancid, fermented hops, watching mindless sitcoms until they're ready for bed.

Until Tuesday morning, when the process starts all over ...

'Til Wednesday morning ...

'Til Thursday morning ...

'Til Friday morning ... thank God it's Friday!

And you know what that means — it's payday. So, at five o'clock, when their boss whistles them over to fetch their meager pittance, they can feel — if for only a few brief moments — like the check is theirs.

Now, of course, that check is already spent, because they have a stack of credit card bills waiting for it. But, for those few glorious moments — it feels like it's theirs. This calls for a celebration. This means tonight they can eat out! So, at least here in America, that means off to Pizza Hut for a stuffed crust, meat-lovers, double-cheese, double-meat pan pizza, which of course they'll wash down with a Diet Pepsi, because they need to "watch their weight."

From dinner, it's off to the neighborhood video store, where they'll stack up 6 to 8 videos — which is just enough to keep them from thinking about their life of quiet desperation all weekend. Until Monday morning, when the alarm clock goes off, and they start the process all over again ...

Do you understand something? You don't need these people. They desperately need and want what you have to offer. So, stop thinking, *who can I get to do this?* Start thinking, *who would I like to offer this opportunity to?*

You may think your product is vitamins, or skin care, or discount long distance service, but it is none of those things. What you have to sell is freedom. Never lose sight of that.

You're offering people the opportunity to become their own boss and control their own destiny. For most of them, it will be the first opportunity they've ever had with unlimited income potential. It's also the first time they've had a chance to become successful by empowering others. Obviously, everyone would be interested in this, right?

No. Actually, many are not.

Why?

Because it means getting out of their comfort zone. Because it takes a belief in one's self that they don't possess. Some of them want success, but not if they have to do any work to get it. They're playing the odds, figuring a rich relative is going to die, or that the next time the phone rings, it will be the Publisher's Clearing House Prize Patrol calling for their cross street. And, many more think they want success — but are actually taking actions to prevent it, because they suffer from "lack" consciousness, and don't even know it. So, while the universe of people who need what you have is vast — the group who will seize the opportunity you're offering them is much smaller. You have to screen out the people who have a dream and are willing to do something about it (the prospects) from those who are waiting to hit the lottery (the suspects).

Of course, the first question to arise is, where do you find these people?

The place to begin is with friends, neighbors and relatives. This is the natural place to start, and it makes the most sense. You won't have to make cold calls or talk to strangers. People who know you will give you the benefit of the doubt and usually at least look at your Pre-Approach Packet, or meet you for a one-on-one over coffee.

A lot of people are reluctant to talk to the people they know, fearing that they'll become the victim of the *can't-be-a-prophet-in-your-own-hometown* syndrome. There is some truth to this. If you've been working alongside Joe for the past ten years, and now come along with this opportunity to get wealthy — Joe is probably going to be a little skeptical. That's okay. This is where edification comes in. Let me explain.

Edification works on the principle that for most people, the *expert* is the guy from out of town with a briefcase. Also known as the fact that many people place much more credibility in strangers than they do in their own daughters, husbands, fathers, etc. After all, they know all their baggage.

Your family and close friends know every mistake you've ever made, from the lemonade stand you had when you were six that lost money, to the time you tried to make money franchising ant farms. They haven't been able to achieve a happy, fulfilling life (and they figure they're a whole lot smarter than you), so they can't understand how you would know.

So, here's how it happens a lot of times. You join a network marketing company, and you're excited about the possibilities. You start to think about whom you would like to help, and naturally your thoughts turn to your parents. You call them up, go over to the house and make your presentation. It's a beauty. You sit back and relax — waiting for the grateful appreciation your parents are about to express — thankful that you've found a way to repay them for all they've done for you over the years.

Mother leans forward, about to speak, "So, Mister Big Shot, you're going to make all this money. Don't you remember when you had the paper route and you couldn't wake up in time? Your father had to deliver all the newspapers ..."

You're devastated. Here you're trying to do some good, trying to help them, and they're reacting like you were offering them a gift certificate for a complimentary office visit with Dr. Jack Kervorkian.

You've just experienced the prophet-in-your-own-hometown syndrome. No one is immune from this. To this day, I still maintain the hardest presentation I've ever given was to my sister Leise. This is the reason most people are afraid to talk to their friends, neighbors, and relatives (their warm market).

There is a solution ...

Edify your sponsorship, line and bring your first people to them. Your warm market is your best market. But, when you first begin the business, you shouldn't be making your own presentations. Your sponsor (or, in cases of fast growth, someone further up your sponsorship line) should be making your initial presentations, while you're taking notes and learning the presentation. This is the time to get to all of your can't-be-a-prophet people. Get them to a one-on-one, or give them the Pre-Approach materials. Make sure you let them know that this is a brand new opportunity for you, you've just discovered it and were introduced to the business by someone with a savvy business mind who's really good at helping people reach financial freedom. By edifying your sponsor in advance like this, you're already building up their credibility in the mind of your prospect.

Your friends and family will hear things from strangers that they cannot hear from you. If you want to start fast and get the best results, get these people in front of your sponsorship line and let them do the presenting. To break through with your warm market, you must take your ego out of the equation and edify your sponsor. This allows your sponsor to give you the most support. If your sponsor is already successful, bill them as "an expert in the business." If they're relatively new, moving up, but not mega-successful yet, refer to them as a "rising star." What you're doing in this scenario is leveraging the credibility you have with your warm market for maximum effect.

Here's why.

If your sponsor were to cold call one of your friends, neighbors or relatives, and try to tell them about an opportunity — they'd probably hang up. If you try to tell your friends about the opportunity, you get the hometown prophet treatment. But, here's the secret ...

Your warm market trusts you enough to review some initial materials, like a Pre-Approach Packet, or meet for coffee. If it looks interesting, they'll be intrigued enough to meet someone with you (or come to your home for a meeting). And, because you said you're new to the business, don't understand it all yet, and you've edified this person as an expert — they will hear things from them that they couldn't hear from you. This is the secret to getting started fast, and it really works!

Over the course of time, while you are learning the presentation from your sponsor (usually a five- to eight-week process), you'll be bringing in all your "chicken list" people. (Your chicken list consists of the people who are the most busy, successful and ambitious people you know — the ones you're "chicken" to make a presentation to.) Just get them in front of your sponsor. And during this time, your own presentation skills will be getting better; and you'll be gaining confidence and getting new distributors into your group. By the end of your first week, you'll be able to do a one-on-one presentation by yourself. By the time your five to eight weeks are up, you'll be quite capable of holding home meetings yourself. Here's the best part:

When you have people that you're still nervous with, or who still give you the hometown prophet treatment, just edify your sponsorship line and bring those people to a second-look meeting, where your sponsorship line is presenting! This is the way huge organizations are built! It's completely warm market, non-threatening, and very easily duplicated. <u>Anyone can build a group this way</u>.

Even if you have no formal education, you're shy, and afraid of making presentations — you can still get started in this business. You simply profess your ignorance, edify your sponsor, and bring your people to them. <u>And, you have as much time as you need to gain confidence and build your presentation skills</u>. Moreover, everyone you talk to will see how they can get involved, and gradually learn the business in a non-threatening way. It's completely duplicatable by everyone.

The first one-on-one presentation you give a prospect is really not designed to get them to immediately sign up, although as you get more experienced in the business, many people will.

As a rule, this presentation is simply a "first look," designed to get the prospect into the sponsoring process, or "pipeline." Your goal is to <u>book the next meeting</u>.

This first look should be non-threatening, and require a short time commitment by the prospect. Do not go into all the details about why the current economic and distribution systems are not working. Begin by mentioning some of the benefits of the business, and then getting right to the part about how the business is built. This does three things:

1. It ensures that the prospect doesn't feel we're attacking his position;

2. It means the prospect's second exposure to the presentation will be a bigger event than this one; and,

3. It allows you to do the presentation in under an hour, which means many more prospects will be willing to sit down and listen to you.

This first presentation can be conducted at a neighborhood coffee shop, your home or the prospect's home. <u>My first choice is the prospect's home</u>. You are much less likely to get stood up this way! Some people, however, are gun shy. They're afraid that if they let you into their house, you won't leave until you sell them something. They will want to come to your house, where they can make a ready escape. Yet, others will be afraid to be trapped in either place. They will feel safer meeting you at a neutral site. If so, select a neighborhood coffee shop and pick a non-meal time. Here's why:

You don't want to meet for a meal, because while this may not be out of your budget, it could be for a lot of other people. You want to keep what you're doing as duplicatable as possible. Make sure that your prospect is aware of this by using such language as, "Let's meet for a cup of coffee and I can show it to you." In addition to scheduling the meeting at a non-rush time, ask for a table out of main traffic paths, so there will be fewer distractions and interruptions for your prospect. Pick up the tab when you're through, and double or triple your usual tip to pay for your "office."

When you're presenting at their home or yours, cut the chitchat and get to the presentation. You probably obtained the appointment by promising not to take more than an hour of their time, so honor your promise. (In addition to keeping your word, this is good business and it allows you time to get in three or four presentations on a night you've set aside to work your business.)

If you're meeting at their house, lose the radio and television, ask them to unplug the phone, and get to the dining room table. Your goal is to expose them to a first look to determine whether or not they really are a prospect and have a dream. Once you determine this, schedule the next meeting. This will be a home or family meeting — a bigger event and their second look at the program. Remember, success is not determined by whether you sold a kit, but by whether you booked the next meeting. Pull out your calendar, and mark the appointment in front of your prospect.

Now, the question always comes up, *Hey, I want to build faster. Why don't I take out ads in magazines and do mail-outs?*

And, the answer is — because they work, but they're harder to duplicate. That doesn't mean you can't do them. I'm just saying that the farther you get from your warm market, the harder it will be for some of your people to duplicate you. A lot of people will not have the necessary skills or investment to do display advertising or direct mail. You can train people to become proficient in these areas, and many groups do. But it just makes sense to start with warm market strategies, and expand from there. Work with your sponsorship line, and they can help you find the right balance of cold market recruiting and duplication. If you'd like to research the subject in more depth, I recommend you get my *Massive Action Marketing* audiotape album and *Study Guide*.

One of the things that concerns me is when new people tell you they don't want to talk to their warm market. Usually, there's one of two variables at work.

One is, they simply don't believe it will work. They say things like, "I don't want to talk to anyone I know yet. I want to take out ads and talk to strangers. Then, when I'm rich and successful, I'll go back to my friends."

Of course, this is craziness. If you really thought you had an opportunity that could bring you wealth, happiness and fulfillment — wouldn't you be burning up the phone lines to tell your friends and family?

These people need to be sponsored all over again, so they really understand the business. And, they need a tough-love sponsor who will guide them, and even prod them into doing the things that are in their own best interests. In later years, I wouldn't spend my time working with someone if they weren't willing to at least approach their warm market. When someone told me that they were not willing to talk to their warm market, I was quick to refund their money and suggest they look elsewhere.

Now, of course, the second variable that can be at play here is that your new distributor has been an "MLM junkie," and they've already been to their warm market 20 times. They're simply too embarrassed to go back one more time. I can relate to this personally, since I went through exactly that.

But, I found a solution to this dilemma ...

Whenever I am faced with a difficult challenge, and there seems to be nowhere to turn — I do something that too few people do. In fact, most people think it's quite radical to even think about it. I tell the truth.

Picture this phone call:

"Rod, this is Randy. You're never going to believe this — you have every right in the world to hang up on me — but I've got to tell you something. I know we thought we were going to make money in that vitamin deal, and the bee pollen thing didn't work out, and the no-run panty hose deal, and I know you still have those water filters I sold you — so you have every right in the world to hang up on me — but, I honestly found something, and I think it's different. Here's why ..."

Now, what if Rod hangs up? He's not a prospect. Remember, all you need is a yes or no. The only thing you can't use is a maybe. So, if Rod does hang up, you can probably assume that you can put him in the no category.

Truth be told, he's really not likely to hang up. When you just tell the truth, and put it out there — most people will give you a listen. And, there will be dozens more people on your list who have never joined any of the programs you ever worked. And, you're meeting new people all the time. You met at least three to five new people this week. So, it would be a mistake to just eliminate all your warm market people without even trying.

Now, let's talk about finding people, and what you say to the ones you would like to sponsor. The reason most people in Network Marketing never make it to the director or breakaway level, is because they don't know how to meet people outside of their sphere of influence. They have a short list, so they need a perfect "invite" every time, or they run out of people. Of course, when they only have a few people left on their list, there's a subconscious tendency to 'save them' for fear that once they're used up — they'll have no one to talk to. This is a self-fulfilling prophecy — one you want to avoid. So, let's talk about how you can meet some new people on a consistent basis.

Here's your mantra: "Two people a day brings freedom my way." Think it and speak it every morning. Put it in a sticky note on your mirror. Then, just go out to live your life with the expectation of meeting new friends every day.

Start the day with two silver dollars in your left pocket. When you meet someone — move one to your right pocket. When you meet the second person, move the next coin over. You'll probably discover, as most people do, that you already meet new people every day. You just haven't been aware of it before, because you just let the moment pass.

Now, instead of just acknowledging new people and moving on — practice the art of conversation. Don't try to sell them anything — don't approach them about your business. Just talk. Be their friend and get to know them. Here are some of my favorite questions:

"You from around here?"

"So, how did you get from _____ to here?"

"What kind of work do you do?"

"Is that a tough business/job?"

"What's the hardest part of that business/job?"

"Are you married?"

"Got a family?"

"So, what does someone do for fun around here?"

These questions get people talking about their favorite subject — themselves. Asking if they're from around here usually gets people going. Almost everyone you talk to is from somewhere else. When I ask them what brought them here — invariably, they tell me it was to take a job or be closer to family or spouse's family. Either way, that leads the conversation to family or what they do for a living — both good lines of conversation to pursue.

Of course, when I ask if that is a tough business or job — 98% of people tell me, yes. Then, when I ask what the toughest part is — in most cases, they give me lots of good reasons why they should be in Network Marketing.

The key here is — you don't bring it up. It's not appropriate, and it wouldn't be effective anyway. At this point, all you want to do is make new friends — two a day. This gives you more than 700 new friends a year! Now, if you're meeting 700 people a year — doesn't it make sense that you'll find a few who are looking for an opportunity?

Of course it does. You'll know which ones by your conversation. Those who seem sharp, ambitious, and who express dissatisfaction with their job or business are your best prospects — the ones you'll want to approach later.

Now, before we talk about that — we need to address two other issues. First, what about if you're speaking to someone you meet and they come back with, "What's it to you — are you writing a book?"

Hey, get away from them as fast as you can. Obviously, they're not a prospect for this business at that point. And, they're certainly not someone you want as a friend.

The second issue is getting the phone number of the good prospects. I have a technique that makes this so simple you're going to be amazed. The most important thing is — never ask for their phone number. Most prospects get nervous here, and don't want to do this. Instead, use my "magic" million-dollar question, the one that never fails.

Simply say, "Ya' got a card?"

Instinctively they reach for a card and give it to you. And you'll be surprised. Most will even write their home phone number on the card. Those who do not have business cards invariably let you know they don't have one, but write their number down on a piece of paper. If you're truly being a friend, just getting to know them and not trying to sell them anything, they'll be happy to give you the number.

That's the main thing. Don't go looking for people to sign up — just go out and make friends. And, remember your mantra: "Two people a day, brings freedom my way."

So, now you're going out each day with the intention of meeting two new friends. As you do this, you're collecting cards and phone numbers. When you get home each day, add these people to your prospect list. When the lines you have are going down in depth, and don't need you doing their presentations anymore, you can now open some new lines. So, you look over your prospect list and decide who is the best of those prospects. I recommend you contact them by phone. This allows you to be brief; get to the point; and control the situation better. The call should go something like this:

"Hey Ray, this is Linda. You probably remember me. We met at Radio Shack when you were buying a cell phone. You seemed like a sharp guy, and from our conversation it seemed you might be open to taking a look at a business opportunity."

Usually now, they'll ask what it is. You respond with something like:

"I run a marketing business, and we're expanding here in the Dallas area. I can't promise you anything, but I'm looking for a couple of key people. If you're interested, I'd like to suggest we meet for a cup of coffee and I'll run it by you. You can't buy anything and you can't sign anything. It will just take 30 minutes, and you can see if it looks like something you want to explore further."

Now, it doesn't have to be this exact script. In fact, you'll find at least a dozen different ones in my *How to Earn at Least $100,000 a Year in Network Marketing* audiotape album. Find one or two that feel comfortable for you. The keys in this situation are:

- ▲ suggesting that they'll probably remember you;
- ▲ telling them you "can't promise them anything"; and,
- ▲ letting them know that they can't buy or sign anything.

Because they remember you, you were friendly, and it's only a 30-minute, no-risk commitment — most people will be more than happy to meet you for a one-on-one. And, because you're out there always meeting two people a day — you will never run out of qualified prospects!

Now, if you still think you don't meet two new people a day, let's look at some places where you can meet good prospects.

First, we can rule out the places you won't meet them. You won't find them in nightclubs and bars. These places are for alcoholics. Go to places where people of higher consciousness gather. Find a church that does lots of classes, like *Unity* or *Science of Mind*. Find some courses that appeal to you, and sign up. People who take courses on prosperity, Tai Chi, meditation and yoga are usually people seeking more, so they're great candidates for your business. And, don't overlook public seminars. It's a safe bet that the people who pay and go to a seminar to see Wayne Dyer, Deepak Chopra or John Gray are looking for more out of life. Just be yourself. Practice the art of conversation and meet new friends.

And then there's my all-time "secret weapon." The #1 best place to go to meet great people all the time. Ready for this? <u>It's the car wash</u>. But not the put-four-quarters-in-and-drive-through-so-they-can-break-off-your-antennae wash. No, I'm talking about the hand car wash.

You know who goes there? People with nice cars. Porches, Vipers, Mercedes and Lexus, among others. People who have nice cars already know something about success. And, the fact they take care of them tells you a lot about them. At the hand wash I go to, I've met numerous company executives (one who owns 47 Ferraris, a couple of Rolls' and a few other cars), a Grammy-winning songwriter, two NBA stars, a minister of a church with 3,000 Sunday worshipers, and a host of other serious people.

The secret to prospecting is having a long, never-ending list. When you practice the strategies we've just talked about, that's exactly what you'll have. Having that long list is the first half of the battle. The second half is how you approach the people on the list — your "invite."

A weak invite can cost you $200,000 a year in lost income. Yet, it's one of the most poorly taught areas of the business. Most people concentrate on learning a good presentation, or they figure they can always bring their prospect to their sponsorship line. What gets lost in all this is the fact that <u>without a good invite, your prospect will never see a presentation</u>.

This is also one of the biggest causes of dropouts. Because new distributors are not trained with a good invite, they blow off some of their best prospects. Not being able to even get their prospects in front of their sponsorship line, they quickly get frustrated, and many call it quits before they ever get started. This is sad, because with the proper training, the invite is simple, effortless, and even fun.

Problem one is that most people in the business only know how to invite people in person — which is much more difficult. Problem two is that most network marketers only know one style of invite — <u>and this style won't work for 90% of the people they approach with it</u>. Once you clear these few things up, people are amazed at how easy inviting prospects to presentations is.

Let's look first at the two ways to approach people:

▲ In person

▲ By telephone

First, let's look at how to do the in-person invitations more effectively.

Here's the scenario most people go through. They go to a ball game with a friend, and during the first inning, they will ask their qualifying question. Right away, their prospect's interest is peaked, and so they spend the rest of the game interrogating our new distributor:

"What is it exactly?"

"Is it Amway?"

"What's the name of the company?"

"What's the product?"

"What do I have to sell?"

And a host of questions like these. The result is that you lose control of the situation. A sure sign of a losing proposition. Remember this. Most of the time, your prospect does not know what's in his best interest. Mention Network Marketing, and he'll tell you he knows all about it, because he was in Herbalife for three weeks, six years ago. Most people make judgments on very limited knowledge, and they don't realize the drastic extent of their own self-imposed limitations. If your prospects really understood your business — they'd already be in it, getting rich.

So, your job is to approach your prospect in a way that ensures they will at least hear about it. If you're inviting in person, here's how that might happen. Let's use our earlier example, where you're at the ball game with your friend. You don't bring up the subject the whole game. Then, when it's over, you're standing in the parking lot ... you have to go, and he has dinner waiting ... only then do you bring up your qualifying question or hand out your info pack. He is now on his way home, an you're on your way, so he is much less likely to ask you a bunch of questions. It's easier to control the situation. The few questions he does have are easy to direct to the one-on-one. You can respond with something along the line of:

"I'd love to show you. What if we meet for a cup of coffee? It will just take 30 minutes — you'll get a good overview of the business — and, you can see if it looks like something you want to explore further."

He is much more likely to agree to this, because he knows that you and he both have places you need to go right then. Serious prospects will sit down and take a serious look. So, when you're doing the inviting in person, stay firm, and direct him into the one-on-one. Most of his questions will be answered in the presentation, and the other ones can be handled after.

If you're using a Pre-Approach Packet, the prospect will review that first, looking for his answers. If they are not answered, he's likely to agree to come to a one-on-one meeting to learn more.

Doing the in-person invitations this way keeps you in control of the process, and ensures that a lot more prospects will actually receive enough information to make an educated decision, rather than a knee-jerk one.

Even better in my mind is inviting by phone. It's simpler, quicker, and it's easier to control the situation. Because you control the timing, and you're not available in person, your prospect is much more likely to agree to meet you.

Now, let's discuss the actual phone invite to use ...

It's not necessary to spend 45 minutes on chitchat to catch up your prospect on everything that has happened since you saw him eighteen months ago. This is the mistake most people make. I recommend against it, because it takes the focus off business, and the prospect is then oftentimes not conducive to receiving a business message. Also, he will often feel manipulated. (And, he's usually right!)

It's actually quite acceptable — and quite effective — to immediately get to the point. Say something like,

"Hey, Chuck. It's Randy Gage. Got a minute?"

"Sure."

"I'm calling about a business matter. Quick question for you ..."

Then, you ask your first question, getting right to the point. You'll find your prospects really appreciate your forthrightness; the calls go much better; and, you can do ten or fifteen of them in an hour's time.

The actual invitation ...

Now, the next thing you need to understand is that there are actually two different styles of invites. Most people in Network Marketing know only one — the "indirect" or "mystery" approach. Some examples of these include:

"Chuck, you seem like a sharp guy. I'm wondering if you ever explore opportunities to make a second income. I'm expanding my business, and I'm looking for a couple of key people. I'd love to sit down and discuss it with you."

"Chuck, I've got a high-volume marketing business (or, I'm working with some people who have a high-volume marketing business). And we're expanding in the (city) area. We're looking for a couple of key people, and I thought you might be interested in taking a look."

"Chuck, have you ever thought about being your own boss? I help people open their own home-based businesses, and I've got something I want you to check out."

Another approach is to offer some teaser information with your question. Some examples:

"I'm involved in a new venture that you may be interested in. You'd be your own boss. There's unlimited income potential, and it's residual income. I have some materials you can review to see if it's right for you ..."

"You consider yourself open-minded, don't you? Well, I'm involved in a marketing business and I'm looking for a couple of key people who want to make money on the side. I'd love to run it by you."

"Jimmy, I'm excited about some new business ideas that I've come across in the financial world. I've discovered how to make some great income with some lucrative tax benefits. I'd really like to share these ideas with you and Brenda and get your opinions on them."

"I'm involved in a marketing business with some large profit potential. I thought I'd call to see if you're interested in making some money on the side. Are you in the market for more money, more time, or both?"

"I have a large volume marketing business ... or, I've recently started working with some people who have a large volume marketing business ... and it's really hot right now. It just so happens we're expanding in (city) and we're in the process of talking to a couple of key people. You impress me as someone who's looking for more out of life. If you're really interested, I can find some time to show it to you."

After any one of these, you would say something to the effect of:

"I'd like to give you a brief overview. It will only take about 30 minutes. If you like what you see, then we can explore it further at a later date. If not, that will be the end of it."

Or, if you're using my Lifestyle Freedom Pack, you would say something like:

"I'd like to drop off some info — to give you a brief overview. Please look it over, and I'll check back with you on [day] to answer any questions you have."

The indirect approach works very well with the casual acquaintances you will meet as you go about your life. However, it's almost destined to fail with close friends and relatives. Unfortunately, this is the only approach most network marketers know. What they are missing is the "direct" approach. This is an approach I was a little hesitant to try, but when I did, gave me a significant increase in positive results. A direct invite looks like this:

"Hey Chuck. It's Randy. Got a minute?"

" Sure."

"Got a quick question for you. What do you know about Network Marketing?"

If you're in an old-line company, you might want to try substituting your company name for the last question: *"What do you know about Amway?"*

Personally, I found the direct approach was a breakthrough for my business, and so has everyone I've taught it to. Now, to do this, however, you might have to make a dramatic paradigm shift in your beliefs. If you still suffer from the belief that "people look down on Network Marketing," or "most people think Network Marketing is a scam," or "most people think Network Marketing is a pyramid," this won't work for you. Try this belief on for size:

Most people are fascinated with Network Marketing.

Now, here's where I get this belief. About two years ago, I started my own unscientific little test. Every time I was on an airplane (which I am a lot), and people asked me, "What do you do?" I began telling people, "I'm in Network Marketing."

Frankly, I was just curious. I wanted to see how many people would give up their seats, go back and sit in coach; how many would run shrieking from the plane and try to jump off without a parachute; and, how many would attack me?

But, a fascinating thing happened. In more than three years, I have never had one negative response — not one. Probably about 20% of the people say something like, *"Oh, is that computers?"* And I'll reply, *No, have you ever heard of companies like Amway, Herbalife and Nu Skin?'* And when they say they have, I say, *"That's Network Marketing."*

And then, invariably, in either case, people will say something like, *"Well, you know, I tried that once. I was in Herbalife a couple years ago, but it never really worked out for me. But I know a lot of people who do really well with that."*

Or, they will come back with something like, *"Well, you know, I was in Amway. I never made any money with it, but I had just had a baby, and I didn't put a lot of time into it, and I never really stuck with it. But, my old sponsor is still in it and he makes a lot of money in the business."*

Or, *"It never worked for me, but I've got some friends. Boy, they have a 20,000-square-foot house and six cars, and man, they're making a fortune with Shaklee."*

All I get is fascination with the industry. Since I wrote the first edition of this book, I've been on countless radio shows all across the country. What I see over and over again is that this is a subject people want to know more about. They're either in Network Marketing; they know someone successful in Network Marketing; they want to be in Network Marketing; or, they used to be in Network Marketing, and they're thinking about getting back in. The amazing success stories they've heard have them very curious what all the fuss is about.

If you're still suffering from the belief that people think it's a pyramid, or it's a chain letter, or most of them will respond negatively — then you're making all of that up yourself. My experience has created nothing but positive reactions, and, in many cases, very qualified leads.

What makes the direct approach so effective is the fact that in reality, almost everybody you know — already knows you're in Network Marketing. So, when you call up with the indirect approach, as a lot of people train, they're thinking, *"Well, why is he being so sneaky about this? Why doesn't he just tell me that it's Herbalife (Or Cell Tech, Amway, etc.)?"*

They know, and because you go with the indirect approach, it insults their intelligence. Just ask the question, *"What do you know about Network Marketing?"* Most of the time, you'll get back answers similar to what I've heard on the plane.

Once in a great while, you may get a negative response. They might say, "Well, I tried that five years ago, and I spent a lot of money on water filters, and it took me two years to sell them." That's not necessarily a bad response. It's good to find out if there is any negativity. So, what you do is give them an opportunity to express whatever it is they know or think they know about Network Marketing. Then, you come back with something like, "Well, you know, the industry has changed a lot over the last couple of years, and I've got an opportunity that I'm very excited about. I'd really love to sit down with you, have a cup of coffee, and have you evaluate it for me. I value your opinion, and I was wondering if you'd be willing to take 30 minutes and take a look at this with me."

Now, imagine if the prospect is really negative. They'll say, "Oh, it's a pyramid; it's a chain letter. If you do that, you are going to go to prison."

Then, you come back with, "Well, you know, I value your opinion, and I've looked at this thing ten ways from Sunday, and I just can't find any faults in it. Would you be willing to sit down and let me give you a 30-minute overview, and then you tell me what you think the flaws are? Because, if you can't find the flaws either, I think it's something you'd be great at."

Now, we're doing a couple of things here. First of all, if they really are convinced that this is a pyramid — how can they resist an offer like this? They've got to sit down with you and show you all the flaws.

In reality, most people don't know anything about Network Marketing. As we said earlier, if they did, they'd be in it, and they'd be millionaires. So, what they have to base it on is their two-week or three-week experience from five years ago, or, perhaps, they were front-loaded in some shady deal — or, more likely — they knew somebody, who knew somebody, who said they had gotten skinned. When they really sit down and take an objective look at it — most people will see the soundness of the business.

127

The direct approach absolutely gets right to the point, and it's very effective. It lets you know exactly what your prospect's perception of the business is, so you can respond appropriately. In actuality though, most people simply don't have a negative opinion of Network Marketing anymore. It has received a wave of positive publicity in many prestigious magazines and newspapers, so many people are quite intrigued by it. Simply by the fact that you're open and bring it up, most are more than willing to sit down and spend 30 minutes with you to take a look at what it's about. The direct invite really has the potential to transform your business.

Using the right approach ...

The secret to all this is knowing which person to use which invite with. Here's my million-dollar secret. For casual acquaintances — use the indirect approach. This works very well with them, because casual acquaintances will take you at your word. If it's somebody you met at Radio Shack that you had a 15-minute conversation with, and you call them up later and let them know that you have a marketing business that's expanding in the area, and you're looking for a couple of key people, they'll simply take you at your word.

Your brother or your neighbor may not take you at your word if you come with the indirect approach. They are much more likely to challenge you. So, with friends, neighbors and relatives — use the direct approach. They appreciate your honesty. They're very intrigued with Network Marketing, and you'll find that this will get you a lot of appointments. Remember, for casual acquaintances, use the indirect invite. For friends, neighbors and relatives, use the direct invite, and you will find that this will allow you to dramatically increase the number of presentations you make. And, when you make a lot of presentations — you're going to get distributors into your organization.

Using a Pre-Approach Packet vs. an Invitation ...

Let's look deeper at this issue of using a Pre-Approach Packet or not, so you can determine which method might be the best for you. Your goal is not to sponsor anybody at this stage, but rather to separate the non-prospects from the real ones.

Going directly to a presentation ...

In this model, you ask the qualifying questions, as we discussed earlier, by phone or in person. The people who don't respond positively are the ones you attempt to get as a customer. The rest, who do respond with some degree of interest, are the ones you want to get to a presentation. This could be a shortened 30-miniute mini-presentation, like I mentioned in the last chapter, or an actual home or hotel meeting. My experience is that it's difficult to get people directly to a meeting, whereas the 30-minute one-on-one seems to be easier. In either case, you are attempting to get someone directly from the qualifying question to a presentation. Once you've been in the business a while, you'll have some success and will develop the skill and confidence you'll need to do this pretty readily.

When you first begin, this may be a challenge. You have to have enough confidence to brush off the inevitable questions prospects bring up, and keep insisting that they get to a presentation and see the whole story. Here are some of the questions you can expect to hear, along with some possible reply scenarios:

"What is it?"

"I can't do business on the phone, but I can tell you it's a chance to diversify your income and make some extra money. If you're serious, let's meet for a cup of coffee, and I'll show you the whole thing."

"What do you do exactly?"

"Well it's impossible to explain over the phone, but there are several scenarios I can put you in. There's a small-business

option, if you're looking to pick up a couple of hundred dollars extra each month — or a big-business option, if you're looking for complete financial independence. Let's meet for a cup of coffee, and I'll show you the whole thing."

"Is it selling?"
"Why? Do you like to sell?"

"Yes."
"Great! You'll like what I've got. There are opportunities in sales and management. When can we get together?"

"Is it selling?"
"Why? Do you like to sell?"

"No."
"Great, you'll like what I've got, because there's opportunities both in sales and management. When can we get together?"

Some other key phrases that you may find helpful:
"I can't promise you anything, but you need to take a look."
"You can't spend any money or sign anything. Just take a look and evaluate it for now."
"An intelligent person looks before they decide anything. I'm sure you'll want to get all the necessary facts before you make a decision."
"If we end up working together, I'll be investing a lot of time and money with you."

If you have a strong training program and culture in your organization, this approach can get prospects into your sponsoring pipeline quickly. The challenge comes with the new distributors who are not forceful enough to deflect questions and get the prospect to a presentation. Which leads us to the second option.

Using A Pre-Approach Packet ...

Here, you begin the process the same way, by first asking qualifying questions, just like the ones above. Like the last case, the people who do not respond positively are the ones you want to get as a retail customer. But, this time, the people who respond with interest are given some materials to study, instead of being asked to attend a meeting.

The reason, of course, is that people are less resistant to studying material than they are to having to go to a meeting somewhere. It is also a lot easier to do with a brief phone call. Once again, you are likely to get some questions raised. And, you'll handle these just as you would if you were doing the direct invitation route. Some examples:

"What is it?"

"I can't do business on the phone, but I can tell you that it's a chance to diversify your income and make some extra money. I need to get some information into your hands."

"What do you do exactly?"

"Well it's impossible to explain over the phone, but there are several scenarios that I can put you in. There's a small-business option, if you're looking to pick up a couple of hundred dollars extra each month — or a big-business option, if you're looking for complete financial independence. Tell me what you think you'd be interested in, and I'll get some information into your hands so you can check it out."

"Is it selling?"

"Why? Do you like to sell?"

"Yes."

"Great! You'll like what I've got. There are opportunities in sales and management. When can I get some information over to you?"

"Is it selling?"

"Why? Do you like to sell?"

"No."

"Great! You'll like what I've got, because there are opportunities both in sales and management. When can I get some information over to you?"

Some other key phrases on the phone that you may find helpful:

"Obviously, I can't explain it on the phone. Why don't you let me get some information into your hands?"

"I just got involved with this myself, so I don't know everything. How about if I bring over the complete information packet, and you can evaluate it for yourself?"

What this approach does is makes it a little easier for new distributors without a lot of experience to recruit faster. The idea is to give them materials that have enough compelling benefits that they will want to come to a meeting after they review it. To facilitate this, I developed the *Lifestyle Freedom Pack* I told you about earlier. This is a small album with a Special Report extolling the benefits of Network Marketing, and a copy of my *Escape the Rat Race* audiotape. Basically, this is an opportunity meeting in an album! It helps you sponsor faster, and duplicate easier.

The tape is a recording of me, conducting a LIVE opportunity meeting. I open with all the benefits of Network Marketing, explain how it works, and establish the credibility of the industry. Most importantly, I do it in a compelling way, with lots of audience response. I paint the picture of the slavery of the regular 45-year plan in a way that prospects understand. I cover all the key elements necessary in a strong presentation, except I don't reveal what the products or company are. This "generic" presentation has proven very compelling, and is working well in a number of different countries around the world. We even see quite a few in countries where English is not the native language.

What we've done with this pack is create a tool that does your initial presentation for you. In real terms, <u>it's meant to disqualify the non-prospects and lead prospects to an appointment.</u>

I recommend that you have ten Pre-Approach Packets — and keep them in constant circulation. They make you no money sitting at home. Keep them circulating, and they can make you wealthy. Get one back from Jim give it to Shawn; get it back from Shawn, and give it to Sherry, etc.

<u>The important part of this process is to creating a sense of urgency.</u> Let your prospect know that other prospects are waiting for this material, and that they may preview it for 48 hours <u>only</u>. Get their commitment that they will review it within that time.

If they balk at 48 hours (saying, for example, that they can't get to it for four days), tell them that you have other people waiting to review it in the meantime, and that you'll bring it back in four days. Don't just say it — mean it. Keep your packs in constant circulation.

Remember, if you're new, you may want to do the qualifying questions on the phone. This is less threatening, and it's easier for you to control the situation. Just like when you prospect in person — when you actually give the materials to your prospect, you must create a sense of urgency. Confirm the prospect's interest on the phone, and then just run by with the materials. You can pull up while you're on your way somewhere — leave the car running the car door open, and honestly say, *"I've got to run. I'm on my way to ——, so I just wanted to drop off the materials I promised you."*

When you return after 48 hours to collect your packet, ask your prospect simply:

"Well, what do you think?"

Their answer should fall into one of three categories:

1) *"That looks very interesting, but it doesn't seem right for me ..."*

2) *"I'm not interested in that pyramid stuff. My brother-in-law has a garage full of water filters, blah, blah, blah!!"*

3) *"Wow! Sounds intriguing. But what's the company? It doesn't say what the products are ..."*

People who respond like the first example are simply not looking for an opportunity. They did not catch the vision, and are best handled by offering them information about your products. If, however, you'd really like to work with them, and you think they didn't really give your pre-approach materials a fair look, you might say something like:

"Hey, it really hurts my feelings that you won't even look at this. Besides that, you're a friend of mine and I was hoping we could work together."

Don't push it after this, however. Remember that you're looking for people who are looking — and are open to new ideas. Not people that you have to twist their arm and sell.

The people who respond in the second manner are closed-minded people who don't want to be confused by the facts. If you're using my *Lifestyle Freedom Pack,* it's obvious they didn't even read the Special Report. You can argue with this type of person, but I don't recommend it. I suggest you get your materials back and get away from them as quickly as possible. If, however, you really want to work with them, and you think they just had a knee-jerk response without really checking things out, you could reply along these lines:

"Hey, I'm hurt that you even think I would be associated with such a thing. I wouldn't be involved with anything that wasn't on the up-and-up. Besides, you're a friend of mine. I'm not looking to rip you off — I was hoping we'd have the opportunity to work together."

Same admonishment as the last time. You want them to at least see a presentation. But, if their mind is totally made up beforehand, don't waste your time.

The *"Wow!"* replies are the keepers. These are the people you want to move to a meeting. If it's possible, do it right then. If it's not, then schedule a specific time and place for this to happen. It's okay to say something like, "Where would you be more comfortable, at your home, or would you like to come to ours?" Then, once you have the appointment, lock it in. Don't be afraid to say something like, "Let me know if you're not going to be there. I'll invite someone else."

I can't emphasize enough how important it is to have both spouses present for your presentation. If I'm prospecting a man, I might say something like, "Like a lot of companies, when we sit down to talk to someone about a business, we want their wife to be there to make sure we're all on the same page." If the man balks, and suggests that he'll relay the information to her, I'll explain why this won't work. "Because, Jimmy, you won't be able to explain it to her. I'll just be doing a quick run-through the first time to see if you're qualified. I'd like you and Brenda there, so you can see it together."

If you're married, you might mention that your spouse is going to be there too. By having both spouses present, you'll dramatically increase your likelihood of success. If you've been using the Pre-Approach Packet long distance, do a presentation on the phone, and send out your company materials packet.

By using a pre-approach in this way, you'll get the best results from the limited amount of time you have to work your business. You'll be making presentations only to qualified prospects, and you'll dramatically reduce the rejection that you and your people will face.

NOTE: As I said earlier, not all lines use Pre-Approach Packets. They ask the qualifying questions, and then go straight to an appointment. Check with your sponsor.

Now, we need to talk about the amount of time you spend doing this. Please understand if you're not out qualifying people, circulating Pre-Approach Packets and / or making appointments — you're really not doing the business.

You need to be open and aware of the messages people are sending you 24 hours a day — not just during the seven to ten hours a week you're doing your business. Here's what I mean.

You hear a co-worker complaining that they don't have enough money to afford a new car, and the old one needs to be replaced. You hear someone at church expressing dissatisfaction with their life because they have a terrible boss. Your friend tells you that she wants to vacation in Hawaii, but has to settle for another trip to Disneyland instead. These are clues. As you go about your day-to-day activities, listen for these kinds of statements. These people are prospects. Make a mental note of this and move them up on your prospecting timetable. And, finally, keep this in mind. This is a business of appointments. If you're not making them and keeping them — you're not doing the business.

Picture a dentist, lawyer, hairstylist or doctor without appointments. They'd be out of business. You are no different. **If you don't have three to five appointments lined up for this week — you don't have a business.** Network Marketing can work for you, but you must really work the business. And working the business means making appointments!

And, while we're on the subject of pre-approaching people, we should talk about when in your relationship with them this approach should happen.

I'm not a big fan of pre-approaching the waitress you just met, or the taxi driver you just had. The odds are long you'll sponsor them, and even longer that you'll get your materials back. It makes more sense to me for you to just put them on your name list and let the relationship develop. As you get to know them better, it will be much more natural, and you will have a greater chance of success when you talk with them.

Now, don't get me wrong. If you meet a flight attendant or hotel desk clerk that just impresses the daylights out of you — you know they're perfect for the business, and you might never see them again — go ahead and approach them. But, for the most part, you will have much greater success prospecting the people that you already have a relationship with.

Now, you're almost ready for the next step — giving powerful presentations. But first, we have to take a side trip — and talk about retailing ...

CHAPTER NINE.

Building Your Consumer Group

O F ALL THE MARKETING STRATEGIES I TEACH — THE WAY YOU acquire retail customers seems to be the most difficult for people to understand. That's because I suggest you do this the exact opposite way that most people do this. It's kind of ironic, but I want you to get your retail customers as a result of the people who choose not to do the business.

I don't want you to build your business in the way most people do — which is to initially sell products to customers — and then try to upgrade them into the business. I'm very much against this approach for two reasons.

REASON 1. IT TAKES WAY TOO LONG.

With some of the products we have in this industry, it can take someone three or four months to have their product "experience." Whereas, with my approach, you can go down four levels in a month. With the product experience approach, that can take a year.

REASON 2. YOU WILL SCARE OFF SOME OF YOUR VERY BEST PROSPECTS.

One of the reasons many people don't join the business is they think they'll have to go out and peddle products door-to-door. Obviously, that's not true, but they don't know that.

138

Here's what happens:

Let's say you work with Phil. And one day Phil is complaining about how tired he gets every afternoon. Your eyes light up, and you begin to lecture him on nutrition, vitamins, minerals and herbs. After your 30-minute sermon on the benefits of healthy supplements, you introduce him to MEGA-POWER-ENERGY-BOOSTER, your company's special herbal formula.

Phil agrees to try a bottle, so you give him one and collect $40.00. Over the next several days or weeks, you talk him through using the product and monitor his progress. He thinks it's improving, so he gets another bottle from you when the first one runs out. You, of course, get another $40.00 from him. A few days later, Phil comes back. "Eureka," he says. "This stuff really works. I have great energy every afternoon. My hair stopped hurting, and my teeth don't itch any more!" Now, you figure you've got him. He's had his *product experience,* so you can safely broach the subject of the business.

"Guess what," you exclaim. "Did you know that you could get these products for free? Even (gasp) make money with them?"

"Really," Phil says. "How do I do that?"

"It's easy," you reply. "You just become a distributor."

"That sounds very interesting," Phil responds. "But I think I'd rather just get them from you, because I don't know how to sell."

You're incredulous. "Sell! Whatever gave you the idea that you have to sell? We never SELL; we just SHARE."

Now, you can talk about SHARING all day long, but the fact is you SOLD Phil a bottle of MEGA-POWER-ENERGY-BOOSTER for $40.00. Then, you sold him another bottle, and took another $40.00. You have unequivocally, without a doubt, proven to Phil that this is a sales business. So, if he's in the 90 percent of the population who are non-sales types — he won't be interested in the business. When you lead with the products, you scare off the non-sales types — many of whom would be great for the business.

It's not that leading with the products doesn't work — it does eventually. But, my experience is that it takes the average person from five to eight years before they get to a livable income when they lead with the products. People who present the way I'm suggesting can get up to a livable income within a two- to four-year period. Unfortunately, people are not as patient and willing to stick to commitments as they once were. If you follow the five- to eight-year program, you'll find that most of your promising people drop out before they achieve any success.

It should be noted that this approach I'm suggesting is not the "business" approach, nor is it the "anti-product" approach. It is the balanced approach — one that includes the products, business, and the entire lifestyle opportunity.

This is not to say that the practice of selling products first — and then trying to upgrade customers to the business — doesn't work. It does to some extent. First, the ten percent who are sales types, if they like the products, will enthusiastically go out and attempt to market them. And, even with the non-sales types, a certain percentage of them will be so impressed with the product results that they will get over their initial fear and reluctance, and go out and market the products. Most, however, will not. And, for the ones who do, you will find this to be a long, delayed process.

They must first try the products, experience some kind of "miracle" results, and then gradually learn how to market the products to others. This process can take months, or even years. My experience is that people who build their businesses by leading with the products — retailing first — take five to eight years to build their businesses up to what I consider a livable income level. On the other hand, distributors who approach on the opportunity and follow the system like the one outlined in this book, can do it in about two to four years.

> **NOTE:** Please understand. I'm referring to the process of building what we'll later describe as a "big business" model, a multi-level money machine. There will be people who choose the "small business" model, which is simply retailing products to people they know. I don't mean to denigrate these people by any means. You must appreciate every person in your network, regardless of the size of his or her business. But, building a few hundred-dollar-a-month income-retailing products is neither the focus nor the intent of this book. It's for that reason that I'm writing specifically on the strategies necessary to build a large network. Make no mistake. I want you to have retail customers. Lots of them. It's just that I want you to get them from the people who don't become distributors.

There are quite a few good reasons to have a large consumer group. First, of course, are the legal ones. Having retail customers is what prevents the program from becoming an illegal, closed system. Customers are one of the things that separates legitimate Network Marketing from pyramid schemes.

Another good reason is the extra income it generates for you. A great part of the population are not prospects for building a business. Depending upon your product, a much larger percentage of people are candidates to be customers. You will buy at wholesale, and provide it to your customer at retail. The difference is your retail profit. This profit will especially come in handy in the lean times, during the first few months you are starting your business.

Another benefit of having retail customers is that they will oftentimes send you people who will become business-builders.

The more happy customers you have out there — the more likely you are to get referrals.

And, finally, your retail customers ensure that your personal volume and/or group volume requirements are always met, so you qualify for all the appropriate bonuses due you in your compensation plan.

So, we know there are lots of good reasons to have a consumer group. Now, let's talk about how to develop one, and then how to manage it.

Let's go back to the initial pre-approach step, and see how that is managed. Suppose you ask someone your qualifying question, "Have you ever thought about opening your own business? Do you ever explore ways of increasing your annual income?" etc., and he or she responds negatively. They maintain they're happy with their job, and they're making what they are worth. (There really are a few of these rare creatures around.)

In this case, you would then go to what I call your "turn" question. This is the question that turns the conversation from business to product. If you were in a nutrition program, for example, you might say something like, "I ask because my business is helping people get healthy (or lose weight). Would you be interested in becoming healthier (burning off excess fat)?" Or, let's suppose you are in a discount long distance service program. Your "turn" question might go something like, "I ask because my business is helping people lower their long distance phone bills. Would you be interested in slashing your phone bill by 40 percent?"

If the prospect responds negatively to both your pre-approach question <u>and</u> your "turn" question — then they simply aren't a prospect for you. Now, if they respond positively about the "turn" question, this is where you present the information about your products (or make an appointment to do this as soon as possible). Of course, at this stage, you'd also present the prospect with the appropriate catalogs, product brochures,

142

videos or audiotapes. Through this process, you should be able to get a fair number of retail customers from the prospects who are not interested in building a business.

You can also pick up customers from the prospects who decide that they are not interested in joining the business during the presentation and follow-up steps. You can do this simply by making a certain statement in their first presentation. At some point, say something to the effect of, "And if you decide not to do this, then we'd love to have you as a customer." By your planting this seed early, many of your prospects who decide they don't want to build a business will select the retail customer option. We'll look at how to facilitate this further when we get to the chapter on presentations.

Now, let's look at some tips on managing your consumer group. Your goals are to keep your customers satisfied with superior service; upgrade their usage through education; and, to do this without taking away from the time needed to work with your business-builders. Ideally, you want to spend 95 percent of your efforts with your builders, and manage your consumer group with the remaining 5 percent. Let's talk about some specifics.

One of the unique benefits you can offer your customers is exemplary customer service. Most everywhere they try to spend their money, they will be confronted with bored order-takers, preoccupied or indifferent clerks, uneducated service people, or downright rude employees. Show your customers you actually care about them. Take a few simple actions to comfort them, and they are likely to turn into customers for life.

Sending a thank-you note after they receive their first order would be a nice start. If you are delivering the products yourself, open up each box or bottle, and get the customer to use the products immediately. Go over the usage instructions completely, and make sure your customer fully understands them. Don't leave until you answer every question they may have. If their products are being shipped from your company, arrange to drop over right after they arrive. If you cannot be there in person, be sure to phone.

There is much to be said about going to the customer's house, being there when they open up their products, and walking them through the usage instructions. You'll find if you don't do this, you'll have a much higher rate of returns. And, when you go to pick up the products — you'll find a lot of people have never even opened the box!

There's bound to be some drop off in excitement, or even buyer's remorse if there's a lag time between the time a prospect orders and then receives his order. If you're over at his house reaffirming the benefits, showing him you care, and explaining how to get the best product results, you'll keep this to an absolute minimum.

After this initial order, stay in touch with your customers. Maintain accurate records of the business they do with you. If your company has an auto-ship option, get as many of your customers on this as possible. This ensures that they have prompt service, a steady supply of the products they like, and that they will never run out.

If your company does not have an auto-ship program – it is your responsibility to call your customers and get their order. Do not expect customers to call you before they run out. Most will not. Then, once they get off your program, their results may suffer, and you may lose them. By keeping good records, you should know when to call them so you can get their order delivered to them before they run out.

Keep them advised of any specific offers and new product introductions. Suggest alternative or complementary products, where appropriate. If any complaints come up, handle them immediately in a courteous manner. If refunds or exchanges are necessary, make them right away. Even customers who are on the auto-ship program should get a once-a-month phone call just to ensure that everything is satisfactory. When you see relevant newspaper articles, or items that would be of interest to your customers, send them a copy. If your company or sponsorship line puts out a newsletter for customers, send that to them, as well as any new product materials that become available.

When your company introduces new products, be sure to keep your customers informed. In certain cases, it may be appropriate to send them a sample. Check with your sponsorship line on this.

, We do need to deal with the question of inventory. Many of today's modern MLM companies have customer-direct programs that ship products directly to the customer, and, in some cases, allow them to order direct via a toll-free number or Website. This has greatly reduced the need to carry a large inventory. Nonetheless, you will still find it helpful to carry a modest inventory. This ensures you have product to compensate for occasional back orders, and allows you to get new customers and distributors started on the products right away.

Good customer service leads you to your next goal — upgrading your customers' usage through education. You'll find that the better educated your customers are — the more products or services they will use. This is where sending out samples, catalogs, newsletters or new marketing materials comes into play.

You may find it useful to have a product seminar or open house in your area once a month. Your upline pin-rank distributor should coordinate this. Check with your sponsorship line on this.

> **NOTE:** These product workshops should be for
> customers and distributors <u>only</u>. You would not want
> to bring a brand new prospect who has not seen an
> opportunity presentation. This would be leading with

the product, which would cause the many problems we discussed earlier.

From time to time, your retail customers may refer other people to you who are interested in your products or services. You will want to ask some qualifying questions to these referrals to ensure that they are not interested in the business. This is because it's likely your customer did not tell them that a business option is even available. There are also two things you need to do for your original customer who made the referral:

1. Be sure to thank them for their thoughtfulness; and,

2. Be sure to again suggest they consider becoming a distributor. Make sure they understand that there is some referral override income available, and by not being a distributor, they will be passing this up. <u>Don't pressure them</u>. It may be that they are still simply not interested in a business. Just remind them of the opportunity.

Following the procedures in this chapter will ensure that you have a steady supply of new customers and a stable consumer base. Make it a goal to get at least ten retail customers as quickly as possible. Just don't confuse them with distributors. <u>Sponsoring five people who want to be customers will not build a large network</u> — <u>only sponsoring business-builders will do this</u>. You need business-builders, and you need customers. Be grateful for both!

CHAPTER TEN

GIVING POWERFUL PRESENTATIONS

B Y NOW, YOU KNOW THAT NETWORKING IS A FABULOUS WAY TO make a wonderful income, help the people you care about, and build residual income security. **But all this will mean nothing if you can't convey this to your prospects.** Establish this, and you will turn prospects into distributors. No matter what your company sales kit or training video tells you — your prospect is only interested in one thing: **how will this benefit me?** You can talk about product research, company stability and million-dollar sales all day long, but if you don't relate them in terms of benefits to your prospect — he's not going to be interested.

> **You must lead with the *benefits*, then substantiate with *features*.**

It sounds so simple that you probably think you already do that. The odds are that you don't. If you're like most distributors — you are talking entirely about features.

What do I mean by that? It means you tell people things like:

We're a debt-free, X-year-old company.

Our products are the best.

I made $5,000 my first month.

We have the strictest quality control standards.

My sponsor is an expert in this.

If you think about it, you'll notice that all of these phrases are about <u>you, your products, or your company</u>. That means they're *features*. Remember, we want to talk about *benefits,* and benefits are always about the <u>prospect</u>.

Find out how much time your prospect has to devote to a business. Is his free time in the evenings or in the daytime, and does he have family obligations to work around? How much money would he be willing to invest in a business, and what would he like to get out of it? Listen. Really listen to the answers, and you will know what benefits your program has that he is looking for. By learning these things in the pre-approach stage — you'll be better able to key in on the appropriate benefits when it comes time to make your presentation.

THE FIVE STEPS TO SUCCESSFUL, EFFECTIVE PRESENTATIONS.

I believe there are five critical areas that need to be addressed in every presentation:

1) **Prospect benefits** (This is where you do the dream-building.)

2) **Network Marketing** (How it works and why it's credible.)

3) **Company** (Why your company is the best fit for the prospect.)

4) **Product** (Why your products are good and their market potential.)

5) **The support structure** (The systems, training and help you will provide the prospect.)

Let's look at each of them in turn.

For the first step of your presentation, begin with the benefits. If you've done your job in the listening department, you'll know what kind of lifestyle benefits your prospect is looking for. For instance, if your prospect is a housewife with child-rearing responsibilities, you may want to stress the flexible hours and the chance for her to work from home. If your prospect were a businessman making good money, but killing himself with a grueling, 90-hour work week, you'd present the quality time and residual income benefits. Mention all the benefits of the networking lifestyle you can think of, but pay particular attention to the ones that fit the desires your prospect expressed earlier. What we're doing here is opening with the benefits to ensure we have the prospect's attention.

There are some key benefits that you should mention in every presentation. They are the:

▲ unlimited income potential;

▲ great tax advantages;

▲ travel opportunities;

▲ ability to choose the people you work with;

▲ minimum start-up costs; and,

▲ the opportunity to become successful while you empower others.

This is probably the most critical point of any presentation — the dream-building. To understand why, it is worth a look at what causes people to make buying decisions.

Most people base their buying decisions on *emotion,* and justify them by *logic.* An example. After I got my first Dodge Viper, I was enraptured with its styling, performance, and the high I got from driving it. Since it was a RT/10 convertible, I decided to buy a hardtop version for the days it rained. Then, I saw a yellow RT/10, and I wanted that one too. So, I bought it. So now, I had three Vipers to go along with my Acura NSX. I told myself that all these sports cars were good investments, because they held their value well. Of course, that's just what I told myself. The reality was I wanted them purely for emotional reasons. I justified buying them with logic, but the logic was not the real reason I bought them.

This is no different than people who vote for a political candidate because he "looks nice," or buy a car from a salesman they like. The woman who accepts a marriage proposal may think she's doing it because she believes that her future husband will be a good provider and father, etc. — but, she won't really make that decision on those grounds. She will do it because of the passion, love and excitement she feels for him.

Now, apply this to Network Marketing. Most people who join will not do so because it looks like the sensible, logical way to build financial security for their future. They will join because they want to be able to travel with friends, buy a big house, get new cars, receive recognition from their peers, and have a lot of fun doing it. For most of these people, these won't be new concepts, but things they dreamed about when they were younger.

Most of the people you prospect will have forgotten or given up on their dreams. To excite them about the business, you must reawaken these dreams. Probably no function is more important to the presentation than this dream-building. For many prospects, it will be the first time they've thought about their dreams in years. Once you rekindle this spark, you'll often find it results in a bonfire of excited expectations. And, because your prospects are hearing about your opportunity at the same time they're seriously thinking about living their dreams again — they'll be motivated to action.

Here's an effective little activity I've woven into my presentations in the past. Near the beginning of your presentation, ask your prospects to think of five things they would like to *do, have* or *become* if money was no object. After you've drawn the circles — or however you show the income potential – ask them if there's anything on their list they could have or do with the income you just showed them. There invariably is. This helps them make a direct, emotional connection between the things they want, and how to get them in your business. Properly done, this can be a powerful tool during the dream-building segment of your presentation.

The other thing you must do in this first step is make sure your prospect realizes that the current economic model we're living under is broken. It doesn't work anymore, and any prospect that thinks it does is likely to end up poor and dependent. Some of the things I'd point out to them include:

▲ The distribution system of jobbers, wholesalers, middlemen and retailers is wasteful and doesn't serve the consumer.

▲ Major corporations are laying off tens of thousands of employees.

▲ The secret to true financial independence is working for yourself.

▲ Half a million jobs a year are eliminated by technology, never to be replaced.

▲ Most jobs are built on trading more hours to get more income — the "trading-time-for- money trap."

You want to make a clear contrast between the futility of working in the broken economic system and the compelling benefits of this business. **Here's the most important part.** Never attack your prospect's situation. This automatically closes their mind and makes them defensive.

Let's say you meet Jimmy at a party, and ask him what he does for a living. He replies that he works for ABC Company. You say, "Oh, I bet that's tough. I hear they've laid off a bunch of people; sales are down ..."

He's going to go into defense mode, even if he hates his job. It's human nature. He'll reply, "No, I haven't been laid off; my boss loves me. I'm a hard worker; they appreciate me ..."

Now, on the other hand, suppose you say something like, "Oh, ABC Company. That must be a great place to work ..."

He'll probably reply, "Great place, my eye! They just laid off 500 people; the benefits are being cut back ..."

You want your prospect to come to her own conclusion that her current job is not going to take her where she wants to go, and that Network Marketing is her best bet. This doesn't necessarily have to happen in her first look at your program. In fact, it may be better if it gradually comes to her over the course of seeing the presentation a few times. Actually, I like to leave out most of the broken economic model information the first time I show a prospect the presentation in a one-on-one situation. This ensures two things:

1. The prospect doesn't think I'm attacking her position.

2. Her second presentation will be a more powerful event than her first.

We will look at this issue in much greater depth in the next chapter, as we look at the sponsoring sequence in the meeting process. (This "first look" is actually just step one in the sponsoring "pipeline.") For now, just know that you don't want to attack what a prospect is doing currently. You want to show him there's a better way, and let him draw his own conclusions about his current plight of quiet desperation. If something's negative — use yourself as the example. Ex: "After 15 years with XYZ Company, I was downsized." If something is positive, use the prospect as the example. Ex: "When you reach Gold Director rank, you'll get a new car for free."

This is also usually the point where you tell your own story — why you got involved. What you want to do here is lay out, in a compelling fashion, the factors that drove you to open your own network marketing business. I always talk about my life in the restaurant business, working 12 to 14 hours a day, 6 or 7 days a week. Regardless of what field you're in — you can usually relate stories of a lifestyle controlled by your income, and an income controlled by the time you spend working.

Most people start their careers at the bottom of the pay. scale, and then pay their dues working for raises until they reach age 35 or 40. Around this time, they're at about the highest level they're going to reach in life. When they reach this zenith, they're still in debt, and their spouse is probably working too. They're paying someone else to raise their kids, and probably don't like what they do. If they own their own traditional business — more than likely, the business owns them.

To the extent your story mirrors this — share your experience in the presentation. By telling your story, many prospects will identify with your plight. This helps them make the connection with the next part of your presentation — how Network Marketing can be a conduit to where they really want to go.

This is the point to start drawing circles, doing the 5 x 5s, or presenting a simplified version of your marketing plan. Please note that I said simplified — and by this, I mean VERY simplified, not a 90-minute recital of percentages, titles and breakaway levels. You have only two objectives in this step. First, you want to demonstrate how exponential growth unfolds. Your prospect needs to understand the general concept of how the business works — not all the specifics of your compensation plan. And, second, you want to show that Network Marketing is the means by which they can get the lifestyle benefits you talked about when you were dream- building. As you explain how the money works in the business, you can tie it to the benefits the prospect will receive.

I'm partial to "drawing the circles" — meaning, I actually draw a diagram with a circle at the top, showing other circles branching off, going down four or five levels. (In one-on-one presentations, this is done on a notepad; in bigger meetings, it's done on an erasable whiteboard.) I have yet to see a more compelling, visual way to get the impact of exponential growth across to a prospect.

To make it more effective, write "YOU" in the top circle to denote the prospect. Then, depending upon how many circles you normally use to show the first level (usually five or six), ask the prospect for names to put in those circles. For example, "Tell me the names of five people you know who are looking for extra money, more free time, or both?" Then, write in the names they give you. So, your diagram might look like this:

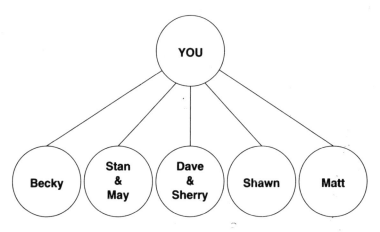

Then, of course, you continue the process, duplicating down a few levels more. Assign an average volume (a conservative estimate of the volume a distributor can actually produce) to each circle, and show the prospect how this grows exponentially. Then, at each stage, give the prospect a breakdown of the type of money he can earn by having an organization producing these volumes.

Designing the presentation to use is an exact science. ("You get six, who get six, who get four, who get two" vs. "you get six, who get five, who get four, who each get three" vs. any one of a dozen possibilities.) For most of you reading this book, your company or your sponsorship line has already determined this.

For the few of you who are responsible for designing the presentation, here are the tips I would give you:

You may have to go through countless variables to get the right one, so be patient. What you are looking for is a sequence where the prospect in the "YOU" circle continues to move up in rank each time you add another level, and also stays at least one rank ahead of the distributors on their first level.

I like to build the presentation so it takes the prospect to about a $50,000- or $60,000-a-year income, plus a few perks (such as a free car, home or travel program, if your company has these). I find this to be the most effective for the following reasons:

If you show massive incomes, like $20,000 or $40,000 a month, two things are going to happen. First, you're going to get into a lot of trouble with government regulators. Second, for a large number of prospects, you will have just lost their belief that this is something they can do. "Joe and Jane Lunchbucket," who've been earning $350 a week or less for the last decade — can't imagine in their wildest dreams pulling down a $20,000-a-month check. They'll just assume your program is for "other people," and begin to tune out the rest of your presentation.

If you show a $50,000- or $60,000-a-year, part-time income, this is enticing to Joe Lunchbucket types — yet, believable enough for them to put themselves in the picture.

Meanwhile, the more sophisticated, professional types will also be attracted. They are smart enough to mentally continue the duplication process and imagine the possibilities. Even though they may be earning $250,000 a year — they are painfully aware of how much time they must trade for that money. They will be quick to figure out that they could replace that income in Network Marketing with a lot less time. More importantly, they will be enticed by the residual income possibilities.

As you construct your presentation, particularly the numbers, keep this formula in mind: it has to be simple enough that they understand the concept — yet, complicated enough that they are afraid to challenge it. Do this, and you probably have a good one. Now, let's go back to the sequence to go through in your presentations.

Next, you must establish why the prospect should join your company. After all, there are dozens of network marketing companies out there. Your prospect will want to know why your company is the best for him. Does your company have a free car plan, profit sharing, incentive trips to Europe, or the like? Lead with these types of benefits.

Use your company's visual aids, like brochures, magazines, etc. **Don't stress the features of your company — stress the benefits to your prospects.** Don't say, "*We've had eight years of steady, stable growth.*" Say, "*You'll be building a business with security. Our eight-year track record ...*" Don't say, "*We spend thousands of dollars on four-color brochures.*" Tell them, "*You will feel proud working with this company, because of the first class, professional materials you have to work with.*" Just as you do in the overall presentation — you want to consider the features of working with your company, and translate them into benefits to the prospect. Talk about conventions, newsletters, conference calls, regional training, and the other aspects of your company's distributor support services, and how they can help your prospect build her business.

The next thing you want to do in your presentation is to introduce your products. You may be accustomed to starting with your products at the beginning of the presentation. Many people advocate selling products first, then coming in the back door with the business opportunity. As you know, I am totally opposed to this. We have found that by doing this, you are scaring away non-sales types, and may be losing a large percentage of your best potential distributors. The top people in this business are not great salespeople, but rather are great teachers and trainers.

Your presentation should show the whole picture — products, lifestyle and opportunity. This will make it easy for the prospect to decide where her interest is. If she is interested in simply being a customer, she will tell you so. But, never prejudge anyone.

Now, you may be wondering, how can anyone start the business without first having a product experience?

Easy. If you've done your presentation properly — they'll assume the products work as you describe them. They'll give you the benefit of the doubt. (This is another example of the advantage of working with your warm market.) And, every reputable company I know has a 100 percent product satisfaction guarantee. Your prospect has nothing to lose and everything to gain.

It's ironic, but one of the main causes of slow growth in an organization is having too much product knowledge. Or, more specifically, assaulting your prospect with it. Distributors are actually talking their way out of the business. It's just not necessary to update your prospect on every use, application and result obtained on your product since Methuselah used the first one.

Does a car salesman demonstrate the side view mirrors, describe every part of the engine, and give you a history of the auto industry since Henry Ford? Or, does he simply let you test drive the car?

I see this "information overload" particularly rampant in the nutrition segment of the industry. Instead of giving presentations, distributors are giving three-hour nutrition lectures. Prospects — overwhelmed by this vast quantity of knowledge in one sitting — correctly determine that they could probably never learn all this information. Based upon this initial impression, they never seriously consider themselves able to do the business. The best you can hope for is a product customer. In this case, your desire to be thorough and professional is making you poor and lonely!

I believe the biggest challenge facing MLM today is that most MLM companies don't really understand the distinction between sales training and duplication. I encounter this very often, as I'm hired to speak at company conventions.

Oftentimes, I've been hired because sales are not increasing, even though their distributors have been trained by some of the world's foremost sales trainers. Of course, all these sales trainers have taught positive mental attitude, mirroring, modeling, closing techniques, and the three-foot rule. And, of course, being non-sales types, most distributors don't perform most of these actions, or they are not congruent when they do perform them. So, in either event, these procedures don't work for them.

This is not to say that most sales trainers are bad, or that what they teach is not good. I imagine that these things work in sales. But, of course, many of those things don't duplicate in Network Marketing. This is usually the point where I'm brought in. My message is simply this:

Good marketing is just a case of identifying qualified prospects — then giving them the information they need to make the correct decision for themselves.

True marketing — with integrity — has nothing to do with closing, convincing or "selling." *You must control the process. You must give the right information, and you must give it in manageable doses that the prospect can digest. But, ultimately, the prospect must determine whether your product, service or opportunity is right for him.* A presentation should be viewed in its proper context. It is simply one step (albeit a very important one) in this information-giving process.

Having said all that, let's go back to the product segment in your presentation ...

When you talk about products, give a general overview of the product line or lines. Don't go into a detailed, product-by-product description. We've seen distributors go into 45-minute descriptions of every individual product, their ingredients, where they come from, proper quantities to use, and what time to take them — then wonder why their prospect ended up in a coma. Give an overview of your product lines, and then just pick one or two of your favorite products to talk about.

Here again, stress the benefits to your prospect. Don't just say, *"These products are unique and exclusive."* Say, *"These products are unique and exclusive, so your customers can only get them from you. You'll make residual income for years to come."*

Special note to distributors in nutritional programs:

Let's suppose that one of your favorite products is one that "cured" you of an "incurable" disease. If this is the case — please don't talk about it in your presentation! I know this may be difficult, and it may sound crazy, but bear with me here.

Personally, I believe the great majority of maladies that send people to the doctor or hospital today are caused by the diets we eat. Ninety-five plus percent of what we consume today is dead, processed food with few or no vitamins, minerals, enzymes or fiber. Ideally, the peristaltic action of your colon should pull your food through your digestive track, taking out the nutrients you need and excreting the rest. However, the reality for most people today is quite different.

Each meal they eat pushes the putrid, rancid, decomposing food that is already blocked up inside their intestine. Because this digestive process is so backed up — many toxins leach through the intestinal wall and enter the bloodstream. The resulting effects may begin with tiredness and lethargy, and advance on to yeast and other bacterial infections, auto toxicity, and even cancer. Who knows what other diseases stem from this breakdown in the digestive process and resulting toxins in the blood?

What we do know is that many people who join network marketing companies — and begin to simply supplement their diets with vitamins, minerals, fiber or enzymes — experience such dramatic and immediate upturns in health, that even so-called incurable diseases are vanquished.

But, here's the sticky part:

You can't say that. The government has legions of regulators whose job is to protect the public from charlatans, false cures and unsafe medical practices. These regulators have been glacially slow in adopting or accepting alternative, and even natural health procedures. They will be quick to close down a company with distributors claiming to have been cured of an "incurable" disease. If you have had a miraculous cure of a supposedly incurable disease — <u>leave that out of your presentation</u>. Save that story for your company convention when there are no prospects — and no regulators — present. Just stick with the benefits that the average person experiences with your products.

The final part of your presentation is where you show your support structure. This is where you show your prospect all the ways you will help her succeed. Let her know she's joining a winning team. Show her all the training programs, meetings, sponsoring tools and company materials available to train her. Tell her about the people in your sponsorship line, and explain how they will be helping her build her business.

This is the time to sell <u>you</u>. No matter how great your company and products look, unless your prospects see <u>you</u> as a benefit, they aren't going to be interested. Stress your personal commitment to their success, and show them exactly how they could get started right now.

Every successful presentation will include all of these five main elements. I don't think the order is critical, as long as the five components are always included — with the exception of the dream-building and benefits. If you don't begin with the benefits, it's unlikely you'll have your prospect's attention through the rest of the presentation.

Keep all these thoughts in mind as you or your sponsorship line design the standardized presentation for your program. Believe it or not, most people will not get involved with your program because your company uses an extra half ounce of this ingredient, or goes to South America for that ingredient. People will get involved because they want a better lifestyle, and they believe they can attain it with you in your program.

Obviously, your company must be credible, and the products must be good. I don't mean to denigrate those things, but people don't buy Ferraris because they have rack and pinion steering and radial tires. They buy them because they want to go fast and look cool. Looking cool is the benefit; the rack and pinion steering is the feature.

Do not take this to mean that your products (or services) are not important — they are critical to your long-term success. In order to have real success, you and your people must be product-centered. But, this is done through use and education, and this takes place after the sponsoring process.

By presenting the opportunity with this approach, you will show the entire picture, and give your prospect the information she needs to make the success decision. You can also bring in people who wouldn't otherwise give your program a second look. Show your prospect the benefits they will get, and you will have the constant benefit of new distributors in your network.

Other thoughts ...

Here's another reality you will have to deal with. Most of the prospects you'll present to won't have the $300 to $800 cash it takes to get started in the business. This includes the people with "good" jobs, and supposedly making "good" salaries. (The average person today is burdened with debt, living on 125 percent of their salary, and subsisting from paycheck to paycheck.)

Most people will be hesitant to tell you this (particularly the ones with those "good" jobs). You will have to try to get a sense of whether this is a problem, and work with those people. They might have to put their initial purchase on their credit card, wait until payday to get started, or buy their introductory materials in several stages. But, take my advice. <u>Never give away a distributor kit to help someone get started</u>. As a rule, people with no investment in their business don't value it, and don't approach it seriously. People who have to stretch and sacrifice a little to get started are much more likely to stay motivated and build a business. That doesn't mean you should encourage them to build their debt, yet deeper. But, it might make sense for them to put their distributor kit and first order on their credit card, if they can get started now, and make back the investment with some fast-start bonuses and other initial products. I've started many a distributor who had fast-start checks back before their first credit card bill arrived.

While I don't believe in closing people, I do go into a presentation with the mindset that I have a business that can help their wants, needs and desires. I also make the assumption that they'll "get it." I have no compunction (and actually feel a responsibility) about guiding them to the next step. I may say something like, "You know, you would be great for this business — here's the next step you need to take ..." or "Hey Doug, let's expose this program to some of the ambitious people you know. Then, it might all come together for you."

I'm really not driving for either a yes or no if the prospect is not ready to make that decision. But, if they're not ready, I want to move them further up the pipeline. The further up the pipeline your prospect gets — the more big events she is exposed to, and the more educated she will become. As a result, she will discover that the business can help her solve her problems and live her dreams.

Even for one-on-one, first-look presentations — show up in business attire. You and your spouse should show up looking like Mr. and Mrs. Success. For professional people (doctors, lawyers, accountants, etc.), you should arrive in a business suit. If your prospect is not a professional, and is likely to be dressed casually, you should wear a business-like dress if you're a woman, or a pressed dress shirt and tie if you're a man. Look like you're going somewhere — don't lower yourself to their standards. Dressing this way gives you more confidence; it increases your credibility with the prospect; and, it lets him know you're serious about the business.

Now, let me go more deeply into this issue of not closing people. I don't want to hard-sell people, <u>but I do want to make sure that they get all the information they need to make the right decision for themselves</u>. If I finish the presentation, and they say something like, "I wouldn't do this in a million years. I hate you. Get out of my house before I kill you," then I will assume that they might not be a prospect. That usually happens only every other time. Just kidding! On the other hand, if they seem non-committed, or casually say they just don't think they're interested, <u>I will persist</u>.

Rather than ask why they're not interested (and get their defenses up), I'll skim right over their objections and let them know that I think they need more information. I might say something like, "I'm sure you want to have all the facts before you make your decision." Then, I'll go through the info pack I want to leave with them, describe what each item is and why it's important they review it. If your packet includes product samples — this would be the time to give them to the prospect and reiterate the benefits of using them. If the packet includes an audiotape, you might plug it into a cassette player and play a minute of it to whet their appetites.

If they will accept the packet, then you arrange one of two scenarios:

1. Set up a time within a couple of days to pick up the packet and answer any questions they will have. *"I know you're going to love these products. Jot down any questions you have, and I'll be back on ..."* or,

2. Edify your sponsorship line in a big way, and get your prospect to commit to a second-look meeting. *"You haven't seen this presentation until you've seen Dennis and Cindy do it. They've helped thousands of people all over the country be successful. You've just got to see them for yourself ..."*

Let me reiterate. I don't want you twisting people's arms to join. But, you do want them to take an honest, open-minded look at the business. In some cases, you have to protect them from their own small-mindedness. You don't want them to have a knee-jerk reaction and disqualify your opportunity because they got front-loaded with water filters five years ago, or because their best friend has a barber whose brother-in-law lost $150 in the hot new fiber cookie deal in 1989. Unless a prospect is determined not to learn the facts, I will always attempt to get them to at least review a packet, so I can follow up two days later — or get them to a second-look meeting.

NOTE: You will find that 6:30 to 7:30 in the evening is the best time for following up and picking up packets. Keep 8:00 to 10:00 p.m. open for making presentations.

If you have people who have seen the presentation, but won't come for a second look, and won't let you follow up — leave them on the back burner. Wait about six months, and then contact them again. You might bring it up again by saying something like, "I just got a check from my marketing business. I need to know if you're serious or not about getting out of your job. I've got one night free this week, but after that, I'm pretty tied up ..."

Other thoughts on your presentation:

I like to open mine by informing the prospects that what they are about to preview is a two- to four-year plan for building financial security in a business that's fun, rewarding, and empowers people. I advise them that to get this result, they need two things: 7 to 10 hours a week, and a dream.

This makes sure that they know the price. They're aware of the time commitment, and this gives me an opening later when I'm ready to do dream-building.

Another important consideration is making sure you're prepared for success before you even begin the presentation. This means expecting a positive outcome, and having the proper materials at hand.

If you're using a flip chart or presentation book — have it with you. If you're going to be drawing out circles — have a notepad and fresh pens or markers handy. Make sure you have the appropriate take-home or follow-up packets handy. And, as hard as it is to believe — there are people who still don't have cassette players. (They don't want to threaten the investment they made in their vinyl record collection.) And, the truth is, today, many have traded their cassettes in for CDs. It pays to have an extra portable cassette player with fresh batteries that you can lend to a prospect if your take-home packet includes an audiotape.

Take control of your own business. Even if you're new, and your sponsor is handling the presentation for you in a two-on-one, be responsible for bringing the supplies. Dress and conduct yourself in a business-like way.

If you're making a lot of presentations, but not getting any sign-ups, it's usually for one of three reasons:

1. **You're not edifying your sponsorship line enough and getting prospects into the pipeline.** If this is you — put your ego in check, and let your sponsorship line go to work for you.

2. **You do a lousy presentation.** If you think this may be the case, ask someone from your sponsorship line to listen to your presentation. They'll be able to tell you how to improve it. Then, practice it over and over ... to the mirror ... to the tape recorder ... to the coffee table. Don't, however, fall into the "getting ready to get ready" syndrome. The distributor who makes lots of lousy presentations will sponsor a lot more people than the distributor who sits at home, waiting to make the perfect presentation!

3. **You're making presentations to the wrong people.** This means you have a good invitation — you're good at getting the presentation in front of people who are not qualified prospects. Don't be tackling prospects on street corners, and begging them to listen to your presentation. Go through the proper pre-approach qualifying questions, and make sure you're presenting to prospects, not suspects.

Finally, I'd be remiss if I didn't talk about objections.

"Your products are too expensive! Besides, pyramids are illegal. Only the people at the top make all the money."

If you haven't heard those words before, chances are you've never made a presentation. It seems that everyone says the same things and has the same objections for not joining Network Marketing. I want to look at how to handle some of these objections, but not in the way that you probably think. Here's why. I'm not going to try to teach you how to sell the prospects, or how to convince them against their convictions, and I'm certainly not going to teach you "guaranteed closing techniques."

Anyone that you have to sell into your program is not the right person. We want to sort people, not sell them. In other words, we want to present enough information for our candidate to make an educated decision, and then STOP. You are looking for people who catch the vision. If they do catch this vision — nothing is going to keep them out of your network.

If they don't — all the cajoling, persuading and arm-twisting in the world will not bring you a distributor. At best, you will have someone who sponsors in just to get you off his or her back, and then leaves the distributor kit in the closet to rot. At worst, you will alienate a good friend or family member. So, please don't fall prey to the misconception that slick presentations and persuasion techniques will build you a huge network — because they won't. They will bring you dozens of front-line, inactive distributors.

The harder you sell someone, the less they will duplicate. Concentrate instead on giving an honest presentation with genuine enthusiasm. OPEN people; don't CLOSE them; and you will be blessed with an ever-growing, profitable and fun business.

Now, with these things in mind, let's go back to handling objections. We don't want to hard-sell anyone. Our purpose is to find out what are legitimate objections and what are merely requests for more information.

If someone tells you that he loves his job, he makes enough money, and he's too busy to open a business — he's probably right. See if he would be interested in buying the products, and leave it there. Now, when someone throws you a lot of objections in the form of questions — it usually means that they are VERY interested in your program, and want to make sure it's the right decision. Questions like, *"Does it cost a lot of money to start? How would I get people? How do I know this will work?"* and, *"Is this legal to do?"* are definite signs of interest, and should be dealt with positively.

<u>Never</u> argue with a prospect. If you win the argument — you lose the distributor. So, when somebody throws an opinion at you — rather than argue the point — pleasantly present the facts. Let's look at some examples:

If someone tells you, "Networking is illegal!" you could respond, "I'm glad you brought that up. I shared your concern, so I did a little research. I found that networking is a 60- to 70-billion-dollar-a-year industry that is not only legal in all 50 states, but is also legal and being done in more than 75 countries and territories around the world."

If they say, "Those products don't work!" you can pleasantly present them with studies or documentation that shows their effectiveness. You can also add any personal testimony of your own. Do this in a way of presenting new, and, perhaps, surprising research, not to discredit what they just told you.

So, in actuality, what you are doing is **accepting** the objection, and then **answering** the objection. Don't be afraid to accept the objection. Say something like, *"Hey, I understand how you feel. I felt the same way. Here's what I found ..."*

By doing this, we discover whether your prospect truly has an objection, or is simply looking for more information. Or, it might be a case of outside influences that they don't want to tell you about. Many times when your prospect says, *"Well, I'll have to think about it some,"* what he or she might really mean is, *"I'll have to check if I have any room on my credit cards,"* or, *"If I do this without asking my wife — she's gonna kill me!"* The key is never to get drawn into arguing your opinion, but rather accepting the objection and simply presenting the facts. If your prospect needs more time, give it to him.

The <u>best</u> way to deal with objections is to answer them right in your presentation, before they even come up. When you see the same objections coming up over and over again, build them into your presentation. Here's an example:

One of the objections I saw come up a lot was people's belief that they didn't have time to start a business. It was a fear I had initially had myself. But, of course, I had come to understand that if I didn't <u>make</u> time for two years — I would forever be out of time. So, I built that right into my presentation. At some point in every presentation, I'd say something like, *"When I first saw this business, dumb as I was — I thought I didn't have time to do it. Can you believe it? I was busy. Of course, I was busy being broke!"* You can do this for virtually any objection that comes up often enough. *"At first I thought these products were expensive. Then, I figured the cost of ..."*

<u>By "clearing" most objections in the presentation, you won't have to deal with them in the follow-up process.</u> This speeds up the prospecting and sponsoring sequence. I wish I could give you answers for all the objections you'll face, but, obviously, that is not possible. The variables will be different for every program. But, by counseling monthly with your sponsorship line, you'll learn the way to handle the most probable objections that come up for your company.

Now, what if your prospect is not moved by the facts to join your program? <u>Thank him and move on down the road!</u> If you've given someone all the information they need to make a decision, and they make one — respect them and honor their decision. It will not serve any purpose to argue or try to manipulate them.

If you follow this approach, you may find that initially, you will sponsor fewer people. However, the people you do sponsor will actually do the business, and, in the long run, you will have thousands more distributors in your group.

Final thoughts:

The most important step in building your business is learning how to make a presentation by yourself as soon as possible. You can never proactively build a group or become duplicated if you have to wait for a meeting, or wait for your sponsor to make your presentations for you. If you wait for big meetings to come around, they could be anywhere from seven to fourteen days away, and you'll lose your prospect in the meantime.

Give them a one-on-one presentation immediately. Then, if they are a real prospect, they'll be much more likely to come to a home or hotel meeting for a second look. Otherwise, you'll find it next to impossible to get a prospect to show up cold for a hotel or home meeting. So, role-play with your spouse. Give presentations to your mirror, your chair or your dog, but learn it as rapidly as possible. In this business,

"He (or she) who does the most presentations wins!"

If you're making a presentation a week, or one or two a month — you're really just doing this as a hobby. If you're serious about your success, even working part-time, then you should be making three to five presentations a week. (Keep in mind that when you're doing one-on-ones, you can actually do two or three in the same night.) Just remember, the person who makes a lot of presentations poorly will become a lot more successful than the guy who's waiting to make the perfect one.

Don't be defeated because you're nervous about making presentations. Just talk fast; raise your voice; and sound successful! Your primary purpose is to see if they have a dream, and to get them thinking about it again. They can see a great presentation on their second or third look at your home meeting, and open, cross-line meetings. For now, <u>you just have to get them into the sponsoring pipeline</u>.

Once you show them there is a better way — it takes their excuses away. If they really want a better life — they must go through the pipeline with you to see if they really have a chance. Just make sure you always book the next meeting, and if you're consistently making presentations, you'll ultimately prevail.

Final, final thoughts:

As you now know, I'm not into "closing" people. However, you do have to bring closure to the process at some point. Don't be afraid to ask your prospects which option is best for them.

Now, let's look at the specifics of doing presentations during home and hotel meetings, and the differences between the two ...

CHAPTER ELEVEN

CONDUCTING DYNAMIC, EFFECTIVE MEETINGS

L ET'S BEGIN BY UNDERSTANDING THE ONLY PURPOSE OF A meeting. Quite simply, it is <u>to schedule the next meeting</u>. A meeting is judged a success — not by whether product or a distributor kit was sold, but — by whether another meeting was scheduled. At every stage of the prospecting and recruiting process, you should pull out your calendar at the conclusion, and book the next meeting.

Give out a Pre-Approach Packet, then make an appointment to get back together — 48 hours later.

When you pick up the Pre-Approach Pack and the prospect is interested — schedule the presentation.

Finish the presentation and give the prospect her take-home package. If she likes the idea, but wants to think about it, schedule the "second-look" meeting.

If you bring someone to a second-look meeting and they seem even more interested, but they're still not quite ready to sign, give them an additional follow-up packet and schedule when you will get back to them.

Do you notice a pattern here? Only a fool makes a presentation and sits by the phone expecting the prospect to call back and join.

At every stage of the process, <u>you</u> must direct the prospect to what should happen next.

Meetings are a critical part of that process. A powerful recruiting meeting can be the difference between just another Tuesday night drawing circles — or going home with eager new distributors in your group. The difference will be determined long before your prospects arrive at the meeting. The preparations you make in advance are what will make the difference. Let's look at some of them.

For home meetings:

Before the meeting, check to see if you have fresh markers for the whiteboard (and make sure they're erasable). Put the whiteboard in the front of the room, away from the door, so that late arrivals will not distract the meeting. If there's a window behind the whiteboard, close the curtains for the same reason.

Before I conduct a house meeting, I instruct the host to make sure that the children are away at the sitter's, pets are put away in the bedroom, and the phone is off the hook at 5:00 p.m. I want the phone off the hook to prevent any last minute cancellations. However, here's what you have to do when you do this. Make sure that everyone you're expecting has clear, precise directions. "Turn at the green house, go down about a mile ..." doesn't make it. They have to say, "Turn right on Elm Street. Go three-tenths of a mile to the second light, which is Fleming Road, and turn right ..." For the larger house meetings, it's a good idea to have someone out front directing traffic and showing people where to park.

For hotel meetings:

If the meeting is to be held in a public location, selecting the site is important. Hotel meeting rooms are usually the best, because they are conveniently located, non-threatening, and have adequate parking and the facilities you need. Your hotel should be a top-of-the-line property. Marriotts, Hiltons and Hyatts are the types you should be using. Do not use Howard Johnson's, Holiday

Inns and motels. Your prospect will judge your program by the caliber of the surroundings in which it is presented. Everything you present to the prospect should be firstclass and professional.

Visit the hotel in person, and look at your potential meeting room. Make sure the carpet, wallpaper and decor are light and attractive. Avoid rooms with baroque, dark, mahogany-type decor. Make sure the ceiling is at least ten feet or higher. It's tough to be grand in a low-ceiling room.

Inquire about parking rates. Some hotels charge $10 or more for parking, while others are free. High parking fees will discourage guests. Check the prices for microphones, screens, and other audio-visual materials you plan to use. Most hotels farm out these services to outside vendors, so they are not negotiable. Sometimes these costs are more than the room rent. In many cases, it's cheaper to buy your own. Some hotels, knowing you need a screen or a chalkboard, will charge you $50, even though they're built into the wall of the room!

What IS negotiable is the room rent. NEVER pay the price first quoted you. These prices are only for neophytes, who don't know better. Let the hotel know that you will be renting rooms regularly. If the price quoted you is $400, tell them your budget is only $150, and ask what they have in that range. Oftentimes, they will then find you a meeting room for about $200. It's the same room they were going to charge you $400 for! If you hold regular meetings, it is sometimes possible to pay only $100 or $125 for a room that lists for $300 or $400.

Now, let's look at the room setup. If possible, put the lectern and/or whiteboard on a raised platform. It gives the speaker more credibility, and provides better visibility for the guests. Just as with home meetings, make sure it is at the opposite end of the room from the door, so late arrivals won't disrupt the meeting.

When I wrote the first edition of this book, I recommended you have a large banner or sign with your company's name at the front of the room. I also asked for an attractive product display table and perhaps a "prosperity" table. (This is like the product table, but features car brochures, pictures of local people winning awards, travel brochures, etc. If your company has award programs, a President's Club, etc., you would have those brochures on this table. The prosperity table can also be combined with the product display table.) I experimented with something right after that edition of the book came out, and I want to share the results of that now.

I began to see the meetings getting grander and grander. It got to the point that each city I visited to do open meetings had a bigger, better setup than the one before. People were making photo boards, collages, and banners, hanging bunting and making the meeting rooms gorgeous. People were racing from work at 5:00 p.m. to have their rooms ready by 8 o'clock. They stopped thinking about getting prospects there, because they were concentrating so much on the room setup. When I saw this happening, I canceled ALL room decorations and displays. We did all future meetings in the rooms exactly as the hotel set them up. Check with your sponsorship line for how this is done in your company. Other set-up notes:

Set up chairs for only three-quarters of the people you expect. Have extras where they can be brought in quickly, but don't set them out. It looks very bad to have empty chairs. The fuller your room, the more likely it is that prospects will join. It's better to be in a smaller room with people standing around the walls than in a large room with empty seats.

Arrive early enough to thoroughly check all the audio-visual equipment. Have extra slide projector bulbs, etc., and check all the volume levels, including the microphone. One hour before meeting time, set the room thermostat to 65 degrees. It needs to be this cool so that when the guests fill up the room, the temperature will remain bearable. If the room is not

<u>kept at a proper temperature, the meeting will suffer</u>. The same can be said for lighting. Make sure the room is brightly lit.

Set up the registration table in the hallway so that late arrivals won't disrupt anything. Encourage all distributors to wear company pins and achievement awards. Pick your friendliest, most positive people for the greeter, registration and door positions. A negative person in one of these positions can end a prospect's career before it ever begins.

Have a tape of upbeat music playing for 45 minutes prior to the meeting. Have another tape of uplifting music to start immediately at the conclusion of the meeting. <u>Studies have shown that the right music increases consumer purchases by as much as 15 percent</u>. Notice that up until now, we haven't even discussed the actual meeting! Because all of these things you do before the meeting are just as important as the meeting itself. Little things are everything!

Here's a checklist of the things you want to do at each meeting:

- ▲ Set thermostat at 65 degrees one hour before the meeting.
- ▲ Test all audio-visual equipment.
- ▲ Make sure display tables are set up (if applicable).
- ▲ Start pre-meeting music 45 minutes before the meeting.
- ▲ Have tape cued for end-of-meeting music.
- ▲ Set up registration table with sign-in sheet.
- ▲ Make sure meeting is posted in the lobby.
- ▲ Check for proper lighting.
- ▲ Have company banners, posters, etc. hanging in a prominent place (if applicable).
- ▲ Check microphone and volume level.
- ▲ Make sure product demonstration area is set up (if applicable).

Now, let's look at the content of the meeting. This is generally the same for both house and hotel meetings, with a few distinctions. Begin by starting on time. If your meeting is scheduled for 7:30 p.m., it should start then, but certainly no later than 7:35 p.m. If you wait for late people, you will set a precedent, and you will have to start later and later every time. In reality, the people who are likely to sponsor in and do the business successfully are the ones who arrive at functions on time! Don't skew your presentation to the losers, who are crying about the traffic, this, that and all the other reasons why they can't be on time.

One way I like to start hotel meetings is with three or four "bullets," which are distributors who each give a one- or two-minute, high-energy testimonial. Examples are:

"Hi. My name is Jim Smith. I just got involved two months ago, and already my organization is taking off!"

"Hi. My name is Joe Johnson, and even though I have a successful law practice, I'm excited about the chance to retire in two to five years."

Following the bullets, the introducer should set the tone. This is just a friendly welcome and edification of the featured speaker. The purpose is to put the guests at ease, build anticipation, and set a positive tone. <u>At some point during the first introductions, remind the people present to turn their cell phones and pagers to off or vibrate mode</u>.

Now, we get into the meeting. This can be done in two ways — either by having only one powerhouse speaker, or by having several. If you are having only one speaker, he or she must be **DYNAMIC.** Another option is to have three or four speakers cover different parts of the presentation. This is a nice way to do it, because it involves more people, and it keeps everyone's attention.

As far as meeting content, essentially you want to take the guests through the five key points we discussed in the presentation chapter.

1. Give them an idea of the lifestyle available.
2. Show them that they can only get it through Network Marketing.
3. Demonstrate why your company is the best one for them.
4. Give them an overview of the product line.
5. Show them how smart and easy it is to get started NOW.

Your prospects are thinking, *"Is this thing for real?"* and, *"Can I do this?"* These questions must be answered. Just like the one-on-one, the emphasis of the presentation should always be on the benefits to the prospect, and not on the speaker and the company. When you explain the marketing plan, don't say, *"We pay five percent on this level. We have a car fund ..."* etc. Say things like, *"Here's how YOU make money. Here's how YOU can win a free car."*

Finally, have the main speaker invite the guests to join. Give reasons for joining NOW, and tell them exactly how to get started. Point out the senior distributors present, who will be available to answer any questions. Explain the literature packs you offer. Wrap it up with a positive statement. Hit the music, and go sign up your new distributors.

For home meetings, most of the variables we mentioned for content are the same. However, there are a few things that you need to do differently. Let's look at them.

Hosts of home meetings should not be flitting around the house fixing things. They should be sitting front and center, paying rapt attention to the speaker. If parking is a problem, have someone out front directing traffic. It isn't going to enhance your business to have a group of neighbors upset because you have lots of guests parking on their lawns. In fact, set a goal that for every meeting you conduct, home or hotel, you will leave the environment in better condition than when you found it.

If you have refreshments, keep them simple, and save them until the end of the meeting. If your company has food products — these should be the refreshments. If your company doesn't have products conducive to being refreshments — offer some light, store-bought snacks, like chips or cookies. You never want to be serving home-baked pies or using fine china, because your guests will think they have to duplicate you.

Usually, you will have just one presenter at a home meeting. Your sponsor will be conducting a meeting for you, or you'll be presenting for one of your distributors. The proper introduction of the speaker is important to the success of the meeting. If you are introducing the speaker, there are four points you want to get across:

1. The speaker is successful.
2. The speaker will show the prospects how they can be successful.
3. The speaker is a friend of yours.
4. You're EXCITED!

Let's look at them in turn:

It's important for you to let the guests know that the speaker is successful, because they will pay more attention if they know this up front. Likewise, tell them the speaker is there to show them how they can be more successful, as well. You mention that the speaker is a friend of yours, because this edifies you in the mind of your prospects. They will feel honored at the chance to sponsor into your group, knowing that you have a direct pipeline to the expert.

Finally, you want to make sure they know that this is not something you're just thinking about, but rather a new venture you are totally committed to and very excited about. You might say something along the lines of, "This is something we're totally committed to, and we're sharing it with our best friends."

And, just like the hotel meetings, you must remind them to turn off their cell phones and pagers.

Now, let's back up and look a little more deeply at some of the critical factors.

Meetings should be fast-paced, intriguing, informational, professional and FUN! I believe that the vast majority of your meetings should be done in people's homes. Personally, I like to see only two hotel meetings a month. One is held by the highest-ranking pin in your sponsorship line. It's a closed family meeting. Closed means that it's only attended by members of their organization (family) and their guests. Other lines in the area wouldn't attend or know about this meeting.

This gives the local pin-rank distributor a chance to have a major event each month to support their group. These are usually much too big to be held in a person's home. It gives that pin rank's distributors a slightly larger event to bring a prospect to for her second or third look at the program.

The other monthly hotel meeting should be an open, cross-line meeting. All of the pin-rank distributorships in the area would join together to create a major monthly event. With all the different lines feeding it — this meeting has a very large attendance, and is quite impressive to the prospect.

The smaller home meetings feed the larger home meetings, which feed the hotel meetings, which feed the large cross-line meetings. Having this structure in place allows distributors to bring their prospects through the gradually expanding process we talked about in earlier chapters.

Here's the sequence:

▲ Two-on-one or one-on-one presentation

▲ Home meeting

▲ Family meeting (this could be in a home or hotel, depending upon size)

▲ Open, cross-line hotel meeting

▲ Major rallies, conventions and events

Open meetings should be used only for a second look at the program. This ensures that there are only positive, qualified prospects in attendance, not someone who's just finding out that it's Network Marketing and which company it is. Now, you probably noticed that a successful pin- rank distributor conducts the larger hotel meetings. There are two reasons for this.

The first reason is how you control your system — by virtue of the meetings. <u>The most sacred position in your organization is whom you allow on the platform.</u> The only people allowed are those who have already built a big business, or people who are moving up in the process of building a big business. Here's why:

The people who speak at your meetings are being edified by doing so. You don't want to edify someone at the March meeting, only to have people hear that they quit and joined another opportunity in April. And, if you have someone up on the platform speaking about things outside of the system — it will negatively influence your group. So, it's very important that the person speaking be someone who has built a group (or is currently doing so) using the system.

The second reason you have pin ranks conduct the open meetings is that <u>they're good</u>! To reach that rank, they've given thousands of presentations. They know how to get and keep a crowd's attention. They tell jokes, weave in stories, and usually tell their own personal stories of success. These meetings are powerful, effective events ... that they won't be if you have them every week.

I know a lot of people believe in weekly hotel meetings, but I am not a proponent of this. My experience is that the people who do weekly hotel meetings are the "super-hype" people who are trying to create momentum. I believe they create a lot of co-dependent people who never learn the presentation and are always waiting for the next meeting. You'll also find that weekly meetings lose their excitement, their sense of being an event, and, as a result, attendance will eventually drop off. *No matter how good a speaker is — if they do the meeting every week, people will get tired of hearing them.*

Here's more:

It sounds strange, but you actually have to train your people how to go to meetings. Teach them that the real meeting is the meeting that takes place before and after the regular meeting.

Before the meeting.

The only way you know for sure that a prospect is coming to the meeting is to pick him up. You can say something like, *"If it's okay, I'll pick you up and we can talk on the way."*

Get your guest to the meeting 15 to 20 minutes early so you can get seats in the front rows. The closer a guest is to the speaker, the more the guest will be impacted. This also gives you a chance to introduce your guest around. Let them meet your sponsor, any other pin ranks in the room, and any other distributors with commonalities (same organization, same occupation, etc.). And definitely be sure to introduce them to that night's speaker. Now, instead of seeing the speaker as a stranger trying to sell them something — the prospect will be listening to what their new friend has to impart.

After the meeting:

After the meeting, you will want to keep the discussion centered on the business. Answer any questions the prospect has, and see if they're ready to join. If not, explain the packet of materials you're sending them home with and <u>schedule the next meeting</u>. Let them know about other upcoming functions.

Other things you'll have to teach your distributors about attending meetings.

▲ It is important to attend every meeting, whether or not they have a guest.

▲ Always be generous with applause and laughter.

▲ Business dress is appropriate. (If they claim their friends won't relate to business dress, explain that maybe that's why they need the business.)

▲ No food, gum or drinks are permitted.

▲ Participate if the speaker calls for it, particularly during the dream-building, as prospects may be very hesitant to get involved in this.

▲ If a handout is passed around, always take one, even if you've seen it before. (If you don't, guests will recognize that only guests are taking them. If there are a lot of distributors, but few guests, they may feel singled out and get defensive.)

▲ Teach spouses who are not presenting meetings that their role is very important.

They need to be watching the crowd, listening to who is the most excited and what their dreams are.

Let's look at how long meetings should be. Of course, this will depend upon what your standardized presentation is, but I'll give you an example of what I do, which will serve as a guide for you to follow.

Even though I follow the same standardized presentation outline for all meetings, my one-on-one presentation will take 25 or 30 minutes, my home meetings will take about 65 minutes, yet I will spend about two hours conducting a large hotel meeting. Here's why:

As I said earlier, I conduct an abbreviated presentation in a one-on-one environment. I will delete the section about the economic system not working so that the prospect does not become defensive. When I do a home meeting, I will conduct the full-size presentation. For a large-size hotel meeting, I will do the same presentation, but I'll go into more depth and add more jokes and stories.

When I do a large hotel meeting — I go to have FUN. It's going to be an event! The bigger the crowd — the more fun I'm going to have. I'll crack a lot of jokes about making money, taking vacations, flying first class, and getting rid of alarm clocks. In a large group environment, these things go over great. People think I'm an incorrigible rascal. Now, were I to say those same things in a small, home meeting — they would come off as egotistical and self-centered. People would be looking at me thinking, *"Boy, is he ever full of himself."* Yet, in a large group, with the social pressures of others laughing and having a good time — they'll thoroughly enjoy it.

Keep in mind that the home and hotel presentations are the same. There are just more jokes and stories in the longer one. The one-on-ones are almost the same — I'll just scale back on the parts that an individual might take personally.

Presentations are where the actual work is done. Meetings are the vehicle that supercharges the presentations. But, before we leave this subject, let's deal with an issue that many people bring up. They claim that prospects are too skeptical, that meetings are outdated, and folks won't go to meetings any more.

Not true.

However, I will be the first to admit that if you walk up to the average person and ask them to meet you at a hotel on Tuesday night at 7:30 — they're likely to run shrieking from the room.

But, that's not what you should be doing ...

Remember, <u>we said open meetings should only be used for a second or third look at the program</u>. It's true, the average person, invited cold, is not going to show up at an opportunity meeting in some hotel. But, if they are truly interested in your Pre-Approach Packet — they will sit down and see a presentation. And, if they like the first presentation enough — they will drive 40 miles in the dead of winter in sub-zero temperatures to learn more. You never want to waste an open meeting. <u>But, the best way to get the prospect to attend one is to give him a one-on-one presentation or a powerful Pre-Approach Packet first</u>.

If you do the early stages correctly — people will come to your meetings. And, when you do the kinds of meetings I suggest, people will actually look forward to attending! The monthly cross-line meetings become such major events that people get prospects into the pipeline just to bring them to the open meetings — knowing that they're almost certain to sign up.

Meetings are extra work, and they take continuous effort. But the rewards are too powerful to ignore. It has become fashionable in the industry to advertise opportunities as "no meetings required." I believe in the old adage that you can find out what kind of a tree it is by the fruit it bears. Here's what I know. In the 50-plus-year history of Network Marketing, no company has <u>ever hit</u> — <u>and survived after</u> — the exponential growth curve without holding public opportunity meetings.

Creating the meeting support structure in an area ensures maximum growth in that area. The one-on-ones feed the home meetings. The home meetings feed the family meetings. And, the family meetings feed the open, cross-line events. This pipeline ensures that there's always an upcoming timely chance for prospects to see the presentation again. And, each time, it is a bigger event, and the prospect receives more social proof that joining is the right thing to do.

Timing is very important. If your family meeting is the first Thursday of every month, schedule the cross-line meeting for the third Thursday. If your cross-line meeting is always held on the first Thursday, schedule the family meeting for the third Thursday. This ensures that there is never more than a two-week wait between a "big event" meeting that you can edify and bring a prospect to. If you get a prospect into the pipeline, take them to a home meeting, and then make them wait three or four weeks for another look — you will likely lose them. Their excitement will fade, and they will move on to other things. Make sure this meeting pipeline is in place so there's always another stage for your prospect to move through.

Final thoughts on meetings.

Some distributors feel that it's the company's place to conduct and pay for meetings. This couldn't be further from the truth. Remember, this is your business and your bonus check. It is your responsibility to set up and hold meetings, and paying for them is just part of the normal cost of doing your business.

The concept of holding meetings to generate interest in a business or product worked in 1970, 1980 and 1990, and it'll still be working in 2010.

If you want to sign up a whole bunch of people fast — prospecting by mail and advertising is faster. But, if you want the long-term security that comes from building depth — there's no better way than the properly structured meeting pipeline. Now, let's delve deeper into how you create lasting security as we explore Building Depth...

CHAPTER TWELVE

BUILDING DEPTH

W HY DO SOME PEOPLE BUILD HUGE ORGANIZATIONS AND receive passive, residual income for decades, while others work furiously to shore up and rebuild lines every few months? The difference comes from **building** lines versus **driving** lines.

People who build strong lines have some sort of system in place, and follow principles like we've outlined in the previous chapters. By spending five to eight weeks working in the living rooms of their lines — then counseling them on a monthly basis — they develop friendships that will last their entire lifetime. When you follow this process, you create an environment of trust and support, so your people come to you when they have challenges. They will seek your advice, and, more importantly, they will build rock-solid lines that create lifetime residual income.

Contrast that with driving a line ...

Here's an example of how that's done. "Heavy-Hitter Harry" discovers that his checks are going down, and many of his distributors are quitting the program he's working. Naturally, he assumes there can only be one cause for this. Obviously, the program has leveled out. So, he starts searching for the next "hot" one. Once he decides what that is, he joins and brings over his leaders from the last deal. He immediately takes out ads in industry trade publications, or starts a direct mail campaign to get new recruits. His headline proclaims:

Find out why the Heavy Hitters are switching to ABC Company!
CATCH THE WAVE!!!
Call now, before your downline calls you!

Of course, Harry manages the whole campaign, even to the point of talking to everyone that calls. So, he's on the phone twelve or fourteen hours a day, working across the time zones. He's overnighting info packs, faxing applications continuously — and sponsoring people all over the country. Eventually, at some point in the process, he'll realize that he simply can't do it all. So, he begins placing people under some of his other distributors. He may do this as a reward for hardworking distributors, or due to their geographical proximity to the new distributors. In either case, this creates a dysfunctional group ...

Many of the distributors who had people placed under them simply don't have Harry's talent for working with people. And, they're a little shy about talking to people they don't know, so they never contact their new distributors. Instead, they wait for the new people to contact them. Which, of course, they never do. These new distributors don't know this new sponsor they've been placed under. They know Harry. So, whenever they have a problem, they call Harry.

So, of course, Heavy-Hitter Harry still works the phones twelve to fourteen hours a day ...

Which befits our hero, because that is exactly what he has become — a hero. In fact, a very un-duplicatable one. Now, this will feel very good to Harry ... at first.

He'll throw up his arms and say things like, *"What can I do? I'm the only one who can make presentations. Everybody always wants to talk to me,"* and other things that make him feel warm and fuzzy all over. Until he discovers something. At

some point, he will realize that he's created an entire organization of co-dependents. And, if he were to take a few weeks off
— his check would go down by 20 percent. If he took off six
weeks — his check would drop by half. And, if he ever were to
take 90 days off — he simply wouldn't have a business to come
back to.

Now, Harry is like a hamster on an exercise wheel. He has
to keep moving to stay in shape, yet he never gets ahead. But,
he can never stop either ...

Because he's grown accustomed to the size of his monthly
bonus check (and has increased his spending proportionately),
he has to keep scrambling to keep the wheel turning. Instead of
escaping the time-for-money trap, he has simply substituted a
different master.

Quite frankly, driving a line like this has nothing to do
with building a long-term, multi-level marketing organization.
But Harry, like a lot of people who don't truly understand the
duplication process, doesn't know any better. People like Harry
just keep spinning on the wheel until they finally burn out and
quit. Then, they'll either give up on Network Marketing, believing it doesn't work, or they'll assume they didn't pick the
right "hot" company. In either case, it's a tragedy. Most of this
disappointment stems from this lack of understanding and training on how the business is truly done.

There are two other problems with driving lines through
cold market campaigns:

First, by the very nature of cold market campaigns, you
end up with distributors spread all over the country. Most of
these areas will have just a few isolated distributors who don't
have the necessary skills to set up and facilitate the meeting
structure. Without this pipeline, they simply can't compete and
build effectively. So, they languish for months, even years, until even the hype and big bonus checks of their sponsors can no
longer keep them motivated. They give up the ghost. We'll talk

about how you can prevent this from happening to you in the chapter on building long distance.

The second problem is that when people are placed under other people, it makes the sponsorship line dysfunctional. Some of the people who have distributors placed under them develop a welfare mentality. You place six people under them in April, and in May, they want to know, "What have you done for me this month?"

Also, because distributors are randomly placed under a sponsor — they have no respect for their sponsor's skills, and thus don't edify them. By not having a sponsorship line they can edify and put to work for them, they lose the single, most powerful part of the support structure necessary to build a business — **edification**.

This is one of the simplest things to do. Yet, most people don't understand it, and even fewer practice it. Edify simply means "to build up," or relate the positive traits and abilities of people. You need to edify your sponsorship line, the people in your group, and even cross lines. (And some other things, as well.)

This doesn't mean be phony. It simply means, look for the positive, and see people as they can become. If you believe that someone is so lacking in redeeming qualities that you simply can't edify them — do a little soul searching. Are they really so worthless that there is nothing good you can say about them? Find what is good about the person, and edify that. Let's look at some specific situations, beginning with your sponsorship line.

The smartest thing you can do to build your business quickly is to massively edify your sponsor and the pin ranks in your sponsorship line. You want to absolutely rave about these people's loyalty, dedication, support and business acumen. You don't do this to make them feel good. You do this for you. Here's why:

The more you edify your sponsor (and the organization you belong to), the more they can help you. Let's look at a couple of different scenarios.

Suppose you're a little jealous of your sponsor's success, so you don't really edify him. In fact, you might even sometimes demean him to your group with the hope that this will elevate you. You say things like, "I'm his number one distributor. Without me, he'd hardly make anything." Or, "I do a better meeting than he does."

In actuality, this lowers your stock with your group. Although they may be impressed initially with your bravado and skills — on a deeper level, they will feel you don't respect and honor people. <u>People don't respect those who don't respect others</u>.

However, the most damage comes from your sponsor's inability to help you. Because you've never talked him up (and have actually talked him down), your group won't turn out in large numbers when your sponsor comes to town. Nor will they work extra hard to get prospects into the pipeline in advance of a visit by your sponsor. And, your people who do go to your sponsor's meeting won't pay as much attention, value the information, or go out and apply it. You've effectively handcuffed your sponsor, and rendered him or her unable to help you. You've built yourself up as a hero, but, in the long run, this makes you unduplicatable, and dramatically increases the amount of effort you will have to expend to move forward.

Now, let's look at the other possible scenario ...

You celebrate your sponsor's success, and edify him at every opportunity. Your distributors almost associate your sponsor's name with a slight degree of awe.

Now, when your sponsor comes to town, distributors are driving in from three and four hours away. They're frantically working to get prospects into the pipeline so they'll be ready for a second or third look when your sponsor comes in to do the meeting. Even better, they'll pay rapt attention, follow his advice, and take action.

But, here's the best part ...

When your sponsor does come to town, he will then edify you. He can say something like, "It's always a pleasure to come to Phoenix and work with Jeannie's group. Jeannie is one of my top leaders, and she's totally committed to her people." Now, your stock really shoots up with your people.

You cannot edify yourself, and your sponsors cannot edify themselves. <u>But, you can edify them</u> — <u>which allows them to edify you</u>. Edifying your sponsorship line allows them to come down and work magic with your group. Some of your people will hear things from them that they cannot hear from you. It liberates you from the hometown prophet syndrome.

Now, the question always comes up: how do you edify your sponsor if they are not moving up?

Simply edify by degrees. If your sponsor isn't actively building the business — don't put them down, and don't let their lack of growth determine your lack of growth. Just love your sponsor and allow them to grow. If someone in your group inquires about them, you can say something along the line of, "Well, Betty and Ricky have other priorities in their lives right now that don't leave them a lot of time for the business. But, I will forever be grateful to them for introducing me to the business. If it were not for them — probably neither you nor I would be having this opportunity."

By the same token, you want to edify everyone on your team. Let's suppose you sponsor Bryan, who sponsors Vicky, then never really does much more. Suppose Vicky then comes to you complaining about the lack of support she's getting from Bryan.

Rather than putting down Bryan, respond instead by telling Vicky that Bryan has gotten busy with other activities at the moment, but you'll be happy to help in the meantime. If Bryan comes to the functions, is on the voice mail system, or participates in the self-development program, it's very likely that he will one day come around and "Go Core." If you have been demeaning him — it will be very hard for him to get back the respect of his group.

Here's the other thing:

If you complain about Bryan to Vicky, she'll be wondering in the back of her mind what you say about her to her group. Negativity has no place in your organization! Edify people by degrees, but do edify them. Talk up your team, and develop a culture of reciprocal edification.

The same thing applies when someone down the group comes up to you looking for advice — usually because they don't like the advice they are getting from their sponsor. When I suspect that this is the case, I'll stop them in mid-sentence and say something like, "Before you go any further, this sounds like something we should be consulting Bob on. As long as you don't have any problem with my going to Bob with this, go ahead."

This ensures I don't de-edify Bob. It also discourages someone who just wants to gossip or whine, on the spot. Don't play games with people. If this person has a legitimate business concern, then they can't object to the matter being discussed with their sponsor. If they just want to complain and moan about their sponsor, but are not willing to.put it out in the open, then they're in the wrong group, and you should let them know it.

It's even important to edify cross-line distributors. While it's nice to create a sense of identity and pride for your group — this should never be done at the expense of other groups. Rather than getting jealous of another line, and making excuses for their success, celebrate it! Here's why: Your sponsorship line may send cross-line, pin-rank distributors to speak at your open meetings, or your distributors may be exposed to them at the company convention. And, sometimes, one of those people will say one little thing that somehow reaches someone in your group — someone you have not been able to get through to. Different people relate to different things. Know that your sponsorship line or company would not send someone to speak to your group, unless they were good. Very good. So, the next time your group is listening to a cross-line speaker, jump up, start clapping, and be sure to thank them afterward.

The end result of edifying all these people is that you are also edifying the system, the company, and even the entire industry. And, of course, that serves you. A strong system, company and industry simply make your job easier. So, be generous with your edification. You don't do it just to help others — you do it because it's good business for you.

One more thought on edification.

Your people will be able to edify you better if you maintain the proper posture with your organization. Here's what I mean:

I love all the people in my organization — but I don't socialize with all of them. I socialize only with the high-level pin ranks. There are two reasons for this: money and time. Not mine. Theirs.

Simply put, most of my distributors simply don't have the time or money to keep up with me on a social basis. Let me give you some examples:

I'm actually doing the final editing of this chapter in the Hyatt Regency in Downtown Indianapolis. I flew in for the weekend to attend the Indy 500. I have the money and the time to pick up and fly anywhere to see a World Series game, a World Cup match, or Stanley Cup Finals Championship game. So, I do.

I eat at fancy restaurants, stay in Five-Star hotels, and fly first class. I spend on a car what some of my beginning distributors spend on a house. Money is simply not an issue with me. If I want something, I buy it and pay cash. If I socialize with distributors at lower ranks, I find that it's very stressful on their cash flow. A simple night's entertainment for me could mean a week's pay for them.

Timewise, it can also be challenging ...

You must be conscious of the time you ask from beginning distributors. They may be doing one-on-ones or home meetings, three or four nights a week. That Friday night social event with you may be the one night of the week your distributor's wife was expecting to spend with him. If you tie him up, she's likely to resent this. This creates negative energy and pressure he doesn't need. You must guard your distributor's time prudently.

As a new distributor begins his or her career, their time and money are tight. They need to invest in their business, and they must carve seven to ten hours a week from somewhere. You don't want them spending limited resources on socializing with you. They will need those funds and that time for their business.

Building a solid network marketing organization, and securing it to the point it provides walk-away residual income, comes from developing relationships. Your relationship with your distributors — even though you're both independent businesspeople — should kind of resemble an employer/employee relationship. It's in your distributor's best interest if you don't allow them to get too close to you. Save the socializing until they reach the high-level pin ranks when they have the time and money to spare.

Now, how do we secure a line, and when do we leave it?

You've probably heard that you don't leave a line until it's three levels or five levels deep, or until they break away. In fact, you should NEVER leave a line. Your role will change. Initially, you will be involved in the day-to-day building of the line as you make presentations during the five- to eight-week process. From there, you will evolve into the counseling stage. This is done when the eight-week process is completed, and your line has now duplicated you (and is doing their own presentations and home meetings). Now, you are out of the day-to-day building, but you play a much more important role — counseling with the leader of the line on a monthly basis. We'll discuss this counseling in more depth in the next chapter. For now, know that this is the stage when massive, exponential growth in the line should begin.

Ultimately, the head of the line should evolve into a top-level pin rank themselves. At this point, counseling may or may not be necessary any longer. You then evolve into more of a motivating presence for the line. You're the living example of someone who's "made it," and simply being who and where you are motivates people in the organization. You will probably be the guest speaker once or twice each year at the cross-line meetings in their area, and you may appear as a guest of honor at the Leadership Conference conducted by that pin-rank distributor.

You should always be supporting the line in one of these capacities. You will move from counseling into motivating after the line is secure.

When we say that a line is secure, we mean that you have walkaway income. If you were to stop working that line — it would continue to develop. This only happens when you have enough core leaders in that line.

By Core leaders, we mean people who are completely self-motivated and practice the Core Qualities we talked about earlier:

▲ Make regular presentations
▲ Develop a customer base

▲ Use all the products

▲ Practice daily self-development time

▲ Attend everything

▲ Are teachable

▲ Edify the sponsorship line

▲ Are accountable

▲ Follow the system

The reason that most people fail in networking is that they fail to identify and work with leaders. They are concerned with the number of people in their group or what their volume is, and they fail to key in on leaders. They are only working their pay levels, or, in many cases, their first levels. To succeed in networking, you must identify and work with your leaders, regardless of what level they are on. This is the only true method to secure lines.

Much of the time when you are building depth, you will be working out of your pay range. This is to build security. But, it will not build you massive income. This can only be done by building width. So, it's not that you don't want to build wide. You do. But, you must <u>secure</u>, then <u>build</u>. Once a line is secure, you begin working more in an inspirational and motivational capacity. You then have the option to stop working and reap your residual income — or, open new lines to expand your income.

Don't be deceived by high volumes, or the number of distributors in a line. High volumes are easily generated by super sales types who are not able to duplicate, and will eventually die off. This same type of salesperson can often sell a large number of people into a program who have no intent to build a business. They basically got involved because they didn't know how to say no. These names may look good on your printout, but they will never duplicate. Counting on these people as distributors is just lying to yourself. The only true barometer of a line's strength is the number of leaders in it who are following the system.

This business is built in the dens and living rooms, and at the kitchen tables. To grow a line, you must be prepared to get into their living rooms and work down the levels with them. It is making these presentations — and properly following through — that builds massive organizations.

Let's look at the entire process of taking a new distributor to a secure line:

First, of course, we're going to do the entire "Getting Started" training we discussed earlier. Say the training is complete. They're using the products; they've purchased the business-building materials they need; they're willing to Go Core; and they have their prospect list of more than 100 people.

They've committed to work at least seven to ten hours a week, so you want to spend that entire time period with them the first week. Schedule two meetings in their house after the first week, and then give them one night a week for the next five to eight weeks. The first week, you have the two meetings scheduled — one is their primary, first home opportunity meeting, and the second is a fall-back night for the people who say they cannot come to the first one. Schedule these first two meetings about seven or eight days from the time they start. Now, get your new distributor furiously pre-approaching their prospect list to get presentations scheduled.

Next, go with your new distributor and conduct two-on-one presentations with them. You want to get in as many two-on-ones as you can possibly squeeze in. The people who get turned on at these two-on-ones will be the ones who come to those first home meetings.

Ideally, your new distributor will learn how to do these short, individual presentations during the first week or two. Once they learn that, they will now continue the process. They will conduct their own one-on-ones to feed their prospects into the home meetings you are conducting.

What I will do is encourage my front-line person to sponsor six people wide their first month. I want them to open six lines, because it is my experience that out of those six, two will become Core lines. The way it seems to work is if you sponsor six people — two will do it <u>now</u>; two will do it <u>later</u>; and, two will do it <u>never</u>.

In order to develop a strong business line with someone who has only seven to ten hours a week to work the business, two lines are about the most they can work with. So, we sponsor six, and we end up getting two. Of course, all six people will tell us that they want to do this business, that they are excited about it, and that they will do what it takes. Unfortunately, history tells us this won't happen.

What usually happens is that when we start to schedule "Getting Started" meetings with them, some of them will drop out, while others won't find time for the meeting. Others will schedule the meeting, but when we get to the actual meeting, and let them know that we are willing to come into their living rooms — they'll immediately take themselves out of the picture. They were okay with the idea of doing the business in the abstract. When they realize it's time to pull the trigger, they bail. End result — you'll have two of the six who will let you come into their living rooms.

Now, why do I say give them two nights a week, and then only one night a week thereafter? This is quite different from what most people in the industry train. They teach that when you sponsor someone who is willing to "Go Core," you should work with them five nights a week and drive the line all way to China. I don't advocate that policy, however. Here's why:

If you get one line and work with it every night of the week, that line will become 90 percent or more of your business. If that should happen, they won't respect you. If they can't

HOW TO BUILD A MULTI-LEVEL MONEY MACHINE

respect you, they can't edify you. And, if they can't edify you, then you can't help them build the business.

The other thing that happens, of course, is that it puts you in a very precarious economic situation. If 90 percent of your income is tied up in one line, and then that line should get seduced away by the hot, new fiber cookie deal that's paying an extra two percent on the fourth level — there goes your entire business. I feel that it's much wiser to diversify your business and build a lot of width, along with building the depth. Width brings you extra income; depth brings you greater security. So, work two lines, giving them each one night a week. You'll be able to diversify your income, and build depth at the same time.

So, let's go back to our example. I've been working with my new line, whose name let's say is Chuck, and Chuck's got two families willing to "Go Core" — the Smiths and the Joneses. The second week, instead of doing the meeting at Chuck's house, I would offer to go do it in the Smiths' or the Jones' house, or, preferably, both. I would instruct Chuck to bring his notes and come to the meetings at the Smiths' and the Jones' houses to learn the presentation. The reason I'm doing the meeting in the second-level people's houses is that it will be easier for them to get guests to come to their own houses than it will be to get them to bring guests to some stranger's house. I'm still teaching the presentation to Chuck, but I'm building depth at the same time.

Give your front-line people a five- to eight-week period, where you'll be working in depth in their organization. Try to go down another level in depth, where you conduct the meetings each week.

During the course of this five- to eight-week period, you'll discover whether or not you really have a Core person who is willing to go all the way, and, in essence, be your partner for life. Or else you'll find out if it is someone who is going to drop out, back off, or just put it on the back burner. Those answers will be determined during this five- to eight-week period.

If you find that you really do have a partner — someone who proactively wants to build the business — expect them to learn the presentation during this time. So, after five weeks, seven weeks, eight weeks, or at whatever time they are ready — push them out of the nest so they can go out and make their own presentations. (You can still spend another night with them just listening to them do their first meeting, and making sure that they're okay to be out there by themselves. If they are, let them fly.)

Next, your level of responsibility will change to the counseling stage. They will still have their family meeting to plug into, and they have their monthly cross-line meeting, as well. This gives them someone to edify and the pipeline structure to plug into, but leaves them the responsibility of getting down in their lines, and duplicating themselves through the one-on-ones and home meetings.

Your next job is to guide this new leader through monthly counseling. You want to make sure he stays true to the system and keeps duplicating. Make sure that he doesn't fall into the "hero" trap by holding weekly opportunity meetings or trainings in his house. Instead, he should be going through the five- to eight-week process — going down the levels in each line.

So, here's what is happening:

After eight weeks, you have broken off a leader, who is now conducting her own meetings. These will be conducted at the homes of the people in her group, going down a level every week or two. By the ninth or tenth week, <u>her front-level people will now be conducting their own meetings</u> — which are now on your tenth level. And, in effect, she has now broken off a leader, so she's out of that process. A few weeks later, <u>those people who were holding the meetings have now worked them-</u>

selves out of a job, and we have another leader, who might be someone on your third, fourth, or fifth level, who is now conducting meetings, breaking off leaders of their own. This is the way you build massive organizations. You work yourself out of a job during this five- to eight-week period, and then teach your people to duplicate the process.

What happens next with this line that you're building depth with? After the distributor has solidified the two lines (meaning that they are now conducting meetings of their own) he's free to go out and prospect six more people — to find the two who will let him come into their living rooms.

Next, he'll duplicate this very same process with these two people. He will give them five to eight weeks in their living rooms, one night a week. And, as time goes on, these people will be learning how to do presentations themselves, and they will work him out of a job. During all of this, of course, you still have your once-a-month family meeting, and there's still a once-a-month cross-line meeting that they can feed into. This allows everybody in the organization the chance to plug into the bigger event meeting sequence, and also to have people that they can edify — to bring their home-town-prophet-syndrome prospects to.

This system — two meetings the first week, then one night meeting per week — is really the best way to do the business. It allows you to become duplicated; it helps you to build width; and it doesn't create co-dependents. It's a very good system that builds level, by level, by level.

The other reason for this system is this:

Your number one obligation in the business is to become successful yourself.

And then, of course, your number two obligation is to build success underneath your people. Most people get this mixed up.

The truth is you cannot show anyone how to attain a pin rank until you attain that pin rank yourself. It doesn't work to think that if you just make a bunch of people successful — then you'll become successful. It sounds good; it looks good; but it just doesn't work. <u>The reality is that you must become successful first.</u> To talk the talk, you must walk the walk. Any distributor you have will lose respect for you if he or she is most of your organization. Your job is to give them that one night a week, for only as long as they need it. One of the rules of building depth is <u>never do for a new distributor (or an existing one) something that they are capable of doing themselves.</u> Your job is to work yourself out of a job.

As you work with new distributors, invest the five to eight weeks to see if you have a builder. Look for the Core Qualities. When you find someone who is willing to "Go Core," and they want to work a two- to four-year plan — then edify the sponsorship line, and plug them into the system.

<u>The key to building depth is to get your sponsor (and, hopefully, others in your sponsorship line) under you, to be making presentations.</u> The most successful people in the business are the ones who learn how to edify their sponsorship line and put them to work. Approach your prospects; do a one-on-one for them; and then get them into the pipeline.

The first thing you do when you bring new distributors to a function is introduce them to your sponsorship line. The sooner your sponsor knows your new distributors, the quicker they can go to work for them. <u>You bring in the new distributors (building width), and then plug them into the support pipeline where your sponsorship line is making presentations (building depth).</u> Then, of course, you duplicate this entire process with your people. Teach them how to sign up new people, and then get down and make presentations in their group.

Your goal should be to build your people up to at least a $5,000-a-year income as quickly as possible. This $5,000 a year is what I consider the break-even point for most distributorships. They'll need that much to buy their marketing materials, finance their self-development program, and attend the functions. Once you can get them to this level, they break even. It doesn't cost them anything to work the business, and anything they do from that point on will put them into profit. The secret is keeping people in the system for two years. Once they are in for this long — they know too much to ever go back.

Most importantly, they can afford to attend the functions and practice their self-development programs. Believe it or not, this is the most important part of the building-depth process. You don't sponsor pin-rank distributors, you grow them.·

People must attend the functions so they can associate with positive, successful people. To hear about them or listen to them on tapes is not enough — they need to meet them. Attending the functions and meeting the leaders builds their belief level in themselves, the company, the products or services, and the industry. Obviously, they need the skills training that the events provide, but the belief they develop is even more important.

Likewise, for the self-development program ...

Here's the reality. Most of the people you sponsor into the business will have a low level of belief in themselves and their spouses. They will be in debt, anxious about the future, and have a very negative view of the world. Their entire life has been spent among the dream-stealers — people who tell them how bad they are, how tough it is, and why they'll never make it.

Once these dream-stealers learn that the new couple you sponsored is on a path to improve themselves, they will intensify their propaganda. Because most people no longer believe in their dreams, they insult, ridicule and beat down anyone who still does. Your self-development program teaches your people that they can dream; it's okay to be healthy, happy and prosperous; and that they really can live their dreams. This is a radical, mind-boggling concept for most people — one that they will need constant, positive reinforcement on before they will be able to accept it. And, once they accept this — they will still need constant, positive reinforcement to counteract the steady barrage of negativity our society exposes them to. The functions and self-development programs promote belief and keep people motivated. The pipeline process gives them the step-by-step system to follow in order to manifest their beliefs into reality.

This five- to eight-week process (two nights the first week, and one night each week thereafter) seems so simple that a lot of people really don't understand its power. This is how to build depth, create walkaway residual income, and build financial security for your front-line people. Just keep replicating this process, working two lines at a time, until your people get to the point of financial security, which, of course, creates your own.

Here's how I like to see the scenario unfold. I ask for seven to ten hours a week from my new people. They commit to that, and I get into their living rooms and take them through the eight- week process. After that, they're working in their people's living rooms. This may go on for six months. At that time, when I counsel with them, they will be evaluating their businesses. At this point, they may be making about half as much from their Network Marketing business as they make on their job. Of course, on their job, they work 40, 50, or even 60 hours a week. Whereas, in their network marketing business, they're only working ten hours a week. I will suggest that they go up to about 15 or 16 hours a week — probably another evening doing meetings. Now, this is more than they bargained for, and more than I asked them for initially. But, based on the progress they've made, and the income they're seeing — I'm wagering that this additional one night a week for another six months to a year will get them to the point where their Network Marketing income matches their job income.

Here's what happens next:

Now, they're at the point where they make as much working 15 hours a week in their Network Marketing business as they do working 50 or 60 hours in their job. However, instead of telling them to retire — I will suggest that they go up to another night a week so they will be out four, or even five nights a week. I want them to do this until they get to the point where they pay off all their debts.

That's one of my goals for them — getting them out of debt as quickly as possible. So, I'm going to encourage them to stay with their jobs even after they've matched the income. This way they will double their income. They'll have their regular income at their job, plus they'll have that same income again from their Network Marketing business. I want them to start paying down their credit cards, paying off their car loans, and even paying off their mortgages. When they get to the point where they are honestly making much more in Network Marketing than they are in their regular jobs and probably have six months worth of income in the bank — or they're completely debt-free — only then will I counsel them that perhaps it's time to leave their jobs and go full time in their Network Marketing business.

Here's the exciting part.

What I consider full time in the Network Marketing business is actually only about 25 hours a week. I believe that you can have a very healthy five-figure (or even six-figure) monthly income and never work more than 25 hours a week. Here's why.

The prime time for the business is during the evenings from 7:00 to 10:00 p.m. Most people are working real jobs from Monday through Friday, so daytimes are not very productive. The best times to work are Tuesday and Thursday nights from 7:00 to 10:00 p.m. The latest you can start a meeting, by the way, is 8:00 p.m., because it can take two hours. So, that would go until 10:00 p.m. Ten o'clock is about as late as you can do meetings. So, Tuesday and Thursday nights are great nights. Wednesday nights are not quite as good, because many people have church, but they are workable. Monday nights are not quite as good, because people have just gotten back to their work-week, but this night can work, as well. Friday and Saturday nights are also not very good, because most people use them to go out and play. Sunday nights have been very bad, but Saturday afternoons work quite well. So, we've got four evenings and one afternoon that are really workable.

Let's assume that they are working three and a half hours a night for four evenings. That would be fourteen hours. Throw in another four hours on Saturday afternoon, and now they are up to eighteen hours. That leaves them with seven hours a week where they might be prospecting, if they are looking for future lines, taking care of minor paperwork; and using the rest of the time to counsel their leaders. So, assuming they are working with three or four lines, which is about the most I would recommend for anyone, they would be working at the most twenty-five hours. The rest of the time during the week, the best thing they can do is live the lifestyle. Wake up at the crack of noon; sit on their balcony, as I do drinking my herbal tea watching the sailboats bobbing in the water. Go out to lunch — dinner — shopping — just live the lifestyle.

This does two things. One — it tremendously motivates the people in your organization, because they would like to have that lifestyle, and, two — it attracts a number of very good prospects to you, because they look at the lifestyle, harmony and balance you've achieved, and want it too. You really do start to attract more and more people to you. <u>The longer you're in the business, the easier it becomes</u>.

> **NOTE:** I must mention here — the suggested nights for meetings are only general guide-lines. I have done meetings on Labor Day, and also once on New Year's Day. If someone has a dream big enough, they will find a way to get people there.

When you work this process with a line, you can build it up to a high-level pin rank (meaning at least ten breakaway or director lines) within a two- to four-year period. In other words, they will have a solid, secure business with ten or more active growing lines. Over a period of time, as those lines develop in depth, leaders will beget leaders, who will beget other leaders. My experience is that once you have 35 to 50 Core leaders in a line — that line is absolutely one hundred percent secure for life. Should you drop dead tomorrow, that line would continue to build and grow forever.

The other area you must take care of in order to build depth and security is the method by which you communicate with your organization. Different organizations do this in different ways. Some people communicate by telephone, and set aside certain hours of the week, during which they are available for phone consultations. Other people communicate only at meetings. They let people know ahead of time that they will be there an hour early or that they will stay two hours late. They expect all of their communication to be done at the functions. Personally, I prefer to communicate by means of a voice mail system.

This, I believe, is the most powerful tool for building your network. I'll go into the specifics I use in a minute, but I must tell you that to begin, you must choose one of these ways to set up a communication link with your organization. What you cannot do is give your number out to every person in your organization, and say that you are available whenever they need you. You will never achieve the twenty-five hour workweek scenario, and you'll find that you'll just be working harder and harder, the more successful you are in the business.

Some of the people I know in this industry, who make the high, five-figure monthly checks, are actually working about 100 hours a week. They place, or take, thousands of phone calls a week. I place only about six to ten calls a week in my organization. The rest of the time, I'm on the voice mail. Voice mail has dramatically enhanced the business. We work a whole lot fewer hours and we're a lot more productive. Your phone bills will go down dramatically, and you'll stop wasting twenty to thirty hours a week or useless chitchat during phone calls that you would normally make.

We don't use the voice mail as an answering machine. We use it as the communication medium for the organization. We strictly follow the sponsorship lines. I send messages to my front-line leaders only. I do not broadcast to the whole group. Now, you're probably wondering why I don't just send messages to everyone. Well, because that wouldn't be duplicatable.

This way, I send just to my front-line people. That's their organization, by the way. They choose whether or not to resend my message, which they resend to their front-line people, who listen to it, and choose whether or not to send it to their front-line people.

The types of messages we send on the voice mail are meeting announcements, new product announcements, any urgent changes or messages from the corporate headquarters, and then mostly training tips and inspirational messages that come up from the organization.

Let's say someone in Gary's line gives his very first home meeting by himself. He'll record a brief (thirty seconds or less) message about it, and send it up to Gary. Then, he will rebroadcast it to me. If I like it, then I will copy it and send it to all of my front-line people. If they like it, then they will copy it and send it to their people. It's very inspiring for the other new people, who haven't yet done their first meeting, or who are about to do their first meeting, or who haven't done a meeting in a while, to hear about someone new who's excited, and is going out and conducting meetings.

We even have messages from people who've held a meeting and nobody showed up! And they came back and sent a message in which they talked about how they conducted the meeting anyway, because they knew that their entire future depended on it. A message like that will inspire thousands of other people.

To really use the system effectively, you must be on it at least three times a day. When you get to the high-level pin ranks, it will be about five times a day. You might be on only five or ten minutes each time, but that way the messages will get through the organization rapidly. If you just check the messages once a day, like most people are inclined to do, it'll take a week for a message to get down four or five levels. Otherwise, someone may check their messages right before you are about to send them one, and then it could sit there for another 24 hours. When everybody is checking voice mail at least three times a day, you can get a message to an organization of thousands of people within 24 to 48 hours.

It is this constant communication, training, guidance and inspiration coming through, in my case the voice mail system, that builds large organizations. Choose the communication method that you prefer, but put it into place. Ideally, you should be using the same method as your sponsorship line uses, so they can be supporting you.

I should take a minute here to discuss some of the newer technologies available to communicate with your organization. This includes satellite TV training, e-mail and the Internet.

Satellite training, due to its cost, is prohibitive (and thus, unduplicatable) for you to use at this time to train your group. Where this works best is when it's used by the parent company for national broadcasts using one central reception site in each area. The reality is that most people still do not have satellite dishes.

If you communicate by e-mail, the people without computers may feel that they are not getting equal support. So, for the time being, use voice mail, contact at meetings, or the standard telephone. Having said that though, I will tell you that the computer and the Internet are transforming the business. There are a lot of ways they can help you build stronger and faster. In fact, I've included a whole chapter on the Internet later in the book.

What you cannot do is allow your people to decide when they want to call you. You will certainly get phone calls from eight o'clock in the morning until eleven o'clock at night. You'll even get a number of phone calls at two, three and five o'clock in the morning from people in faraway places who haven't figured out that you are in a different time zone. The only way to manage your organization is for you to manage the communication structure that you set up with your people.

Manage the communication structure; have a complete duplicatable system in place; and follow the five- to eight-week period to bring new distributors up to speed, and you'll build an ever-expanding, ever-deepening, massive organization. Now, let's look at the leadership strategies you'll need once that happens ...

CHAPTER THIRTEEN

DEVELOPING LEADERS
IN YOUR GROUP

A COUPLE FRIENDS OF MINE, **ART BURLEIGH AND JAN RUHE,** put together a book on leadership, and asked me to write a chapter. This was good timing for me, because I had just spent a week in Los Angeles, interviewing CEO candidates for a venture I was involved in. In 95% of the cases, I was able to disqualify the applicant within one interview. The reason: <u>weak leadership skills</u>.

Many of these people were in what would be considered leadership positions in the companies they work for now. They knew all the buzzwords: leading by example, developing team-work, creating vision, delegation and values. They spoke of managing resources and leading people. Yet, I really believe they didn't understand the real essence of leadership. Most people don't.

I believe that <u>a true leader is someone who is capable of getting people to willingly do things they wouldn't ordinarily do</u>. They are able to do this by helping them believe in them-selves, and by teaching them not *what* to think, but *how* to think.

In the military environment, a leader might inspire troops to get out of a foxhole and charge an enemy encampment. In a corporate environment, a leader may empower an employee to take immediate action to save an important account. A leader in a network marketing organization might inspire someone to speak in front of a group for their first time, or it might simply be causing a new distributor to buy a suit and tie for his first time.

In each case, the person wouldn't normally want to do these actions, <u>but they willingly do them</u>. They exercise leadership qualities, because of the leadership influence of the leader they follow.

I believe this is possible, <u>because of the increase in belief and esteem they have achieved as a result of their exposure to a leader</u>. That leader has done much more than demonstrate leadership skills and qualities — they have helped develop positive growth in the individuals they lead.

The old leadership model was to teach people what to think. In the military model, examples of this would be the secret police, the many civilian massacres and the Third Reich. The belief was that you simply indoctrinate people into thinking what you want them to think (and one of those thoughts was to never question authority). The examples above prove the dangers of this way of leadership.

The fact is, many people are actively looking to be shown what to think. They search the globe for gurus to follow, and movements to join. The strong growth today of gangs, religions and cults is a manifestation of this. People watch ESPN and other sports programs to learn what they should think about their local quarterback; they listen to bombastic buffoons on talk radio stations to know what to think about political issues, and they read the social columns so they can know who is hip, hot and trendy. The education system around the world is moving from institutions that teach people how to think — into places that disseminate facts to memorize.

Although this environment exists — real leaders do not exploit it. They carefully choose the people they lead, and select only those who are interested in thinking for themselves. They create situations where people develop problem-solving skills — which fosters thought and builds belief in themselves.

True leaders don't develop people's beliefs in the leader; they develop the belief *in the follower.* They foster growing confidence and esteem in those who follow them and help them think independently. This freethinking and newfound confidence causes the follower to empower themselves into leadership ways of their own. Leaders beget more leaders — the real test of leadership.

I've said the biggest cause of failure for most people in Network Marketing is their failure to identify and work with the leaders in their organization. By the same token — you need to identify and work with the leaders in your sponsorship line. They are your best source of help. When you create partnerships with the leaders in your sponsorship line — you are now demonstrating the leadership traits that will develop more leaders in your group.

Never be at cross-purpose with your sponsor or sponsorship line. If the person(s) right above you is unwilling or unable to help you, keep going up until you find someone who needs the security of depth. Find out how he or she communicates (voice mail, after meetings, or whatever), and then replicate this throughout your organization. However your sponsorship line is communicating, is the way you want to communicate with your organization.

One of the strongest parts of the support structure that your sponsorship line and your company have in place for you is the **function calendar.** Find out what is being provided by them so you can tie your events around them. I'll give you an idea of how this works.

Let's say you're given every Tuesday night to do a home meeting for a new line that you have. On the night that your sponsor has their cross-line or family meeting — your home meeting should be canceled and rolled into the bigger meeting. The same thing would happen if you were having a family meeting, but the open, cross-line meeting is scheduled for the same night. You would roll your meeting up into that meeting.

> **NOTE:** This always holds true if your meeting and the larger meeting are scheduled for the exact same night. Other meetings scheduled for that week would go on as planned.

You always roll your meetings up into the sponsorship line's functions, because then you have a stronger function, a larger event, and there are lots more people. You must always defer to your sponsorship line in this area. Doing that will create the same reality in your organization and they will duplicate the same process with you.

One of the important leadership strategies is making sure that there is an adequate and effective support structure of meetings and trainings in place. So, I'd like to spend some time going over that with you now.

I'd like to emphasize again my belief that you should only have a once-a-month open, cross-line meeting in each area. Now, if your home meetings are getting so big that they won't fit into living rooms, it doesn't mean that you need to do them in a hotel. It means that you're not doing them in the true "pipeline" fashion (with the exception of family meetings, which will eventually get too big to be held in people's homes).

It means that you've set yourself up as a "hero," and everyone is coming to your house for meetings (or they're all going to someone else's house to see you do meetings). In the proper pipeline sequence, you're doing the home meetings in a line for only five to eight weeks — then replacing yourself. Each time the meetings go down a level, the home meetings should split off.

So, if you sponsor Gary and Vicki — and help them open three front-line builders — there should be three different home meetings going within several weeks. Several weeks later, there should be a couple dozen different home meetings going. Eventually, there will be hundreds of home meetings in an area!

The secret is to not go to a large, weekly hotel meeting, but rather to keep expanding this network of home meetings. Save the hotel meetings for the larger, family meetings that will no longer fit in people's homes, and the monthly open, cross-line meetings. The more home meetings you conduct — the bigger the cross-line meetings become. The bigger the cross-line meetings become, the more home meetings spin off. It is a self-perpetuating growth cycle.

Follow the system of two meetings for a new distributor their first week, one night a week each week thereafter, and your people will duplicate. This will create the network of home meetings you need for your pipeline. Then, have your area family meeting and your cross-line meeting each once a month.

Now, let's say you're the highest level pin rank in your town — that would mean you hold the family meeting. If you are a mid-level pin rank, and you have a sponsor who is the highest level pin rank in your town, and they are doing a once-a-month family meeting — then you would plug into their family meeting. If you have a sponsorship line, a big organization above you, in town — then feed into their meeting. If you don't have the sponsorship line there, it then becomes your job to set up and conduct the family meeting. Once a month, you have the open, cross-line meeting, as we discussed earlier.

There's another level you should go up to from there. This should be a quarterly event, and this should be a <u>major</u> event. Now, again, the important thing is for you to tie into the functions of your sponsorship line and/or the company. If your company is having a convention once a year, that would be one of your major functions. If that's in the summertime, then it would be your summer function. If the company has some type of leadership conference, institute or retreat once a year — that would be the major event for that quarter. Likewise, if they have launches or rallies at certain times of the year, those would be major quarterly events.

Here are some ideas to help you figure out which events would qualify for your calendar.

I believe that the average distributor can generally only afford to go to one "destination" event a year. A "destination" event is an event to which they need to buy tickets, get on a plane, rent hotel rooms, and spend a couple of days there. A once-a-year event like this is going to be about all the average distributor can pay for. There can be another "destination" event each year, however, that's geared only for leaders. For instance, one of the things I did for my organization was a yearly Leadership Institute, usually in the wintertime, and usually someplace nice like Hawaii. This is also a destination event, but it's only for the pin-rank leaders who are making more money, so they can handle it. But, I would also schedule something during the same quarter (that would be done on a regional basis) for the average distributor who would not be attending the Leadership Conference.

It's the same thing with the other two quarters of the year. You want to have events that people can get to. It's okay that they have to pay a little money; and, it's okay that they have to travel a little. It might even be one night in a hotel, but, preferably, it should be an event that they can drive to — even if it means driving three or four hours to get there. This does involve some expense and commitment on our distributor's part, but not a major commitment like the annual convention. We've said that to "Go Core" takes approximately $5,000 a year. That will work if you have only one destination event. If the events are all hosted by the company, and they have four major destination events a year — that may work for the leaders, but it won't work for the masses. In order to develop a massive orga-

217

nization, you're going to need quarterly events in every area where you have a large organization.

Here's an example of how I set up my calendar:

In January, I have a Leadership Institute, which is for pin-level ranks and above. We also schedule goal-setting weekends around the country for the lower ranks. These are Friday night/ Saturday day events. Friday night is more of a vision and goal-setting type of an evening where they're making their plans for the upcoming year, and then Saturday is nuts-and-bolts training on how they can achieve some of the goals they set the night before. The pin ranks will be going to the Leadership Institute, which is high-level leadership strategy training, and the lower ranks will attend the regional events with the basic goal-setting training.

In the spring, I schedule regional rallies. These take place around the country in every major city where there is a large presence of distributors. In the summer, there is a company convention, which we tie into. We make that the once-a-year destination event that all distributors attend. Then, in the fall, we do another rally, which again is a Friday night/Saturday day thing. The Friday night program might be a second look type of opportunity meeting where we would have high-level, pin rank distributors speaking (so distributors might bring a guest), and then Saturday would be an all-day, nuts-and-bolts training.

If you are the highest ranking pin in your area, there are a couple of other things that I would recommend you do. One is some type of a product workshop once a month, and possibly some type of builder's meeting once a month. Personally, I don't do these as separate events. I tie them together with other events. I might bill the builder's meeting as a "night owl training," and schedule it either after the family meeting or the open, cross-line meeting. We might have an opportunity meeting from 7:30 to 9:30 p.m., take a break, and then have a "night owl training" for the distributors.

Product training workshops might tie in the same way, or we might hold them on another night. This would be an informal event — maybe 30 to 45 minutes — just touching on some of the benefits of the products, making sure people know how to use them, and talking about what makes them unique from a marketing standpoint. We want to make sure that they really understand them, which creates excitement and builds volume.

> **NOTE:** The product training and builder's meetings are the only local training events that I recommend — and only if they are conducted by the **highest ranking pin-rank distributor in the area.** It's important that you don't let yourself get drawn into the role of a "hero." This can easily happen if you conduct weekly trainings, or bring all of your people to your home once a month to teach "how to do presentations." Your people start to think they have to <u>learn</u> the business, and only then can they <u>do</u> the business. In reality, this is not necessary.

Actually, they should be learning the business as they are doing it. The secret of the business is getting your people to <u>study, do and teach</u>, all simultaneously. Instead of doing training sessions on how to do one-on-ones — get with your new distributor and do two-on-ones with him. Instead of conducting training on how to do home meetings — get into your new distributor's living room and hold meetings for him.

Having this steady, regularly scheduled stream of functions keeps your people motivated; it provides them the training they need; it drives growth; and, it creates tremendous momentum. One of the most important things you'll do as a leader is make sure that this function system is in place. Again, <u>it's very important to be in contact with your sponsorship line, and tie in with the events that they and your company are doing (to make sure that there isn't duplication of effort, or that people aren't being</u>

encouraged to attend too many functions). If there are too many functions that cost too much money — people stop attending, and their network will begin to suffer. Set up the sequence properly, and you'll have a structure that fosters steady growth.

Now, let's look at another critical leadership strategy:

Monthly Counseling. This is the monthly process you do with the leaders and potential leaders in your organization, to keep them growing on a consistent basis. Here's how counseling works. Let's say you're a Bronze Director with your company, and the next rank up is Silver Director. You would counsel with the first Silver Director in your sponsorship line. Now, once you become a Silver Director, if your sponsor is still a Silver Director, you would no longer counsel with her. You would go, instead, to her sponsor, who is a Gold Director. (As we discussed earlier, if you want to know how to be a Gold Director, you have to talk to somebody who has already done it. If you want to be a Diamond Director, you need to be counseled by a Diamond Director.) You should counsel with the next upline person who is at the rank above you.

This ensures everyone has someone to counsel with, and also ensures that the top ranks don't have thousands of people looking to them for counseling. Just like the sponsorship lines work, you work with your front-line leaders, who work with their front-line leaders, who work with their front-line leaders. In the event you're in a sponsorship line with a level or two at the same rank as you — go up the organization. You will find someone who will be willing to work with you.

It should be noted that just because your sponsor is the same rank as you does not mean that they are a bad leader, or that they don't know the business. It simply means that they've helped you achieve fast growth — and what quite often happens — they've brought people up to their own rank slightly before they moved up a rank themselves. So, don't judge them or hold that against them. Celebrate the fact that they've helped you get this far, and counsel with the appropriate person in your sponsorship line. Your job is to learn from their experience. They will already have made the same mistakes that you are headed toward, which means they can cut many years off your learning curve. Be open-minded and coachable, for they have a vested interest in your success.

> **NOTE:** A counseling can only help you if you do a real one. Your sponsor can only help you if he or she has real information to work with. Don't draw out twelve lines if you really have only two active, core lines. Otherwise, the counseling is a lie.

Now, let's look at how to do the actual counseling. We collect the relevant information we need. (You'll find several samples of generic counseling forms in my *MLM Power Weekend Home Study Program.*) When you counsel someone, you need to know their rank, how many distributors are in their group, how many lines they have, what their average volume is, and a number of other variables.

Probably two of the most important variables you should be concerned with are the number of lines with a leader, and the total number of leaders in the organization. To me, these are the two most critical statistics that determine all future growth. We know that a line could have fifteen people in it, but, if none of them are leaders — within three months, the line will probably have diminished to one or two people. We can have another line with only two people in it, but if they're both leaders — people willing to "Go Core" — in a month or two, that line will probably have forty or fifty people in it. Leaders produce leaders. That's the number one factor we want to watch when we are counseling — the leaders in the organization.

Then, duplicate the process with your people. Here are some guidelines on how to counsel:

The first question I like to ask is, "So, in the past week, whose living rooms have you been in?" This is the million-dollar question, because it drives right to the heart of the system. If someone hasn't been doing home meetings for anyone in the last seven days — then they have a complete breakdown in the duplication process. If this is the case, you need to dig deeper and uncover the cause.

If they don't have anyone in the five- to eight-week process — it usually means they haven't been working. Which, of course, is their option, because it is their business, after all. But, if they come to you for counseling, it is your job to call them on this, and let them know that they cannot expect you or the company to help them if they don't put out effort. You can also bring them back to the goals they set in their "Getting Started" training, and ask whether or not they were really serious about them.

Now, it is possible (although not likely) that they will have been working, but still without having been in the living rooms in the past week. Exploring in more depth, you will usually find one of the following two problems:

1. Their people are calling them to cancel the home meetings, because they have no guests coming. Or,

2. Their people won't commit to home meetings, or they keep promising to do them in the near future.

In the first instance, this is easy to fix. <u>Usually, it means that they are not doing the one-on-ones,</u> and are trying to get prospects to come to a home meeting cold. This is next to impossible, and virtually guarantees lots of no-shows, canceled reservations and "secret meetings." Putting the one-on-ones back into place eliminates this problem.

The other cause of having no guests may be that the distributor is simply not doing effective one-on-ones. They're presenting to lots of people, but none of them want to take a second look. If this is happening, <u>then it means that they were probably pushed out of the nest too early</u>. It may be necessary to go back and do some two-on-ones or role-play with them in order to find the weak points in their presentation. Once this is done, get right back into the five- to eight-week process.

Now, in the second instance — where new distributors won't commit to or keep postponing their home meetings — this answer is also simple. <u>It means they are not a "big business" distributor</u>. They may be a tourist — someone who talks about building a business, but just watches others. Or, they may be someone who really just wants to retail products, and be a "small business" builder.

Once you point this out to the person you're counseling with, they can come out of denial. Instead of thinking that they have "big business" builders, they can actually go out and get some.

There are several things I should point out here:

The situation I've just described ("small business" builders posing as "big business" ones) is one of the most frequent occurrences I see when I counsel people. When this is cleared up for a new distributor (and even an experienced one), they feel the weight of the world is lifted off their shoulders. They've been begging, pleading, brow-beating, and desperately trying to drag people across the finish line who don't want to be there. Once they realize this, they can then move on to take the proactive steps that actually build their business. Meaning, of course, that they can then get some real "big business" builders, and get them plugged into the five- to eight-week process.

The other point I want to mention concerns what we do with the "tourists" and "small business" builders. <u>Love them</u>! "Small business" distributors are the lifeblood of your business. They create volume, bring you "big business" builders, and many will grow into "big business" distributors themselves. And the "tourists," believe it or not, are doing the best they can with what they have to work with. Instead of berating them into letting you do meetings for them, back off. Let them know that you're always available to help them when they're ready. If you let them know about the functions, get them into the self-development program, and plug them into your communication system — it's very possible that some of them will grow into productive distributors down the road. Just love them, and let them grow at their own pace.

This process I've just taken you through is one of the primary functions of counseling — namely, <u>to direct your people on how and where to spend their time</u>. This facilitates the action I mentioned at the start of the chapter — identifying leaders. Only by doing this can you intelligently work depth in your organization.

Last thoughts ...

The last leadership strategy I want to go into is honoring the system. By this point, you have probably discovered that I'm a fanatic about following a duplicatable system, and I think you can see why. The things that grow your business — getting your people involved in a self-development program, getting them in regular communication with you, and setting up the sponsoring pipeline — really work effectively <u>only</u> if you're following a system. All of these things should be inherently built into your ultimate system. This should be a completely duplicatable, step-by-step-by-step system that anyone in your organization, at any level, will be able to duplicate. The system must remain sacred with you, as a leader. If you change the system, even only slightly, you will send a message to the organization that it's okay to change the system. Of course, from time to time, market conditions will dictate that you change the system. Let me give you an idea of how you might go about that if you need to do so.

Let's say you have reached the top-rank pin level in your company, and you have fifteen top-rank pin levels on your front line, and you're thinking about changing something in your system. Suppose you want to take out one book that you're currently using at one part of the sponsoring process, and substitute another in its place. Well, I would bring that up at your annual Leadership Conference or at another event that you have from time to time with your top leaders attending.

In my case, it was called a "Diamond Weekend." This is a weekend where each Diamond distributorship pays its own way. It was not an official company event, but it was just a chance for the Diamonds to get together, talk shop and interact on an informal basis. Before the weekend takes place, you would send out to every one of them a copy of the new book you are proposing, and ask them to read it. They would come to the weekend; you'd talk about it; and a decision would be made.

Let's say that you chose to go with the new book. Well, then you would set a specific date when that would take place. You would announce that on March 1st, the system officially changes from book "A" to book "B." So, anybody you sponsor or prospect on the night of February 28th would get book "A," but anyone starting March 1st would then get book "B." That is the message you would be sending out in the voice mail, or through whatever means you communicate with your people. <u>The system can only be changed from the inside as an entire organization, and when you do it that way, it protects the integrity of the system</u>. Then the system protects the integrity of your residual income.

Now, let's look at how to diversify that residual income, by sponsoring long distance lines ...

CHAPTER FOURTEEN

BUILDING LONG DISTANCE LINES

O NE OF THE FIRST THINGS YOUR NEW DISTRIBUTORS ARE LIKELY to ask you is, *"Hey, when are you going to have meetings in XYZ city? I know lots of people there."* This is an escapist mentality. Instead of building their businesses locally, which they can actively do right now, they're fantasizing about a faraway city, because that gives them a chance to procrastinate.

Here's what you need to know and make sure each of your people knows. <u>Your local lines should be your primary sources of income.</u> You need to have a strong, sound, local organization that grows on a continuous basis. This is the easiest, most cost-effective way to build. As you begin to develop depth, lines will start to expand into other states. By the time you get down seven or eight levels, it will not be unusual for you to be in eight or ten different states. But, first you must develop a strong, local foundation.

There are lots of good reasons to build long distance, but there are also some drawbacks if it's not done correctly. Let's talk about that.

Some of the reasons you want to sponsor long distance include overzealous government regulators, negative publicity, economic conditions, loss of key people, and natural disasters.

All of these things are factors that can dramatically affect your income if it is all tied up in one local group.

Let's suppose that you have an overzealous attorney general who wants to run for governor, and he's looking for some extra free publicity. He figures the best way is to take on one of those evil, mean, nasty MLM companies, and he picks yours. So, he's holding press conferences every day for two weeks, as he attacks your company. What do you think that would do to your income if it were on the late news on television every night at ten or eleven o'clock? The same thing can happen if the local newspaper does an investigative journalism series with a slant that Network Marketing is a rip-off, and your company is on the front page of the local newspaper every day for two weeks.

If your whole line is local and all tied under one or two people, where would you be if they should leave for another opportunity? Here in South Florida, where I live, we saw massive attrition that took years to rebuild after Hurricane Andrew struck. All of these things are very good reasons to protect yourself, and diversify your income by sponsoring long distance.

There are some other benefits, as well. If you are like me and enjoy traveling, you'll like having groups around the country (or the world) in beautiful destinations. Long distance sponsoring is a wonderful way to finance your travel and get great tax breaks. It allows you to see some beautiful cities and/or countries, while developing new friends along the way.

Now, some of the drawbacks.

First, of course, it costs more money. Take a prospect to an open meeting in your town ,and it will cost you only five to ten dollars. Fly 1,500 miles to spend a weekend with a new line, and you can easily spend $1,000. For that reason, you need to first have a solid, local group. You can use the income from your local lines to invest in developing long distance lines.

> **NOTE:** This is also one of the reasons why I don't encourage people to quit their jobs right away. Most people want to do this as soon as they are making $2,000 to $3,000 a month. Instead, I counsel them to reinvest that income into working with the long distance lines that branch off as they begin to get depth in their organizations. This diversifies their income at the same time income is increasing ... giving them a much more lucrative opportunity, so they can ultimately leave their jobs for good.

Another drawback of working with long distance lines is that you cannot be there to look them in the eye on a day-to-day basis when they experience challenges, or celebrate victories. A good voice mail system will help a great deal in this area. Which naturally leads us to the question of whether or not you can effectively sponsor long distance simply by phone, FAX and mail. I really don't believe so.

And, just to be totally up front, I should tell you that I cash a check every month that is the result of lines I sponsored five to eight years ago through direct mail and advertising. These lines were initially opened on the telephone. So, know that I'm making money from having done something I recommend you don't do. I'm not being hypocritical — I'm simply trying to encourage you to learn from my mistakes and build upon them.

Of the dozens and dozens of long distance lines I've sponsored by telephone, there are only eight left that give me residual income. And, there are two things you should know about that.

1. I personally traveled to and worked with each of those eight lines a number of times.

2. Those lines do not regularly grow. They are, for the most part, static, bringing in only enough people each month to replace those who drop out. The vast majority

of people in those lines are satisfied customers who use the products each month, but do not actively build the business.

In fact, a number of them love the products enough to buy them regularly — but, are actually successfully building organizations in *other* network marketing companies. This happened because they found someone local in another company to join as a partner with and build a business. I take personal responsibility for this. You will find that your lines that experience large, consistent growth will be the ones you work intimately and directly with. This means local lines — <u>or long distance lines that you develop in the same manner as the local lines</u>. We'll look at the specifics of that in a moment. For now, let's just accept that there are lots of reasons you should sponsor long distance, but you want to do it in a functional, duplicatable way.

In fact, I've always maintained that the best-kept secret in Network Marketing is that your long distance lines are your strongest ones. Most people think it's just the opposite. They think that their local group is stronger, because they have the most people there. They see more people, more often. There are people coming by their house, picking up products, borrowing sales tools, and making lots of calls. In actuality, that's your strongest <u>co-dependent</u> line. You'll notice that a line 3,000 miles away doesn't call you when they need products; the line doesn't call to see if you have an extra distributor kit they can borrow; and they don't call to ask you to do a presentation for their hot new prospect. Because they are 3,000 miles away, they have learned the art of self-sufficiency. That's one of the benefits of working long distance — **it forces you to do what you should be doing anyway with your local lines ... which is to work yourself out of a job.**

Before we go any further, however, let's define what we mean by a long distance line. If you can leave your work at five o'clock, drive to your new distributor, be there to make an 8:00 p.m. presentation, finish at 10:00 p.m., and be back home by 1:00 a.m. — then that's considered a <u>local</u> line. It's only when you can't get back home the same night I consider it a long distance line.

Now, you're probably saying, "Hey, you're working me too hard. I get home at 1:00 a.m.! By the time I get to sleep, it's 2:00 a.m. I have to get up at 6:30 a.m. to go to my job." Yes, that's true, so perhaps that's probably not the best line to start with. You would be better to start with the people who live right in your hometown. But, if you have a prospect that is really serious, they're looking for an opportunity, and they're three hours away — it's worth your time to make the investment. Remember, you'll be doing that for just a five- to eight-week period. You'll know that one night a week you're going to get less sleep, but you're building your dream. That's the payoff.

Now, if you cannot get there in three hours, then we're talking about a long distance line. Many times these lines will be in places where you need to get on a plane and fly hours to get there. So, here's the formula for working with them. I wouldn't recommend you sponsor anyone long distance unless you're willing to follow this formula.

<u>You must be willing to travel to their city at least two times, and perhaps three, the first month they are in the business.</u> You must then be prepared to go back once a month for five to eight months. We're making a schedule much like we do with our local group, only instead of weeks, we're using months. So, we go there two times the first month, and then once a month for five to eight months. Now, you're probably wondering, "Hey, how do I know this is a good investment? I'm spending all of my money on a plane ticket, hotel, travel, meals and expenses. What if they quit?" That's one of the risks you take. However, there are some things you could do to make it more sensible and reduce the risk.

I wouldn't even think of traveling somewhere to build a line with someone who was not core. I mean completely Core ... using the products themselves, willing to make presentations, on the self-development program, on the voice mail system, attending all functions (if there are any) in their town. They have to be willing to do all these things. I will get on a plane and go there if they've done all of those things; if I have done the entire "Getting Started" training with them, by telephone; if I know they have their list of 100+ prospects; if they have circulated Pre-Approach Packets and have people committed to come to a presentation.

It's for their benefit that I get there at least twice, or, ideally, even three times the first month. What I've got to do in that first month is teach them how to do a presentation themselves, be-cause I won't be able to be there in their living rooms one night a week like I could a local line. So, they've got to learn the presen-tation quickly. If I get there two or three times and stay a couple of days (usually a weekend), then I can role-play and practice with them. I'll do as many two-on-one presentations as I can with them. They'll take notes, and learn it as quickly as they can. That's the most important goal for month one — learning how to do the presentation by themselves.

We may have to supplement that with some telephone role-playing, as well. But, once that's done, they will be able to go out and start building their businesses. Now, their confidence is probably not that strong at this point, and neither are their pre-sentation skills. That's why I'm willing to come back once a month. What I'm doing on those return trips is a meeting that gives them an opportunity to have someone they can edify. They'll have a bigger event that they can excite their people about, and bring their "home town prophet" syndrome pros-pects to, as well.

I'm hoping to bring them up to a high-level pin rank over the five- to eight-month period. You want to get them where they have enough confidence, success and leaders of their own that they can do monthly functions in their area. Then, it's just not necessary for you to be there any longer. You will still drop back from time to time, probably a couple of times a year, to be their special speaker at a monthly open, cross-line meeting, as a way of supporting the group.

When you've gotten a long distance line to this level, you've built walkaway residual income with this line just as you have in the local lines. This is even more powerful than the local lines, because it gives you places to travel to; it makes you friends all over the country, and often the world; and it protects your income by diversifying it. You have income coming from a number of different lines and different cities, so you're in a much stronger position financially.

I might also mention that you should check with your sponsorship line for cities in which there are already open, cross-line meetings scheduled. You may have — or your people may have on their prospect list — a number of people who live in cities where open meetings are already being conducted. This is the fastest way to build and gain security, because it won't be necessary for you or your people to spend a lot to fly there once a month. If there is a solid open, cross-line meeting that you can plug into, it's simply a question of getting your people started right, grounding them in the basics with the "Get Started" training and then turning them loose with an open meeting they can plug into.

Once you develop a number of long distance lines, it allows you to go to the next level "leadership-wise" in providing the functions. Let's say you've got Jimmy in Dallas, who is a high-level pin rank; you've got Nancy and Ben in Arizona, who are high-level pin ranks; and you've got the Johnsons in New York, who are high-level pin ranks. Each of these distributorships has a large organization based in their hometown. They might have some smaller long distance lines, but they have huge organizations in their hometowns. You can now arrange to have these pins speak at each other's meetings. So, there is always a different speaker for their monthly open, cross-line meeting. The Johnsons can speak in January and July at the meeting in Dallas, and in February and August at the meeting in Arizona. Likewise, their people in Arizona can travel to Dallas, and they can travel to New York. You, of course, could speak once or twice a year at each of these meetings, as well.

This creates the best kind of open, cross-line meetings. There will be different, powerful, successful speakers every month, so people really will look forward to going to the meetings, and it makes them major events that they can edify. Once you have a number of long distance lines in many cities then you will be able to orchestrate this network. By getting people trading meetings back and forth, there's always something new — someone different, exciting and fresh speaking at every open, cross-line meeting for all of your long distance lines.

The key to successfully working long distance is working profitably. You want to look at everything you do as an investment, rather than as an expense. An expense is something you simply spend money on. An investment is something you spend money on, because you know you are going to get a return. Work smart before you go somewhere.

I'm not opposed to you sponsoring the first person in a long distance area by phone, by FAX and by mail. You'd start by sending them the Pre-Approach Packet, following up with a phone call, sending them out the company materials packets, and making a presentation on the telephone. It's very likely that some of this can be done over the Internet, as well. But, one of the big things I always say about building a line long distance is if you can't afford it, don't do it. Now, let's suppose you do get the first distributor in an area started by phone, fax, mail or computer. You can do the "Get Started" training by phone. Simply have them fax you their list of prospects.

NOTE: You can get them started by phone. You will
need to travel there to get them duplicated, however.

Okay, let's suppose you're ready to go and work with this
line long distance. Here are some things I would do if I were in
that situation. I'd make sure that I had seen their list, and that
they had faxed it to me. I'd want to know whom they had invited to the presentation I was coming to. And, I would ask
them how they had gone about inviting people. I've gone to
places and meetings where someone's idea of inviting people
was to take out a classified ad in the newspaper, or go out and
hand out 8 ¹/₂" x 11" photocopied flyers on street corners. My
experience is that you would have to hand out 10,500,000 flyers to get three people to come to a meeting. As soon as I've
found out that that's how they have been looking to invite people,
I know that it's certainly not worth the plane ticket. But, if I
find out that they've done the "Get Started" training with me;
they've got their list; they've circulated the Pre-Approach Packets, and they seriously have some people scheduled, then I'm
willing to travel there.

I go there for the weekend. I would fly in on Friday. I will
ask both the husband and wife to take the day off. *"Huh? Wait,"*
they're saying, *"and miss our check from Burger King?"* Yes.
Listen. I'm going to get on a plane. I'm going to spend a thousand or two thousand dollars going to work with them — they
can afford to miss a day's work.

I want them to pick me up at the airport. We'll spend the
day doing one-on-one meetings and two-on-one meetings, and
I'll train them and get them ready. We'll probably have a Friday night home meeting. On Saturday, I'll schedule more
one-on-ones and two-on-ones maybe, and we'll do a builder's
meeting and some kind of basic training for the people who've
gotten involved. On Sunday, before I go home, we'll do a great
big "Get Started" training for everyone who may have joined

over the weekend. I may not stop there. Sometimes, I'll take a list of the new people who've joined over the weekend, and, when I get back to Miami, I'll send them out a welcome card or a brief welcome note. I may take some phone numbers of prospects that we talked to with my new people who weren't quite ready to decide, and might need a follow-up call. I want to do everything I can to maximize my trip there, and support my new distributor in the best possible way. And, of course, I'll have scheduled the next meeting before I left.

Doing this kind of activity in a weekend is a good investment — one that will pay you dividends for years, or even decades.

Some final thoughts on building long distance — it's kind of nice to have our local lines. We get so much attention; we seem so indispensable; we can seem like the "hero" in the area. In actuality, we have to be careful we are not creating co-dependents, and hurting our prospects for duplication and long-term income. Locally, as well as long distance, our goal has to be to work ourselves out of a job. Working long distance lines forces you to do this more effectively.

CHAPTER FIFTEEN

THE POWER OF THE INTERNET

IN THE COURSE OF HUMAN HISTORY, NOTHING THUS FAR HAS MADE A bigger impact on humankind then the Internet has. I believe it is bigger than the Agricultural Revolution, the Industrial Revolution, the telephone, the telegraph and personal computer all put together. It is completely transforming three of the most important things in the world. The way we communicate; the way we buy products and services; and, the way we learn and acquire information.

It's amazing how many parallels there are between Network Marketing and the Internet. Both are considered revolutions in the way business is done. Both are about educating the consumer. And, both are pioneers in eliminating the middleman and empowering the consumer to buy direct from the manufacturer. So, you have to figure when you combine the two mediums — amazing things will happen.

Some of the technologies the Internet brings us as I write this are not yet widely adopted enough to be duplicatable. But, change is accelerating so exponentially that it won't be long before they are commonplace. Other technology is widely available now, and can be harnessed for your business today. Let's look at some of the possibilities.

Prospecting.

Enough people who are getting online know that the Internet is a great place to meet people and make new friends.

And, we know from earlier chapters that the best way to prospect, is to meet people and make new friends. The same rules from the physical realm apply in the cyberspace realm.

If you meet someone in line at the supermarket and immediately try to pitch them about your opportunity, you're not going to impress many people. It's no different than if you assault someone you've just met in a chat room. You demonstrate no concern for the other person, no manners, and you come across as desperate. (Which you probably are!) <u>Approach your online relationships the same way you do your offline ones</u>. Go out and look to make new friends. As you meet new friends, add them to your prospect list. Then, when it's time to open a couple of new lines — go over your prospect list, select the best candidates, and approach them in a businesslike way.

The best place to meet people online is also like meeting people offline. <u>Go where you will find people with commonalities with you</u>. AOL, Yahoo, Geocities and e-groups all have communities or sub-groups of people with similar interests. You'll find groups from stamp collectors to car enthusiasts, from belly dancers to racquetball players. Join the communities that interest you.

Next, look for actual stand-alone sites that are devoted to your interests. Simply type a keyword search of your hobbies, and you're likely to pull up hundreds of sites. You may have several that you already visit now. Look for the ones that have community features, like chat rooms, newsgroups and message posting boards. Then participate. Offer information, start dialogue and just get to know people. You will develop some online relationships that can develop into deeper ones. Then, just like offline, the time will come when it makes sense to approach your friends about your opportunity.

E-mail marketing campaigns.

The next option is e-mailing out mass offers, doing the online equivalent of direct mail. The difference here is no one gets upset if you mail him or her an advertisement. People get very upset when they get unsolicited e-mails in their in-box. This is what they mean by Spamming, and it is also illegal in many jurisdictions. Don't ever buy e-mail lists from questionable sources. (The same advice goes for fax lists, by the way. That's another route that can get you into legal trouble.) If you want to prospect by e-mail, you should only be doing permission-based marketing.

A lot of hype is going around about marketing via e-mail. And with that hype, a lot of misconceptions. And, some outright falsehoods. So, let's look a little closer and see what you should be doing in this area.

A number of clients are coming to me lately saying things like, "Why do we have to spend all this money on mailing? Why can't we just send e-mails? Someone told me I can reach 5 million prospects on the Internet for free. Or a few cents a name, instead of 50 cents in the mail."

Ah, if only this were true. The reality:

Most of the people making these claims are people who sell e-mail lists. Lists of e-mail addresses that they got through deception; or sending out viruses, chain letters and phony alerts. Or lists that they bought, which the recipients don't know were sold. And, won't know until they get your offer from you ... and become enraged that you're spamming them.

The only lists you want to use are "opt-in" lists. Meaning lists where people have elected to receive offers in a certain area, such as yours. There are two list houses I can recommend for getting opt-in lists. They are www.yesmail.com and www.postmasterdirect.com.

Even so, this approach is not always a good idea.

Postmasterdirect claims to have 8.5 million opt-in names, as of this writing. Yet, in the big scheme of things, this is miniscule. Because, when you want to mail a specialized category, the selection is quite sparse indeed. In the recent Direct

Marketing Days seminar held in New York, **Bob Hacker** related a story like I'm hearing over and over. He had a seminar company for a client, and they wanted to fill 40,000 seats in the Midwest. The seminars were geared to CFOs, CIOs and MIS Directors. Bob did some research, and came up with some list recommendations, creating a universe of 240,000 names.

The company didn't like this. Feeling they were a high-tech company, they felt the offer should go out via e-mail. When Hacker went looking for e-mail addresses for this same group, the most he could muster was 10,000 names. Of the specialized lists I see, most have a few hundred, or at best, a few thousand names.

Even worse, even though these lists are primitive, the owners are often asking for 25 to 35 cents a name. Some are asking even more for transmission. And, the big lists available are not that impressive to me. First of all, anyone who asks for e-mail commercials is a little suspect to me. I mean, can you picture the lonely boob who actually asks for solicitations?

Another issue is getting names that are truly MLM-seeker names — not business-opportunity names. There is sometimes a big difference. People who are interested in buying a McDonald's or Hilton franchise are not necessarily good candidates for your MLM offer.

A better bet ...

Model exactly what I do. Create e-zines in your area of expertise. Give people value and you can work in Recommended Resources and links to products or services. As long as you are providing information that helps them, and the product or service is related to what you're teaching — people will not only not mind your advertising, they will welcome it.

When I check the stats for my www.gagedirect.com Website, I always get the same results. There are always two large spikes in the traffic each month.

Those two spikes always occur at exactly the times I had sent out e-zines that month. The e-zines contain links back to featured products and features that I had mentioned in the message. And people click through them in droves. The e-zine subscriber list on that site grows every single day. Often, many issues are passed on to dozens of friends or acquaintances — many of whom subscribe. So, there is a strong "viral marketing" action that takes place from well-written e-zines. And best of all, you are building a strong database of real names — qualified prospects, who cost you nothing, and will welcome the offers you send them. That's marketing!

This doesn't mean opt-in bulk e-mailings won't work or the price won't come down. Lists are getting better all the time, and the price is dropping. It may be dramatically better, even by the time you're reading this. The thing to keep in mind, however, is staying as duplicatable as possible. That's why you should always check with your sponsorship line before embarking on any kind of marketing campaign.

And, keep in mind, if you're going to promote this way — the rules of normal direct mail marketing still apply. You need to start with a strong headline; lead with benefits and substantiate with features; use "bucket brigade" copy; utilize an internal message; and use post scripts effectively. For tips on doing all this, get a copy of my *Massive Action Marketing* audiotape album with the *Study Guide,* and a copy of my *Million Dollar Mailbox* book.

Like direct mail, you will send out many messages, in the hopes of getting a response from a very small percentage. But, even a small percentage can be profitable. Follow the strategies mentioned, and you can do well.

Now, let's talk about actually having a Web site. Many companies are creating home sites for the company, then creating links to individual distributors' homepages. If you have an opportunity to do this, I would certainly recommend it.

240

Oftentimes a prospect may be attracted to a particular company or product, and then want to link up with a distributor in their area.

Other times, your company may not offer the option above, so you might create a stand-alone Web site. Here's the thing you should know about that. Simply putting up a Web page does not bring one single penny of business. Not one. Most people, even experienced businesspeople somehow suffer from the delusion that once they put up a Web page, customers are going to flock to them. This couldn't be further from the truth. Your site simply exists, in the void of cyberspace, unseen by no one, except you and your mother. You only make money with a Web site if you have a plan to drive traffic to the site. So, if you're going to go this route, let me give you some pointers on driving traffic to your site. We'll begin with some design considerations for when you're actually building your Website. It's important that it not contain design flaws that will drive away the traffic you develop. So here are some quick tips.

Make it text-driven and photo/graphic complemented. This is one of the simplest lessons — and the one that is most ignored by dimwitted marketers. If you make your home page a big photo of you or your product, it will take too long to load, and you'll lose visitors. If you want to market effectively on the Web, you must make your pages text-driven and use photos, graphics and special effects to complement them.

This is no different than what I've been saying about your space ads for years. Photos and graphics are great for getting the prospect's attention. But, copy is what causes people to buy. Set up your site so that the second people view a page, the copy loads and gives them something to read while the pictures load. Which leads us to the next consideration …

Make your headlines and copy benefit-driven. I could write a whole chapter on this topic, but I will leave it at what I mentioned in the earlier chapter. But, remember, if it's about you, your product or company — it's a feature. If it's about your prospect — it's a benefit.

Build your pages with no dead ends. Don't let a prospect scroll down to the bottom of a page and have nowhere to go. It's amazing how many sites do this. Put a navigation bar at the top, left side and bottom of <u>every</u> page.

Make everything "clickable." Build links crisscrossing all over your site. Make sure every photo, graphic or description of something links to the appropriate place on your site.

Keep the creativity of your designer in check. You can't swing a dead cat without hitting ten people who claim to be Web site designers today. Most of these people know how to make pretty pages, but have never actually sold anything. (Not counting selling their services to gullible people like you!) Some of them bought $69 Web design software from Office Depot; others trained for ten years in design school. It doesn't matter. Most people in both groups suffer from "multiple paint bucket" disease. Now that they've discovered how many colors and fonts are available, they want to use every one of them on your Web site. <u>Take it easy on multiple colors and fonts</u>. More than two or three fonts on a page gives your site a circus type feel, and doesn't build trust and warmth with the visitor. Same thing with color. Use these judiciously. Which leads us to the next consideration ...

Make the tech stuff serve the marketing function! The problem with most Web designers is they get seduced by the dark side of the force. Meaning they get excited every time they learn about a new bell or whistle. They immediately want to put this on your site because it's fun, it looks cool, or no one else has it yet. The one thing they never seem to consider is — how does this help us sell?

Make your site as "organic" as possible. Now, by organic, I mean living, breathing and changing. If possible, you want the site to have something different each time someone visits it. And, don't think you or your people are going to change it regularly, because you're not. It takes too much time. <u>Look at applications where the visitors do the work</u>. Things like surveys, chat rooms, and message posting boards build community, but, just as importantly, give a site a heartbeat, so it's not the same static pages every time someone visits.

Keep your site clean and easy to navigate. Don't go for design ideas that look pretty, but make it difficult to buy. The sites that actually make money (MSN, eBay, Yahoo) are all ugly, text-driven sites — but, you know how to get around them.

Use <META> tags effectively. This is another subject I could do a whole chapter on, but this is not an Internet book. So, for now, see <u>www.rankthis.com</u> or <u>www.websitegarage.com</u>.

If you're selling clothing, décor or certain luxury items — color on your site is critical. There are two companies that I know that specialize in improving color accuracy. I won't go into all the technical stuff, check them out for yourself at <u>www.imation.com</u> and <u>www.ecolor.com</u>.

Following these simple suggestions will make your site a lot more likely to make you money when people get to it. <u>Now let's look at some quick 'n' dirty things you should be doing to promote your site inexpensively</u>. Here are 24 quick tips:

▲ Mention your URL on your telephone voice mail message and answering systems. People who call when you are out will often go right to the site...and buy.

▲ Put your URL on everything you print. Everything.

▲ Utilize "viral marketing." Create rewards and reasons for visitors to your site to spread the word to their circle of influence.

▲ Have links from related sites.

▲ Register "Keywords" and your company name with www.RealNames.com.

▲ Have a "Refer This Site" box. This is the very best viral marketing — and better than any marketing you can buy. The endorsement of your site comes from someone the prospect knows and trusts.

▲ Have a "Send a Copy of This Article to a Friend" function. This is more of the same. You can assume that if you operate a site on nutrition — and someone e-mails a copy of a nutrition article to someone — that someone is a good prospect for your site.

▲ Install a signature file in your e-mail program for outgoing messages. I've been amazed how many friends and acquaintances of mine didn't know I had a site, and went to it, because they saw the signature at the end of my e-mail.

▲ Submit your sites to search engines & portals like Yahoo (not more than once a month).

▲ Publish an e-mail newsletter or e-zine. We've already discussed this. This is a very strong way to foster community, build your database and cross-sell your Web site. You need to be doing this now.

▲ Get linked from appropriate associations.

▲ Set up an affiliate program. You can do it all through outside brokers, like Commission Junction, and get all the benefits without having to worry about all the technical details.

▲ Use text links — inbound from other sites.

▲ Mail to opt-in e-mail lists. We've already talked about this, as well. Just remember the keyword here is opt-in. NEVER "Spam" a list of names you buy or rent unless they asked for this type of offer.

▲ Utilize Usenet postings for groups in your target markets.

▲ Participate in discussion groups and chat rooms on your subject.

▲ Get involved with list sponsorship. There are thousands of these lists.

▲ Install pop-up ads and new pop-up browser windows on your site.

▲ Offer related giveaways — everyone loves freebies.

▲ Don't overlook your middle pages — promote these in the search engines, too.

▲ Use audio ads on your site. Tell prospects about your new offer.

▲ Syndicate your content. Have your articles placed in other newsletters with a plug for your site.

▲ Create e-coupons. Tests have shown these really do work. Use already-in-place coupon systems. And, finally,

▲ Sign up for my Free Marketing Report E-zine at www.gagedirect.com. You'll get a steady stream of new promotional ideas.

These are just some simple steps you can take to promote your site, if you do one. Remember to check with your sponsorship line about the advisability of doing a site. Being duplicatable is an issue. But, technology is progressing so fast that things that may not be very duplicatable today will be quite duplicatable in six months. Now, let's look at the other ways the Internet can help you grow your business, with ...

Communication and Training.

The Internet transforms the entire world into a village. Everyone in the community is accessible and in easy contact with one another. In days past, people met in the town square. Today, it has moved to shopping centers and pedestrian malls. For Network Marketing, the "town square" is the www.mlm-metro.com

site I mentioned a few chapters ago. This is where you can meet and interact with your peers, purchase goods and services, and even connect with your long distance lines. Here are some of the features on the site, and ways you can use them to build your business.

Training:

Each Friday at 8:00 p.m. Eastern Time, there is a guest expert in the Live Chat. I've appeared a number of times myself. I suggest you get your group on each Friday, and let them ask questions of the guest expert. Then, once the session is over, you can open your own chat room. You can create a room, name it anything you want (Amway, Usana, Herbalife, etc.), and create a password so only your group can enter. Then, you can do a mini-training, and discuss any topics that came up with the guest expert and how they apply to your business.

There is also a video conferencing reflector on the mlm-metro site. This means you can purchase a small camera kit, and actually see the people you are talking to real time. The big benefit of the chat training and the video one is that everyone can get on the site for the price of a local phone call. This is what makes the whole globe the equivalent of a village. And, it saves you and your people a lot of money, and lets you communicate better.

Another training feature of the site is the e-zines. Sign up for the "tip of the day" and the weekly training e-zine. The tip of the day sends you an inspirational, motivational or "how to" message into your in box each morning. It's a great way to focus you and your people on their business. The e-zine is longer and comes out once a week. It's packed with business-building strategies and techniques. You'll get lots of good ideas to grow your business.

Another helpful area is the Forum section. These are discussion threads, on many different topics. If you have a question in an area, you can post it and start a discussion. Then, network marketers from all over the world can weigh in with their answers. It's a powerful way to enlist the support of your peers.

The www.mlm-metro.com site also has all the past training articles, and, if you subscribe to the newsletter, you can also access the subscriber-only area with the current issue. In addition to the things we've discussed, you can send e-cards to your group, peruse or place classified ads, study survey results, and keep up-to-date on the industry news. If you're serious about the business, then this is a site you should be on at least three to five times a week.

The other way the Internet will impact your business is through ordering and management. Many companies are setting up their sites so you can order online. The savvy ones have sites that allow your retail customers to order online, and you get the credit. Some companies have sites where you can track your volume and the growth of your network. Soon, all companies will have to have these kinds of sites. And, sites that do lots, lots more.

So all told, the Internet will change the way you do the business forever. Prospecting, communication, business management and training will all become easier through the power of the Net. It's simply a question of how fast you adopt the various technologies. One more time, I'll advise you to check with your sponsorship line — so you can balance the issue of remaining duplicatable, yet growing your business at the optimal rate.

Next, we'll talk about another resource, one more powerful than even the Internet — you!

CHAPTER SIXTEEN

DEVELOPING YOUR MOST IMPORTANT RESOURCE

VIRTUALLY EVERY PERSON IN THE WORLD HAS THE ABILITY TO create a massive network marketing organization. Yet, most people never will.

Now, this would seem completely crazy. Because, realistically, who wouldn't want to be their own boss, set their own hours, pick the people they work with, have unlimited income potential, and go to bed every night knowing that what they do empowers others?

So, why doesn't everyone do this?

I believe it's because they are not willing to do the necessary work on themselves that would allow them to accept success. Put another way — they won't let themselves become the kind of person who is a high-level, pin-rank distributor.

Even before I began this project, I knew that no how-to book on Network Marketing would be complete without addressing the issue of self-development. I've learned that how fast your organization grows is directly related to the speed at which you yourself grow.

Frankly, I don't know why this is, or how it works. But, I do know that this is exactly what happens. Your network will grow only as fast as you do. This was a lesson I learned the hard way.

I often joke with seminar audiences that I got into this business for three reasons:

1) To make money.

2) To make money.

3) To make money.

They laugh and I laugh, but that was no joke. I entered the business solely because I saw it as my only chance to get rich. And, thus, I began my career with a mercenary zeal to make lots of money. Every action I took was calculated to make me money. As a result, I made none.

I couldn't see it at the time, but my selfish, narrow-minded focus alienated people, and actually prevented me from making money. What happened instead was a lot of frustration, rejection and lost money. Which, fortunately, ultimately led to a greater good.

My total lack of success humbled me, and finally caused me to come to the conclusion that I could learn from others. Or, more importantly, that I had no other choice if I wanted to be successful in the business.

As a result, I made a conscious effort to befriend successful people in the business. I wanted to learn what the "secret" of building a business was — what they knew that I didn't. It was quite disconcerting, at first ...

It seemed that every leader I spoke with had a different way of doing the business. Some held meetings; some built by mail; others only did one-on-ones; and, yet, some concentrated mostly on retail.

It was only after extensive study that I learned that most of these people really couldn't put their finger on what caused them to be successful. But, more importantly, I came to the realization that they had achieved their own brand of success, but not the kind I was looking for.

These people had what I considered large incomes at the time, but none of them seemed to be retired or have true, residual income. Most of them had nice bonus checks, but were working ten to fourteen hours a day. It was this revelation that made me understand the importance of true duplication (and, ultimately caused me to create my own duplicatable system). Having that duplicatable system in later years gave me the freedom of having true, residual income.

But, creating that system has not been the primary reason for my success, nor the success of the people who follow my system ...

Success in this business comes from something much deeper. Something I learned from all of those leaders I had befriended. For, although they all seemed to approach the business in a different way, I did discover a commonality that each of them possessed:

A passion for learning, self-development and personal growth.

These people listened to tapes, read books and went to seminars. They spent a specific portion of each day on self-development. And, it seemed that the more successful they were — the more time they spent working on themselves.

This was an amazing new concept for me. I had never been to a seminar in my life. I didn't even know they existed. I read mystery novels and political books, but I had no idea that there was such a category as self-help literature.

When I hung around those leaders, they all talked about books like, *Think and Grow Rich, How to Win Friends and Influence People,* and *The Magic of Thinking Big.* They spoke of these in revered tones. These books were old friends they had visited with again and again. At last, I had found "the secret!"

This was the one thing that all leaders — with all different approaches — had in common. This was something I could model, and my people could duplicate.

I learned that if there really were any secrets to the business, it was this. If you want to reach a certain status, or certain goal — <u>you have to become the kind of person who would reach that status or that goal</u>. The talents are hidden within you, waiting to be unleashed. What you have to do is let them come forth.

You must eliminate all the negative and lack programming· you've been exposed to, almost since birth, and get back to your natural essence. The doubts, fears and uncertainties you have were learned — now, you must unlearn them.

Do you believe in universal laws?

If you're like most people, you do. You've come to believe that things are controlled by cause and effect, and you understand that gravity, centrifugal force, and other such laws, are governed by immutable, unshakable principles. If you hit a baseball, it will project forward. If you throw an object into the air, it will fall back down to the ground. You must plant a seed and nurture it to grow a plant.

Next question ...

Do you believe the same universal laws govern your own life? Now, here's where it gets interesting. Most people believe these laws govern the entire universe — but things that happen in their own life are *coincidence, chance,* and *luck.*

Fascinating.

When they see someone else get hit by a car, they think, "Why didn't that dummy look where he was going?" Yet, if *they* fail to look before they step into the road and get hit by a car, they attribute it to "bad luck." They believe the moon, stars, planets' rotation, climates, nature, evolution, mathematics and physics are all controlled by universal laws. But, when they get fired, have dysfunctional relationships, addictions, or bad business — these things get explained as bad luck, coincidence, tough breaks and other names — *all of which denote them as an innocent victim.*

251

Just how often are you a victim? And, just how innocent are you, really?

It's a fascinating subject. The lament I hear most from people in the direct selling industry is, "I wish I could find more people like me." Unfortunately, their problem is actually quite the opposite. They have attracted leaders exactly like them.

I know this from first-hand experience. When I joined the business, I was very excited, and leveraged that excitement to sponsor a few people. Then, when the excitement wore off, I stopped sponsoring, and instead devoted my efforts to calling up my three or four people and encouraging them to make me rich.

And, for some reason, they didn't share my enthusiasm. I couldn't understand this at all. I felt I had done my part, since I had introduced them to the business and sponsored them in. Now, I felt they weren't living up to their part of the bargain. They were supposed to duplicate this process and ensure *my* success. Then, it would be up to their people to take care of their success.

I felt as long as they got a few serious people — like me — who understood the system, duplication would be assured. These new people — if they were like me — would recognize that their job was to go with the program, reward their sponsor, and trust that they would receive their own reward in the end.

My whole strategy was based upon two elements: **fear** and **entitlement.**

The fear was my fear of rejection and fear of failure — both of which had prevented me from approaching anyone who was even moderately successful. Because of this, I had only approached people like me. Fearful people, who were easy targets for a message of getting rich quick. I was naïve, gullible, and not even remotely aware of the principles that success was founded upon. I thought Network Marketing was a shortcut to success, a way to cheat the system and get rich without having to do all the work.

My thinking was, "I see this shortcut. Now, I shared it with you. Your job is to find other people to duplicate this, and give me the reward due me for introducing it to you in the first place."

Unfortunately, because my whole approach was based around my own fears, I attracted people just like me — fearful. And, although they were just like me, they didn't duplicate the same results. (If they had, I still would have made money. Even though I would have had a fearful group, the growth would have kept coming.) What actually happened was they duplicated the actions they were seeing from me. Or more accurately, the lack of action.

I sponsored the initial people in, and then went into management mode. You know, trainings at my house, lots of calls, plenty of busywork, but no actual sponsoring. This is what duplicated in my group. My organization had the best briefcases, file systems, plastic page protectors and training meetings in the company. Unfortunately, by the third month, there were only about 11 of us left. My bonus check was in the neighborhood of $18, and I was spending about $80 a month on meetings, gas and expenses.

I whined and moaned about why I couldn't attract more people just like me. The truth was — I had. I had an organization full of scared people, doing busywork all day, afraid to talk to any credible people. I felt ripped off from my entitlement, and bemoaned the unfairness of it all.

Ah, yes, entitlement. It's a funny thing. I read something yesterday about entitlement, though I can't remember who said it. They stated, "Don't think the world owes you a living. It was here before you were."

All I knew at that point, however, was that things weren't working out, and somebody was responsible. It never occurred that it could be me ...

I thought perhaps the products were too expensive, my sponsor was too stupid or too lazy, or maybe I lived in a city where Network Marketing didn't resonate well with the local population.

I looked everywhere, but in the mirror ...

I went to training seminars where people talked about investing in your business and learning new skills, but I discounted them, figuring that they were just trying to sell me books and tapes.

I went to company functions where leaders spoke of sponsoring activities and follow-up, but I discounted them, figuring they were holding back the real "secrets" because they just wanted to make money off of me.

I went to motivational programs on getting out of my comfort zone, but sat in the back row on the aisle — so I could leave when they started all that "rah-rah" stuff I was too good for.

I talked with the most successful people in my sponsorship line. They told me to read positive books, listen to tapes, and use affirmations and visualizations every morning. I discounted them, because obviously they were under the influence of soymilk and tofu burgers.

I had it all figured out. The one thing I couldn't understand was why I always got so many bad breaks — and why I didn't get more empathy and sympathy from all those "lucky" people who had more success than me. I assumed they must have forgotten what it was like to be broke.

Actually, it was just the opposite. Many of them had come from the lack and limitation that I was in, and refused to let me drag them back into it. Since they correctly assumed that I was not open to change, they smiled sadly and acknowledged my poor "victim" state of affairs, and then couldn't wait to get away from me. Which just proved my conspiracy theory about them withholding the magic secrets of success from me.

As you've probably surmised, a transformation took place. Which is why I can write you this book today. I won't go into the drama of it all — since that would be (and may be) a book all its own. Suffice it to say, it involved a string of dysfunctional relationships, near bankruptcy, therapy, and a lot of setbacks before I finally got the clue that there was ONE person who was always at the scene of the crime.

When I changed ME, I changed my group, my company, and the world. Or, so it seemed. All I know is that when I changed, so did my results. Whenever I grew as a person, I saw an even bigger growth in my business and my happiness.

I discovered that Network Marketing was not a shortcut to success. I realized that the corporate rat-eat-rat mentality was a fraud, and Network Marketing was the real way to build security. But that true security came when you worked hard, acted with integrity, and grew as a person.

What's the bottom line in all this?

Network Marketing is not the shortcut to success, because there isn't any shortcut. However, MLM is a vehicle that if you practice the principles of work, fairness and giving value — you can reach extraordinary success and help lots of others to reach this same success. But, it all begins with self-development. Being willing to become the kind of person successful people are.

It starts, of course, with a dream, and then from there, I think you need to have what I call the $25,000 attitude. Here's what I mean by that. The $25,000 attitude simply means that you approach every decision you make in your business as though you were already making $25,000 a month in your bonus check. For example, suppose you decide to buy business cards. You could get the cheap ones for ten dollars that come with black ink on white paper from Office Depot, or you could get the firstclass, professional ones provided by your company. Well, if you were making $25,000 a month, which ones would you choose?

When your company develops some new marketing materials, a new presentation kit or new catalogs, what will you do?

Will you discard your old ones, and make sure that you have the latest, most current, up-to-date, effective materials? Or will you try to milk life from outdated ones? How would you make that decision? As you work with your long distance lines and your phone bill rises, and you have to decide whether or not to travel there, what is the decision you would make if you were making $25,000 a month in your check?

Here's an exercise that I learned some time ago from networker **Tony Regina.** He suggests that you think of one of the most successful people in your program. Maybe you haven't even met that person. You've seen them at a convention, or you've heard them on a tape, but they're one of the most successful people in your program. Now, ask yourself, "If they had and did all of the things that I have and do, would they be where they are today?" In other words, if they had your business cards, your inventory of products, the marketing materials that you use, and they made the same number of presentations a week that you make ... would they be where they are today? Now, if the answer is no, then you are going to want to reevaluate the things you have and do. That's the $25,000 attitude.

It's important that you work on self-development, because as you reach different levels of success in the business — the skills necessary to perform the business will change. When you first begin, listening and being coachable are the first steps to success in this business. Being proficient in these areas will help you develop the next set of skills — which are the prospecting skills.

Prospecting skills will take you to the next level — becoming a sponsor. By having a group under you, you'll need to learn teaching skills. This is what allows you to go duplicate yourself. As you duplicate, you will develop the need for other skills.

Time management will become an important skill in your life. Later, as your group grows more, you'll need to develop leadership skills. This is kind of a catch 22. You need some leadership skills to develop, but, as you develop, you will need more of them. **Richard Brooke** from Oxyfresh was speaking at a program with me, and he said something that I thought was probably the most profound thing of the entire weekend. I'm paraphrasing him here, because I don't have the exact words, but, in essence, he described his company as a leadership factory — disguised as a personal care products company.

That's what I mean when I say that the personal development is the stealth ingredient of this business. A lot of people don't recognize or understand that that's really the ultimate benefit they receive from Network Marketing. Yes, the money is nice, the cars are nice, the trips and the friendships are nice, as are the status and camaraderie — but, what really sets this apart, head and shoulders above any other business — is the personal growth. The leadership skills you develop are a tremendous part of that personal growth.

You'll also learn to develop management skills. You'll be managing a very large, and, in many cases, million-dollar or multi-million-dollar company. Now, you won't have employees; you won't have so much paperwork; and, you won't have a lot of the traditional headaches that go with a multi-million-dollar business, but you will still have a million-dollar business that needs to be managed on a daily basis. There are skills that make that easier.

Probably the most important step you can take in building your business is to make and keep a commitment to set aside time daily for self-development. Now, if your company has some type of book-of-the-month, or tape-of-the-week program, this would be the perfect thing to plug into. It's better for you to work with the program that your sponsorship line has, if it's available, because you'll be able to create some synergy and mastermind with other people in the organization. If, however, your company or sponsorship line does not have one, it's critical that you set up your own. Here's how this worked with me:

I started with fifteen minutes a day of self-development time. I recorded a tape for myself (which, today, has become a best seller) called *Secrets of a Dynamic Day*. It was just a tape designed to get me focused before I left the house. In fact, I believe your day is created before you ever leave the house in the morning. So, I listened to the tape, and spent fifteen minutes reviewing my goal card; thinking about where I was going and what I wanted to accomplish; remembering who I had packets out with; thinking of new people I could get packets out to; and just generally organizing what I would like to do throughout the day.

Now, I have to tell you, it was really difficult for me to listen to that tape every morning. I was one of those people who always woke up at the last possible second, late for everywhere I was going, and desperate to jump on the highway and make up time to get to where I was already supposed to be. I had to force myself to listen to that tape each morning in order to become focused. It was very difficult at first, but what I found was that after a few days, I was more organized. I started to have more time; and, I was getting more things accomplished. When I saw what this was doing for my productivity, I went up to thirty minutes a day for self-development.

I listened to that tape, and then I might meditate, pray, exercise — anything for my self-development — mind, body and spirit. What that did, in essence, was double my income. I was so much more productive. I had so much more self-confidence, and such a great sense of purpose that magical things started to happen.

What that did to my income, my relationships, my spirituality, and every other area of my life, prompted me to increase it even further. Nowadays, I will often take an hour or more for self-development. I don't answer the phone; I don't answer the door; I don't check my e-mail. I do my 30-minute cardio workout, which also serves as prayer and meditation time. Then, I do a little exercise, read my Daily Word, and possibly some stretching. The result is I don't interact with people until my consciousness is up at its peak level. Now, an interesting thing happens.

As I go forth into the world — I attract people who have the same level of consciousness. Whereas, in the past, when I was a victim, I always attracted people with a victim mentality. Now that I have a higher consciousness — I attract people who have a higher consciousness, as well.

In essence, what I did with this self-development program was make myself over. I was not happy with the person I had become, so I worked on me everyday — consistently and persistently. Just a little bit — to get a little bit better each day. I figure it took me about two years, but I was a completely new person by that time. Then, from that point, I became a completely new person in another year. And, from that point, I felt that within another six months, I had completely "made over" myself again. I have found that the personal growth starts to build exponentially, just like your network does. As you grow personally, your network grows at the same time. If you learn to speak German, it will improve your network. If you study Yoga, it will help your business. If you take continuing education courses in mathematics or carpentry or basket weaving, it will help your business. Anything you do that gets you out of your comfort zone will make you a stronger, better person, and, thus, you will have a stronger, better business.

Now, I do mine in the morning. You may like it at night; you may like to split it. The morning works better for me, because it motivates me to go out and be productive each day. Do what works best for you.

It took me a while to learn this, but success doesn't come from changing the people in your organization, changing your sponsorship line, or changing your company. <u>Success comes from changing you</u>. Would you like to have a growing, dynamic, empowering organization? It's easy. Simply become a growing, dynamic, empowering individual! Now, let's really get serious about the topic, as we explore the amazing power of your mind ...

CHAPTER SEVENTEEN

THE POWER OF THOUGHT

"As a man thinketh in his heart, so is he."

J AMES ALLEN BEGAN HIS BOOK WITH THAT APHORISM MORE THAN
seventy years ago. As a big champion of the book — and
a long-time student of the power of thought — I believe
the book is likely more relevant today, than it was when it was
written. I used to think the most important things to teach my
people were prospecting and training strategies. Now, I work
on helping them discover and implement their innate personal
power. This is what has the power to transform your business
and life.

It's pleasing to your ego to assume you're poor because of
your virtues. Like it's convenient to assume your group is not
growing because of outside factors and other circumstances.
It's very convenient to blame your lack of progress on the compensation plan, the price of the products, timing, the area you
live in, and a host of other external factors.

But the truth is, *you are reaping the results of your
thoughts.* Your suffering is the result of your negative, greedy
or lazy thoughts, just as the blessings in your life are the results
of your positive, kind and loving thoughts. This is an immutable, unshakable, universal law.

You cannot change your thoughts without changing your
life. In either direction. Fortunately, you can pick the direction.

You follow the thoughts you allow yourself to be dominated with. Program your mind with Jerry Springer, Drew Carey, UPN, and the FOX Network, and you're certain to lead a life of victimhood, lack and limitation.

Program your mind with the fertile stuff of *As a Man Thinketh*, *The Magic of Thinking Big*, and *Think and Grow Rich*, and you'll be walking the highway of strong and high endeavor. Just as planting an acorn will grow an oak tree, planting positive thoughts into your subconscious mind will grow a life of wonder, harmony, happiness and success.

It is common for people to think that they will attract what they want. Unfortunately, this is not true. You actually attract what you <u>are</u>. And, of course, you are what you think about.

The whims, desires, and even strong passions you have can quite easily be thwarted by the thoughts you have about them. I had a breakthrough about this one day when I was out doing my morning cardio work.

This is a special time for me each morning. I jog along the causeway that links several islands in the bay, so it turns into a meditation for me. This is also the time I do my morning prayers. During my prayers, I always give thanks for the skills, talents and abilities I've been blessed with.

On this particular morning, I was still contemplating a line of thinking I had been pursuing for several days. The extent to which I apply myself; what I accomplish; and what I'm doing to give back.

It had begun the week before when I had done a speech to help raise money for a charitable organization I belong to. The talk had gone great, and I knew that I had really impacted those people, and helped them to make a meaningful difference in their lives. Since I had semi-retired about a year earlier, I hadn't had much cause to do this.

Around the same time, other things seemed to all converge. I ran into **Bill Gove** (the first president of the National

Speakers Association), and he beseeched me to get back on the platform. And, while all this was going on, **Ford Saeks,** from Prime Concepts, called to ask if I would do a few speeches, provided he booked them.

I agreed to do a few, so he asked me to put together a demo video. I flew to California, spent many hours in the studio editing tapes of my past programs, and the fire grew! I realized how much I missed being on the platform and contributing to others. And, I knew that not speaking was wasting the talent that God had given me.

I knew that I still had a message that had to get out. I also knew that I had to do programs on human achievement. How you overcome adversity, negative programming, and doubt — and build the belief to do great things.

I came to understand that all those years in MLM — while I thought I was teaching how to do the business — I was really teaching people how to shatter their self-limiting beliefs and give themselves permission to succeed.

If you see my later works — the *Prosperity* album, *Dynamic Development Series*, and the *MLM Power Weekend* — you'll see they are a lot more self-development-oriented.

As I was jogging along on that fateful morning, I estimated that I was probably operating my life at about 15 to 20 percent capacity. Here's the funny thing.

I believe most people operate at about three to five percent. I had always figured that because I operated at ten or twenty times the rate of most people, I must be doing great. I've built successful businesses; made a lot of money; done a lot of charitable and spiritual work; helped a lot of people; and, built a solid résumé of accomplishments. By society's standards, I'm a super achiever.

But, while the world thought this — I knew the truth. I knew that God had blessed me with an incredible arsenal of skills, talents and abilities — and frankly, *it was a sin for me not to be using them.* Right then, I made a promise to God and myself — that I was going forward from that day — and unleash the tremendous power He had given me, and use it for the highest good.

Some pretty amazing things happened ...

A lot of people think because I'm so successful and teach prosperity, I never have lack thoughts anymore. Well I have a lot. Fortunately I recognize most of them for what they are, and dispel them accordingly. Even so, in a tight softball game, in the back of my mind, I would be thinking, *"If that guy hits the ball to me, I hope I don't make an error. The game's on the line."*

But, after my revelation, I just simply detonated any thought with the slightest degree of doubt, lack or limitation. I would not even consider the possibility that I would accept anything less than Divine order in any area of my life. That meant that all activities, projects, relationships, and everything else would be great. And, if it wasn't great — it was the next step in my development, and on the path to my highest good.

And the second I started believing that, it became true. In every area of my life.

My softball team won the league championship and qualified for the World Series. Which we then won! I played better than I have ever played in my life. The second I started to think, *"Well what if..."* I stopped, and just reminded myself that God had given me extraordinary abilities — and I was now going to use them. My thoughts switched to, *"I hope he hits that ball to me, because if he does, it's over."* And that's exactly what happened.

I've since done some consulting projects and the results have been extraordinary. I practically had to scrape clients off the ceiling. They have been so excited about the concepts I developed for them. It seems that my creativity is busting out all over the place. I've been on a creative binge, writing until 5:00 a.m. — then getting up at ten and starting again.

Relationships are getting positively euphoric, and new clients are lining up to throw money at me — a lot of which I will turn down, so as not to interfere with my softball schedule and other personal time.

Every single element of my life — and I've had a great one — has gone over the moon since I made a slight, simple adjustment in my belief — which changed my thoughts — which changed who I was.

Last night, I ran into a friend who works as a clerk on the graveyard shift. He attended a program I did at a church not long ago on the power of thought. He mentioned that he was trying to create a vision for the future — but all he could see were cracked mirrors. He asked me what I thought would cause that.

I replied that the likely causes were watching too much TV (he nodded); reading the daily newspaper instead of positive books (he nodded again); hanging around with negative people (now he's nodding furiously); or, all three. *"Busted,"* he says.

Like a lot of people I know, he wants a better life, and often asks me for advice on how to get it. I used to give these people copies of *As a Man Thinketh,* and suggest they read it. I discovered they never found the time. Then, I switched to giving them the name, and suggesting they buy it themselves. Most never get it. They spend so much time in thoughts of negativity — being a victim — they don't release those thoughts and replace them with thoughts of self-improvement.

It's a chicken or egg thing. They don't buy the book because they don't have positive thoughts. They don't have positive thoughts, because they don't have the book.

You see a lot of parallels in Network Marketing. You need to believe you'll be successful or you won't be. But you have to believe it before it happens. Most people fail because they can't keep this positive frame of mind until they actually manifest success.

They start out believing it, or at least thinking they do. Then, one of their people drops out, a presentation goes bad, or their first guests never show up for the presentation. <u>This is the absolute turning point of their career</u>. They will see these things as a challenge to be overcome — or an insurmountable obstacle — and quit.

If they accept it as a challenge, they build character and persevere. Until they get a little success. Which gives them some more positive thoughts — that build their belief — that lead them to their next success — which builds their belief stronger. They are on a win/succeed cycle.

If they view the situation as an insurmountable obstacle, subconsciously, they will look for validation to fail. The economy is too bad/good, the town they live in is too big/small, or it can't work because their sponsor is a no good bum who just wants to make money off them — a superstar with special powers that can't be duplicated. They are on a lose/fail cycle.

Each of these cycles will provide evidence to support these views. Which is one reason why it is so critical to feed your new people positive programming and protect them from lack programming their first few weeks in the business.

Because of the negative programming they receive from TV, radio, movies, other media and their families — most people will doubt their beliefs. <u>I teach my people to doubt their doubts</u>.

When I made my mental shift, I knew I'd have to get even more serious about policing my thoughts. I used to occasionally play subliminal programming CDs when I went to sleep at night. Now, I do it every night. I increased the time I was spending reading self-development books. I haven't seen a prime time television show in months. I put my negative thought radar on "maximum," and I won't let it down again.

To really understand all this, **you must accept that you are exactly where you are by the law of your being**. As James

Allen tells us, <u>the thoughts you have built into your character have brought you to where you are</u>.

He says, "Man is buffeted by circumstance, so long as he believes himself to be the creature of outside conditions, but when he realizes that he is a creative power, and that he may command the hidden soil and seeds of his being out of which circumstances grow, he then becomes the rightful master of himself."

Translated to today and your business ...

This means you may attribute your problems, challenges and setbacks to "outside" circumstances. This is escape mentality, and keeps you in victim mode forever. Once you realize that <u>you</u> control what you attract — and you do this by the thoughts you give precedence to — you can and will achieve true freedom and prosperity.

CHAPTER EIGHTEEN

PUTTING IT ALL TOGETHER

I'D LIKE TO SHARE MY THOUGHTS ON HOW YOU PUT ALL OF THESE pieces together, and go out to build a massive network — your personal multi-level money machine. But, before I do that, I'd like to share something else — call it what you <u>don't</u> want to do to be successful. It's very much a tongue-in-cheek article I wrote a few years back that was published in *Upline* magazine under the pseudonym Ydnar Egag.

I received more response from this article than anything I've ever written. Astute readers figured out what the byline spelled backward, and called, wrote or faxed to express their appreciation and amusement. It's since been reprinted in at least five or six other trade publications.

Sad to say, many readers accepted it as gospel. They are so tied to the MLM-junkie, look-for-the-next-hot-deal syndrome, that they simply don't know there's another way. They've spent so long *getting ready to get ready* that they've lost touch with what building a network actually entails.

So, before we look at creating your action plan, here's my gift to you, *The Lazy Man's Guide to MLM Success.*

> *Stop working so hard. You're training your group, following through, going to meetings, investing a lot of time in new distributor orientations, etc. Don't you realize that you could be spending that time,*

instead, in your very own home, sipping a cold drink and watching, "The Simpsons?"

If you wanted to work, you'd stay with your regular job. The reason you got into networking was to kick back and let other people make you rich. So, let's look at the proper way to do that.

First of all, you want to choose the right companies. Now, it's hard to stay focused, so you definitely don't want to have more than say, fifteen. A lot of the best HOT companies have a habit of closing up, so if you don't have some spare ones, you will lose credibility with your downline.

Look for companies that you can build by just mailing postcards or tapes to multi-level junkies. They already know how to mail postcards to other MLM junkies, so you won't have to waste any time training them.

Avoid any companies that have anything to do with selling products, buying products or holding meetings. If you must buy products, try to find a company where you can buy your way into the car fund, directorship, etc. You can always unload the stuff on your new distributors. Any companies over 90 days old are already "over the hill," so avoid them like the plague. Try to find "no-brainers," where they build your downline for you.

Another pitfall to avoid is companies with beautiful four-color literature. That stuff costs a fortune! Find a company that uses economical Xerox copies and tenth generation videotapes.

Try to find corporate leaders who have bounced around from one company to another, and who've been shut down by the attorney general once or twice. These are the seasoned pros who know their way around. They've learned from the school of hard knocks, so you don't have to.

*Once you have this portfolio of companies selected, it's time to begin the **analyzation stage**. This is a critical time for your business, so don't rush it. Basically, what you want to do here is review every single piece of literature from every single program. Then, watch all the videos, listen to all the audios, and go to any trainings. Read all the John Kalench books, Big Al books, and everything from Randy Gage.*

Now that you're well-versed in the industry, start analyzing your marketing plan. Compute all the percentages to make sure that the company didn't make any errors. Then, figure out how much money you're going to make with 10,000 people in your downline. Do the same thing with 20,000, 30,000, and so forth up to a million people. Now, you figure a plan to accomplish this.

Example:
You will mail out 100 postcards. Seventy-five people will join your program. They will each mail out 100 postcards the next month, after which 75 will join, so you will have 5,700 distributors by the end of the second month. In the third month, they repeat the process, so you will have 40,000 and so on and so on. Now compute your volume if they each buy just $30 worth of products. Now, figure your volume with $50, then $75, and so on. Deduct a small percentage

for the deadbeats who don't want to work and you can get an accurate picture of your income. Call your sponsor and see if he has sponsored anybody under you yet.

*After you have properly analyzed, pontificated and meditated for at least three months, it's time to move on to the **preparation stage**.*

First of all, go out and rent the biggest office you can find. Rent some swanky office furniture, as well. Try to find the same desk and chair that Blake Carrington used in "Dynasty." You want to show people you're serious about success. Don't get nervous about the costs — remember those income projections you've got on paper.

If your spouse is giving you a hard time, explain that this is not "another one of those deals." This is different. Anyway you'll close their trap when you pull up in your new Rolls.

Put up some diplomas, degrees, plaques and other status indicators around the office. Let people know that networking is not for the average slob — you need to be an experienced professional like yourself. Besides, it's nice when your downline has the proper hero worship for you.

*Another important step in the preparation process is **Starter Kit Preservation**. NEVER OVERLOOK THIS STEP!!!*

Get some Avery brand (don't settle for cheap imitations) white reinforcements, and put one on the front and one on the back of each hole of each page in your binder. Make sure that you don't miss any, or the page could come loose, and then what would you do?

After the reinforcements are applied, enclose every single page of the kit in plastic page protectors. Otherwise, you never know when a careless slip from somebody's coffee cup could bring your networking career to a screeching halt!

Once your starter kit is protected, you can begin printing stationery, business cards, postcards, etc. Buy a new briefcase, appointment book, electric pencil sharpener, and get yourself a new wardrobe. Get a large file cabinet and stapler, and buy a computer system for doing your newsletter. You don't want people to see you driving that old beater, so rent a Lincoln to hold you until your company car comes in. If all of this is taxing your spouse's take-home pay, just tap those credit cards. Remember, "Fake it until you make it."

Next, you want to study your sponsor's presentation and find the weaknesses. Create your own special, unique presentation that can be changed weekly. Also, develop some tapes, brochures, and flip charts on your own. These are always better than the company's, and it allows you to exercise your creative abilities. It's important that you set this example. You want leaders, not sheep!

After these first stages are completed, only then are you ready to talk to anyone about your business. If you tried to sponsor anyone before this four- to six-month process was completed — they might have asked a question you couldn't answer, and you would have lost credibility.

Unfortunately, by the time you've reached this stage — probably several of your companies have closed down. But don't worry. That's what the spares are for.

*You are now ready for the **Postcards to Strangers stage**. Don't talk to your friends, neighbors or relatives. They're all skeptics and losers! Besides, think how much time it would take to train them. Let them see how much money you'll be making in a couple of months, and they'll come crawling to you, begging to join. Just get yourself a list of fully-trained, serious MLM junkies, and mail out those 100 postcards!*

*Once your 75 distributors sign up, you can move into the **Hot Bath Hype Stage**. Since these lightweights don't understand the big picture like you do, it's important to keep them motivated. Get some copies of big checks from the heavy hitters and wave them under their noses.*

The biggest problem you will face is that most of these people are sluggards and procrastinators. They want to analyze everything to death when they should be out making you money. They think money grows on trees; they don't realize that it has to be earned.

Call them daily and check up to see if they've sponsored anybody. Let 'em know that if they want to make the big bucks, they'd better get off their butts. At the end of the month, call everybody and remind them to order or you won't get a check. Let 'em know that if they don't tow the line — you've got a new distributor just a postage stamp away.

If the majority of your people aren't producing, it can mean one of two things. Your programs have all peaked and are over the hill, or these just weren't hot programs worthy of somebody of your caliber. Either way, it's time to chuck those turkeys and start looking for the next HOT deal. Let the losers work those programs that take time, money and commitment – a heavy hitter like you has no need of such things. Just get out there and get RICH!!

*   *   *

Don't you wish it were that easy? Well, the truth is, this business is not that difficult. If you have a big dream, you're coachable, and you're willing to trade seven to ten hours a week to get it — you really can become successful in Network Marketing.

You can be a Ph.D. or a high school dropout, like me. You can have a healthy war chest, or you may have to borrow the money to get started, as I did.

You can analyze your compensation plan, and you can research the industry and do a due diligence on your company, but, ultimately, those things won't mean as much as who you are and what you do.

Believe it or not, your company, and even the industry, is not the opportunity. You are. Your company and Network Marketing are simply the vehicles that allow you to express your own inherent opportunity.

You are that opportunity, but you have to take the necessary steps to manifest it. It's very easy to fall into the procrastinate-and-analyze trap. Most of us have a lot of negative programming that lets us easily fall prey to such thinking. The reality is that Network Marketing has proven itself to be a viable business entity, a state-of-the-art distribution system, and an empowering vehicle for personal growth and lifestyle fulfillment.

The new cars paid for, the dream houses built, and the millionaires created are simply too numerous to calculate. More importantly, how many relationships were strengthened or saved because spouses came together to work toward a common goal? How many mothers (and fathers) got to go back home and raise their own kids, instead of paying someone else to do it?

How many millions of people — who have never even been a distributor — have had their lives enhanced because of products supplied by a network marketing company? What about the pounds lost, the nutritional deficiencies alleviated, the energy restored, or maybe just the money saved on the monthly phone bills that was put to better use?

How many more people support charities, because of the money and freedom they've earned from Network Marketing? A future president, the doctor who finds a cure for disease, or the person who creates the starship that can take us to Jupiter — may be the person who gets a college education on the money their parents are earning today in Network Marketing.

Yes, there are tens of thousands of people who are in the business, but will never get rich with Network Marketing. I'm okay with that. Because I know the potential is there. It is their choice whether or not to accept it. If they find products that enhance their lives — if they develop a sense of community with positive, goal-setting, dream-building people — then their lives will be better than when they joined.

Most people will benefit from the products; some will benefit from the personal growth; and, the serious ones will become wealthy. I'm hoping that <u>you</u> will do all three. That's why I wrote this book. To share and give back, in the best way I know how, for all of the many blessings I've received.

You can really build a massive, empowering and exponentially-growing organization if you follow the specific steps I've outlined here. Network Marketing and the systems I teach are not unknown commodities. They work. Everywhere. I've done "Getting Started" meetings in Skopje, Macedonia; conducted Leadership Institutes in Zagreb, Croatia; done training seminars in Nassau, Bahamas; and, held opportunity meetings in Ljubliana, Slovenia — not to mention virtually every U.S. state and Canadian province. Thousands have done it. Millions more are doing it.

The principles are the same everywhere. They transcend cultures, economic situations, and even time. The power of a dream is the most awesome force that humankind can harness. Electrical generators, nuclear power plants, even the atomic bomb are minuscule by comparison. The only obstacles that can stop you are the ones you see in the mirror every morning. Make three investments in yourself.

First, invest in a commitment. A commitment that you really are worthy of success and that you'll do whatever it takes to achieve it. Second, invest your time. Of course, it's not easy to find seven to ten hours a week. If it were, everybody would be doing it. But, if you tell yourself, "I'll do it after school's out" or "after the holidays," you're in denial — lying to yourself. If you really believe you're worthy — you'll act NOW.

I know that finding the time involves sacrifice. But, making a sacrifice for two to four years – for a lifetime of freedom — is a pretty good investment in my book.

Do me a favor — don't ever use your kids as an excuse not to do the business. Use them as the reason to do the business. It would be worth missing one more evening a week with them for two years — to then be with them every day, and make all the PTA meetings, school plays, soccer matches and little league games after that.

And, please. Don't use your spirituality as an excuse not to do the business. I must tell you. I missed some nights in church. And, some Sundays too, when I was on the road working long distance. I held my own service. Because, in my faith, we believe that there's nothing spiritual about being poor. In fact, we teach that being poor is a sin. I believe that your Creator wants you to be healthy, happy and prosperous — it is your birthright.

I have prosperity now, because I made choices along the way. And, you know what? I serve on my church's committees; I've been the president of the Board of Trustees; and, I tithe more than most people make. Because I didn't use my spiritual identity as an excuse for inaction, but rather, as a reason for action.

Third, invest your money. I don't think you'll find a more disproportionate reward or return on an investment in any business today than what's possible with Network Marketing. But, you still have to invest something.

You need business-building materials; you need self-development materials; and, you have to attend functions. If you don't have enough money — sell your television! You'll probably be better off without it anyway. If you don't invest in you — who will?

Another thought on investment. Please don't live out of your business if you want a big business. Keep your day job in the beginning — as distasteful as that sounds — so you can reinvest everything you make back into your business. Like everything else, a little sacrifice early will pay much greater rewards down the road. Network Marketing works on the principle of delayed gratification. Invest in yourself for two to four years, and then reap the rewards for a lifetime.

Finally, set the example for your group. Work hard; support your people; use the products; and, have fun! Set an example of integrity and work ethic that your group can duplicate. Because, you know what? They will!

As you approach any decision in your business, ask yourself this simple question. Will this bring me closer to my dream — or take me further away from it?

You must be willing to pay the price — and that means taking action. Building a large network is not easy — but it <u>is</u> simple. Each day, you must make consistent, persistent, positive movement toward your dream. If you keep Pre-Approach Packets in circulation; practice self-development; attend the functions; are teachable; and always make your two to four presentations a week — you really will live your dreams.

I didn't write this book to challenge your dreams — but, rather, to help you realize them. And, I certainly didn't write it to change you — but, rather — to help you discover and unfold who you really are. Relish the journey my friend. You're about to take a magic carpet ride of challenge, adventure and growth. Enjoy the ride!

ABOUT THE AUTHOR

RANDY GAGE IS REGARDED BY MANY AS THE PREEMINENT EXPERT on Network Marketing in the world today. Tens of thousands of people around the globe credit Randy with helping them reach higher levels of success. For more than 15 years, Randy has been helping people in the direct selling industry break through self-limiting beliefs and achieve their dreams.

Rather than "rah-rah" hype, Randy focuses on specific, how-to training you can use to build your business faster. He has emerged as the highest paid, most sought-after speaker and consultant in the industry. His *How to Earn at Least $100,000 a Year in Network Marketing* audiotape series is the #1 selling album in network marketing history. Randy has conducted training in almost all the fifty United States and in many other countries around the world.

Born in 1959 in Madison, Wisconsin, Randy now lives in Miami Beach, Florida. His hobbies include car racing, baseball and collecting comic books.